YOU
HAD ME at
HALLOUMI

Ginger Jones is a fiery redhead with a love for chocolate, spicy food and swimming al fresco. She collects chintzy china teacups, drinks loose leaf Darjeeling and loves fifties fashion. Most of her writing time is spent in the company of Lulu, her Schnoodle who has helped and hindered the creation of her books in equal measure.

Ginger loves comic writing. Her influences are Caitlin Moran, Helen Fielding and Nora Ephron. Having previously written for the stage, she finds the live buzz of theatre exhilarating and enjoys nothing more than finding fringe venues she never knew existed.

She and Lulu look forward to penning many more novels together. You can find them both via:

🐦 @GingerJ53270983
📷 @redhotscribbler
f @GingerJonesRedHotScribbler

YOU HAD ME at HALLOUMI

Ginger Jones

ZAFFRE

First published in the UK in 2022 by
ZAFFRE
An imprint of Bonnier Books UK
4th Floor, Victoria House, Bloomsbury Square,
London, England, WC1B 4DA
Owned by Bonnier Books
Sveavägen 56, Stockholm, Sweden

A CIP catalogue record for this book is
available from the British Library.

ISBN: 978-1-83877-846-0

Also available as an ebook and an audiobook

1 3 5 7 9 10 8 6 4 2

Typeset by Envy Design Ltd
Printed and bound in Great Britain by Clays Ltd, Elcograf S.p.A.

MIX
Paper from
responsible sources
FSC® C018072

Zaffre is an imprint of Bonnier Books UK
www.bonnierbooks.co.uk

To my Dearest Juliet,
a true friend and free spirit,
who loved cheese and will stay forever in our hearts

PART ONE

PART ONE

CHAPTER ONE

A Taste of the Mediterranean

'Yes, chef!' Freya grabs the handle of a frying pan and gives it a flick and a shake whilst spooning cranberry confit over a row of equally spaced tuna and citrus fishcakes with her slow hand. The hairnet still itches after all these years, her flaming red tresses bursting to escape the confines of a tight bun. It's 8 p.m., dinner service is at its peak and although she should focus, all she can think about is whether Charlie has opened the link to The Golden Spoon cookery competition she has applied for and whether he has enough remaining annual leave for a fortnight in Cyprus.

Drizzle. Flick. Drizzle. Flick. Drizzle . . . Too much confit? Not enough? She twists the tray this way and that to examine the fishcakes from all angles and then panics that she's becoming too much like her mother. Wasn't obsession-compulsion one of the first symptoms? Filling her lungs with hot air, she exhales sharply through her nostrils and counts to five, repeating twice until every thought in her head is dispelled until next time.

The kitchen is at full tilt. Plates rattle. Pans clank. Water hisses from the cold tap, sizzling against the piping-hot baking tray as it clatters into the sink. Freya looks up as the thud of something solid hits the worktop and a tub of frozen God-knows-what gathers speed across the smooth stainless-steel. Plop. It falls off the end and into the food waste bin.

'Grab it then!' Courtney barks through a curtain of sweaty dreadlocks.

Peering into the bin, Freya wavers. 'Don't you think—'

'Quickly!'

Against her better judgement, she plunges her hand into the damp mush of potato peelings, capsicum seeds and fish heads to retrieve what is labelled COURTNEY'S ROULADE – DO NOT EAT and gives it a rinse under the overhanging hose. The lid is a bitch to peel open even with her good hand, its seal frozen along with its contents and Freya having to lever it out with the handle of a serving spoon which takes off two fingernails in the process.

'Microwave instructions on the bottom!' Courtney roars.

Freya turns the frozen tub upside down, sets the microwave to 'defrost' and keys in the requisite minutes.

'Three lamb chops!' Courtney flings his oven glove onto a bloodstained tray of rapidly diminishing sardines.

'Yes, chef,' she yells, grabbing another lamb chop from the meat station and returning to sauté a handful of king prawns.

Sweat pools at the base of her spine. If only she could cook everything from raw ingredients instead of microwaving the shit out of food that has lived in the freezer for over a month. How she'd love to take over the running of this place for a day and give both the menu and décor an overhaul, restoring A Taste of the Mediterranean to its former glory when it opened three decades ago to rave reviews, or better still: start afresh, putting her own stamp on it. She peers through to the dining area with its dated wallpaper and frayed carpet and is reminded of the way her mum described herself three months after giving birth to her: worn out, tired and suffering a complete loss of identity.

Strip the wallpaper. Paint the ceiling. Get rid of the statue – who the hell wants to guzzle *polpette alla bolognese* under the lustful gaze of a God with disproportionately large, lumpy meatballs of his own? Well maybe Zeus can stay, but as for the rest: take everything back to basics, replace the signage and let the food do the talking. If Freya were head chef (or executive chef as Courtney likes to call himself; a title that apparently affords him the freedom of ditching his hairnet), the menu would be simple yet delicious, fancy yet unfussy, allowing each dish to be tried, tested and perfected; the focus on flavour rather than volume, giving diners the Mediterranean taste sensation they crave without needing to fly to sun-kissed coastal Europe.

She looks down at the jagged pink scar running across the flesh between the thumb and forefinger of her right hand and sighs. One day, she will leave this place and set up solo – she didn't spend a whole year studying for that ball-breakingly difficult exam and writing a ten-thousand-word dissertation on Mediterranean menu plans for nothing. One day (soon, fingers crossed) she will cash in her advanced chef accreditation for a chance of winning The Golden Spoon – a little-known but highly prestigious award that has gained gravitas over the years, originating in Cyprus and producing some of the most talented chefs in the world, and something she can only dream of right now. Draining a panful of spinach, she wonders what it might feel like to be part of that small, revered clique of super-chefs. The microwave bleeps, the reality of the here and now slapping her in the face. Still, Golden Spoon or no Golden Spoon, she's getting too old (and too frustrated) to be somebody else's sous-chef.

'How long for lamb chops?' Courtney plucks a yellow ticket off the ballooning row of orders.

'Seven minutes, chef!' Freya shouts over the clangour of falling saucepans.

André maître de whatever-it-is-he-does, glowers from the serving counter, the vein in his temple pulsating. 'Seven?'

Freya looks at his smart black suit and crisp white shirt, the side parting of his hair an immaculate straight line and imagines what his bathroom would be like. High-end men's toiletries perfectly aligned on flawless polished glass; each label positioned at the same angle. Impeccable. Pristine. Befitting of a psychopath. 'One-minute prep, two point five minutes on each side, unless you want them rare, one minute to garnish and present,' she says on the exhale.

'For fuck's sake!' André clenches his fists, his knuckles rage-white.

In his eighteen months of running the place, André Cobb has only ever taken three days off – one day for his mother's funeral and two days for his honeymoon – and it shows. Since buying into the business last year (his co-owner a silent investor based in French Guyana) he has become a stress ball of knitted nerves. His mere presence in a room serves only to conduct anxiety and tension amongst diners and kitchen staff alike, the pronounced lines etched into his forehead and constant tremble in his left leg testament to a decade of restaurant kitchen PTSD. They've all tried talking to him, but he won't listen. Not to Freya. Not to Courtney. Not to his saint of a wife. If he doesn't get everything yesterday, it's not good enough.

He shoots a death-stare at Freya. 'Any slower and you'd be in a fucking coma!'

The scar on Freya's hand starts to itch. Short of a miracle or buying twenty microwaves to heat up defrosted gunk, food preparation takes time. Cookery is beholden to rules; not to stifle or prohibit but to provide a failsafe method; heat at the right temperature and dough will rise, bake for too long and cake will burn. You can't boil an egg or pan-fry a lamb chop in three seconds and that's the way it should be, otherwise where would be the joy in it all coming together? The sweet honey fragrance of slow-cooked, marinated pork. The anticipation of rising sourdough. The gratification of roasting flaked almonds for long enough to give them that sweet, nutty flavour without them becoming too oaky and brittle. These are moments to be savoured, not rushed. How she would love to tell André what she thinks of him right now and return his volley of abusive comments with a tirade of her own. Fuck him and fuck him some more. She looks down at the baby-leaf salad she is drizzling with dressing, her stomach dropping with the stark realisation that the bottle she is clutching is soy sauce rather than balsamic vinegar. Shit. So stressed she's seeing double, she slides the salad towards the bin only for it to be immediately scooped up by Courtney who shoves it under the tap, washes off the brown residue and sets the leaves aside to dry.

The temperature soars, the oven behind her belching out heat until the air is so hot and humid that they could be in a Turkish bath. She pulls at her collar, sweat trickling between her breasts, and repeats the mantra she learned from her Home Economics teacher at school, Mrs Kyriakedes: *Breathe. Stay focused. Happy is the heart that cooks with all its soul. Move deliberately and with efficiency. But above all, enjoy the process.*

'Enjoy the process.' She smiles to herself, remembering Mrs Kyriakedes' olive skin and amber eyes, her birdlike frame and mass of unruly thick, black hair. She thinks back to the low-fat yoghurt cheesecake she enjoyed making this afternoon when Charlie disappeared to watch Spurs v Liverpool – with time on your hands and room to fail, it's easy to enjoy the process, but let's be honest, a Saturday night dinner service is an altogether different kettle of fish. The pressure on the five of them – herself, Courtney, two line cooks and a plongeur – to deliver two hundred covers in an evening is heart-attack fodder as it is, without being under the hot-headed, fist-slamming, acid-tongued scrutiny of a stress cadet like André.

She throws her head back, enjoying the way her clothes stick to her when the kitchen is furnace-hot, her skin feeling alive, her senses heightened. Hot air swirls with the aroma of garlic, chilli and lemon, everything coming to life with a splash of olive oil. Breathing in the vapour, a cooling sensation passes over her as a waft of cold air blasts in from the backstreets of Nottingham through the fire door which has been wedged open with a crate of Peroni. The smell of rosemary-infused lamb intermingles with the fragrance of garlic prawns and, like songs sung in rounds, the aroma of starters mixes with that of mains and desserts until they all overlap; a harmony of gourmet food. A smile plays on her lips as another rush of heat rockets from the oven. Maybe she *is* enjoying the process.

An hour later and at last the kitchen falls silent save for the hum of the fridge and the cracking open of beer bottles. Service is over and André reverts to the human he actually is, offering everyone a Peroni fresh out of the fridge. Freya presses the cold bottle against her cheek, enjoying its touch against her hot skin and watches Courtney cast his latex gloves into the bin, the rest of the team already halfway out of the door.

André looks from Courtney to Freya with bloodshot eyes. 'Sorry for being an arsehole.'

She shrugs her shoulders and says nothing.

And so the cycle continues; a slow build of pressure from Monday to Thursday as their patronage gradually increases, tension mounting as week becomes weekend, culminating in a wall of stress which hits fever pitch each Saturday night, followed by a comedown of reason and regret washed down with beer, André's kitchen PTSD resurfacing like clockwork on Sunday in preparation for the next cycle.

Freya takes a swig of Peroni, relishing the coolness of the light, crisp liquid in her mouth. 'You know what would go well with this?'

'A shot of tequila?' Courtney laughs.

'I was thinking *this*.' She heads to the fridge and gets out the two-tone cheesecake she made earlier, plonking it down in front of them, its smooth, pink surface glistening like fresh snow upon a layer of pistachio. She hands them both a spoon and drives a serrated knife through the cherry yoghurt topping and into the biscuit base, manoeuvring half of it into a take-away carton for Charlie. He'll enjoy that later.

'Love the pink and green layering.' André plunges his spoon into the cheesecake and takes a mouthful, his facial expression transforming from one of hunger and exhaustion to one of full-blown ecstasy. Spoon poised mid-air, he closes his eyes and chews slowly. 'Light. Tangy. Fluffy. And the crust . . . It's delicious.' His eyes burst open. 'Who made it?'

'I did.' Freya swells with satisfaction. There is no better feeling in the world than someone finding her food delicious – not only has she excelled herself in the field she loves, but she has also given someone a sensual experience, and all without getting naked.

'That needs to go on the menu,' André says to Courtney, pointing his spoon at the cheesecake.

Freya can barely control her excitement. She claps her hands together with glee, wondering if she can remember exactly how much of everything she threw in, today's recipe more about experimentation than exact science.

'We'll start it tomorrow.' Courtney reaches for another slice, and a warm, fuzzy feeling spreads through Freya. Not only has she hit the culinary jackpot, but she has also scored her name in lights on the menu; something that has taken her three years, two months and eight days – not that she's counting.

@UtterlyButterly
My cheesecake is going on the menu @TasteoftheMed
#fameatlast #cooking #recipes #ninjainthekitchen

It's finally happening. Freya Butterly is on the path to culinary greatness.

CHAPTER TWO

The Cheesecake

An hour later.

The path to culinary greatness is, of course, not the Google Maps-recommended fastest route, but a meandering one prone to diversion and procrastination. Missing the bus home and having to spend half an hour killing time in a 24-hour Sainsbury's Local before getting on the City Clipper which only goes as far as West Bridgford, has kind of taken the edge off Freya's cheesecake euphoria. With the rain hammering relentlessly, she lifts the collar of her coat to tramp up the hill towards Gamston, and a lorry ploughs through a gargantuan puddle of rainwater, drenching her from head to toe. Spring supposedly became summer last week, but that's Britain for you!

When she finally arrives home shivering, the lights are on, but in spite of ringing the doorbell twice, Charlie doesn't answer. Emptying her shoes of rainwater, she rings for a third time. Charlie eventually appearing with a mouthful of fries and a fistful of burger.

'Did you not find the coq au vin I left you?' She kisses him on the cheek, avoiding his MSG lips.

'Coq au what?' He throws her a bath towel fresh off the radiator and walks back to the living room. 'I thought it would be easier to get an Uber Eats. Good night?'

She peels off her coat, a smile igniting her face. 'Really good night. They're going to put my cheesecake on the menu!'

Charlie resumes his place on the sofa and un-pauses the football.

'Did you hear what I said?' she says excitedly. 'They're going to put my cheesecake on the menu. They loved it and . . .'

Charlie has zoned out and clearly can't hear a word she's saying.

'Charlie?'

'Sorry?' he says, pausing the football with an air of exasperation.

'It doesn't matter.' She wanders out of the room to take off her wet clothes, Charlie letting out a 'Whoa, referee!'

Her annoyance rises; the match isn't even live so he can watch it whenever. Must he really pick the moment of her cheesecake triumph? She pokes her head around the door, water dripping from her hair onto the wooden floorboards. 'Did you look at the link I sent?'

'You donkey!' he screams at the television and reaches for another swig of Coke.

'Charlie?'

'What?' His eyes remain glued to the plasma screen that takes up most of the living room.

'The Golden Spoon Cyprus holiday?' she repeats.

'Huh?' he grunts.

'I just thought it could be a good compromise. You know, the foodie stuff for me. The water sports for you.'

'No way was that a foul!' He throws himself backwards on the sofa and folds his arms behind his head.

Hitching up her towel, she pads over to their bearded dragon's glass tank and lets Arteta out, scooping him up for a cuddle and administering his deworming medicine using the syringe supplied by the vet. With Arteta draped across her shoulder, she wanders back over to Charlie and pulls her best seductive pose. 'I guess I'll see you in bed then, my hot hunk of burning love.'

'Hey, don't be like that,' Charlie says, turning back to her now that the game has stopped while a player gets stretchered off the pitch to hisses and boos. He pats the sofa beside him, suggesting that she should take a seat next to his discarded burger box with a slice of gherkin slopped in the corner. 'I thought we might go out tomorrow.'

'I have to go into work,' she says, letting Arteta climb over the sofa.

He looks up at her. 'I thought tomorrow was your day off?'

'It is, but I have to make three cheesecakes and take them in before the restaurant opens.'

'André takes the piss. He really does.'

'It's actually an honour, Charlie. If I'm ever to become head chef, I need to show willing.'

He takes her hand and squeezes it. 'That's what I love about you, Frey; you always give it your all. Cyprus sounds good. Let me check it out properly later.'

And for a moment, she feels like the centre of Charlie's universe, his faithful grey eyes gazing into hers beneath his floppy, light brown fringe – his hair the same colour as his freckles – his strong, warm hand wrapped around hers, until the match resumes, Charlie's attention disappearing with it.

Gathering up Arteta in her arms, she climbs the stairs to bed. Maybe it's her, not him. Maybe getting your cheesecake on a menu isn't anything to make a song and dance about – at least not whilst Arsenal are playing. Still, he could have at least looked up. It may not have meant anything to him, but he must have seen that it meant something to her. She places Arteta down on the carpet and reaches for her phone.

Freya

> I'm seriously evaluating my relationship with Charlie.

Khady

> Whassup?

Freya

> It'll sound stupid. It's about a cheesecake.

Khady

Is this a sex thing?

Freya mulls this over, thumbs poised. Maybe this is a sex thing without her knowing it's a sex thing. An unconscious sex thing. Maybe the fact that it's not a sex thing but should be a sex thing is a problem. She glances at the bed covered with clothes, Charlie's jeans twisted around her stripy jumper, three of his T-shirts strewn across the pillows next to her discarded floral dress, her pyjama bottoms wedged somewhere between the two, and then it hits her: Their clothes are more intimate than she and Charlie are.

It should be *she* who is draped across the pillows in carefree abandon, not her leggings. It should be *her* naked body pressed up against his shirt, not the gusset of her knickers. It should be the pair of them entwined on top of the duvet, a tangle of post-coital sweat and elation, rather than a bunch of mismatched socks and an inside-out Arsenal football shirt. She picks up Charlie's boxer shorts and throws them into the laundry basket. This is where they are going wrong: they are not having enough sex. And when they do, it's perfunctory, she, mentally compiling the shopping list whilst staring at the ceiling, and he, reaching for the remote as soon as it's over. They need to spice things up a bit. When was the last time they had sex which wasn't in the missionary position? In fact, when was the last time they had sex at all?

It's not his fault – if anything the fault lies with her; she often feels too sweaty and revolting to strip off and initiate anything after a shift at work, and by the time she's washed, dried and feeling human again, sex has taken a back seat to Google – Charlie looking at aspirational sports cars whilst Freya favours holidays and any cookery posts by her idol, Talia Drakos, founder of The Golden Spoon.

She takes a shower, towels off and moisturises, then moves the clothes off the bed and searches the room for inspiration to create 'the mood'. In the absence of scented candles or a dimmer switch, she lights a bundle of sage and stands it in a glass on her bedside table, watching the leaves glow as they burns. Sultry.

Reaching into her bag, her fingers run across the empty miniature bottle of l'eau d'Issey eau de toilette she carries around everywhere, before finding the large slice of cheesecake she has saved for Charlie. Glancing at the dark-red pitted cherries decorating the top, she's reminded of a YouTube channel called Peaches & Cream she once came across when browsing food preparation techniques, Peaches turning out to be a platinum blonde who loves smothering herself in whipped cream. It certainly got Charlie's attention when Peaches, all wet parted lips and heavy panting, was spoon-fed maraschino cherries and quivering jelly by a statuesque milkman, and although Freya doesn't really fancy the thought of lowering her tongue like a pornographic drawbridge for someone to drip cherry coulis onto, she does wonder whether she's onto something here. She may not do sex very well, but something she does do well is food . . . If only she could somehow . . . She looks at the cherry cheesecake and wonders what it would look like smeared across her naked body. Opening the lid, she's not sure she can actually do it. It's not so much about lack of confidence, it's more about ruining a perfectly good cheesecake, but then again, isn't fresh snow there to be spoiled?

Tentatively, she dips her finger into the mousse-like froth and wipes it across her chest, a cherry rolling into her cleavage. It feels cold and sticky. Still, you have to work at these things. She dabs another blob onto her nipple. And another blob. And then fully committing, she grabs the whole slice by its biscuit base and, as though it is soap on a string, smothers the cheesecake all over her stomach, the topping sliding over her skin, the base crumbling over her crotch. It's tacky. It's itchy. It's deeply uncomfortable, but if this doesn't get her cheesecake noticed, what will?

'Charlie!' she calls downstairs.

The muffled hum of the television continues.

'Charlie?'

A chunk of biscuit rolls off her breast and embeds itself in the crease of her elbow, the burning sage starting to billow out smoke.

'CHARLIE!' She begins to feel less sexy now that the cheese-cake has started to congeal, and she can't move in case it goes all over the bed sheets.

The hum of the television is replaced by the sound of foot-steps on creaky stairs.

'What's that smell?' Charlie enters the room, the expression on his face akin to someone who has stumbled across a ticking bomb. 'Is something on fire?'

'I am,' she growls, forming a tiger's claw with her hand, raising one knee and flicking back her hair, thrusting forward her chest and lifting her cheekbones towards the ceiling in a practised look of longing. 'Come to bed.'

'What are you doing?' He looks at her like ... she's no connoisseur but it doesn't look like lust. Maybe indigestion.

She swishes her hair back over her shoulders and licks her lips. 'Eat me.'

'Are you OK? You look ...'

'Horny? Hungry?' she says, not daring to move her head lest the big clump of yoghurt on her neck slide onto the pillow.

'I was going to say *ill*.'

'Ill?'

'Mentally ill.'

'Thanks!' She sits upright, a bolt of horror flashing through her (maybe she really is becoming like her mother) the cheesecake slowly slipping onto the sheets. 'I was trying to be alluring.'

Charlie chuckles, wafting smoke out of his eyes and gingerly lowering himself onto the edge of the bed. 'You do make me laugh.'

She sighs from within, wiping cheesecake off her face with the pillowcase. 'I want you to desire me, not find me laughable.'

'Of course, I "desire" you.' He stares at his feet and picks a strand of cotton off his left trainer.

She props herself up on her elbows, annoyed that he is wearing his shoes upstairs *again*. Did he not learn from the dog poo incident last week? 'I brought this home for you.' She nods at the congealed mess on her chest. 'You could at least indulge me with a lick!'

'And suffer indigestion for the rest of the night? Come on, Frey, I'd never be able to perform after eating half a chuffing cheesecake!'

'Just one lick?' She pouts, determined to see this out.

He turns towards her and for a moment she thinks he is going to scrape it off her layer by layer with his tongue, but instead he wipes his finger through a blob of mousse and lifts it to his lips. 'Not bad!'

Not bad? NOT BAD? Cordon fucking bleu is what it is! Menu-worthy. Heavenly. Scrumptious. Divine. She feels as though her lungs have been popped by a pin. Unsure whether she's more hurt by Charlie's nonplussed reaction to her food seduction attempts or by his apathetic appraisal of her cheese-cake, she becomes aware of the smell of singeing and wonders what the crackling noise close to her ears is. The next thing she knows, Charlie has grabbed the pint glass of water he keeps on his bedside table and is launching it over her head.

'You're on fire!' he shouts.

'I told you that, but you were more interested—'

'No, you're really on fire!' He pats at her hair which fizzles and burns as the smoke alarm lets out a high-pitched screech.

'*Aaargh!*' she shrieks.

'Saved by the bell,' he declares, offering his arm to give her a hand up. 'You grab a shower and I'll sort out the alarm.'

Singed and humiliated, Freya slumps back onto the bed and absent-mindedly runs her finger over the scar on her hand. Could that have gone any worse? Back in the day they would have at least had a laugh about it, but laughter doesn't seem to be a thing anymore and here they are again, back to division of duty, each of them doing their own thing. Each of them in separate worlds. Saved by the bell? The smoke alarm cuts out. She knows she fucked up – mixing food and sex is like mixing spirits and wine and expecting not to get a hangover. But shouldn't she get points for trying?

Khady

> You should totally get points for trying! This is where it pays to be bi. Men have their strengths, but women are so much more creative between the sheets. And most other places.

Freya bends down to pick up her underwear from the floor and sees that Arteta is merrily tucking into a chunk of biscuit base. At least someone is having fun.

Bundling bed linen into the washing machine and slamming it onto a hot wash does nothing to improve her mood. Sheets spin, pillowcases whirl, and so does her head. She thinks about the burger boxes all over the living room floor and the uneaten coq au vin in the fridge, her mind wandering back to meeting Charlie online. He'd certainly ticked all the boxes on Tinder, professing to be both a foodie and a fitness junkie, his profile describing him as having the ambition of Steve Jobs and the wanderlust of Michael Palin. She lets out a laugh. The furthest they have ventured since they got together two years ago is Blackpool. A shimmy up the tower, a stick of rock at the top and a sugar rush headache in the arcade to boot. Funny how two people can be on completely different wavelengths. She closes her eyes and runs her hands through her hair, her fingers sticking to something cold and congealed. She examines the blob of cheesecake on her fingertip and stuffs it into her mouth. Light. Tangy. Creamy. Buttery biscuit perfection. Charlie's missing out.

The hallway clock strikes midnight. She looks down at her soiled stomach and wonders how she can be starting a new day in this dishevelled state. Tomorrow will be different. A new dawn will bring change. A new day will bring fresh perspective, but first she should probably take another shower and go to bed.

The next day, a storm is brewing. Rain pounds against the patio, Freya soaked to the skin within seconds as she ventures into the back yard to bring in the washing. A ferocious wind howls, swooshing laundry across the garden, the clothes horse clattering to the ground and Charlie's underwear scattering across next door's clematis. Plucking pants out of the hedgerow, Freya is nearly blown over as another gust of wind knocks over the bistro chairs and detaches a bird feeder from the lower branch of the silver birch, spewing sunflower seeds and grain over the grass. What she'd do for some summer sun right now. Still, today is the day her cheesecake makes its debut, and nothing can take that away from her.

A few hours later, she and Charlie sit at the window table of A Taste of the Mediterranean, the menu laid out in front of them. Condensation clings to the glass panels and a draught of cold air blows out of the vent next to their feet. Eating at the restaurant you work in is like dating your friend's brother (something she did when she was seventeen and still regrets) it's all too familiar and incestuous. The kitchen should be a chamber of mystery, not a dungeon of familiarity, and when you're eating, you don't want to visualise your chef picking dandruff out of his dreadlocks over your plate of *gambas al ajillo*, or coughing up phlegm over your freshly defrosted roulade. However, today is different, as she explained to Charlie this morning. Today is all about selecting her cheesecake from the menu and giving it the inaugural moment it deserves.

The door swings open and a fresh gust of cold air whooshes through the restaurant. Khady, all fake fur and bluster, grabs the small, brass bell before it can signal her arrival with a ding and, primping her new hair – a choppy burgundy bob wig which offsets the streak of bronzer accentuating her beautiful ebony skin – makes a beeline for Freya.

'Can you take this, so it looks like I've been here a while?' Khady says, bundling her coat and belongings into Freya's arms and glancing across the room at André who lingers behind the counter.

Freya hangs the faux mink coat on the back of her chair and watches as Khady flattens her apron down over her thighs, peels a notebook out of her pocket, and gestures to the Specials on the board, aware that André is watching her every move.

Charlie grins. 'We're here for Freya Butterly's amazing cheesecake, please.'

Khady smiles broadly. 'And a damned fine cheesecake it is! Would you like a dessert wine to accompany said damned fine cheesecake?'

Charlie looks over at Freya. 'I think this calls for Prosecco,' he says proudly.

Freya swells with pride.

Khady scribbles in her notebook, tears out the order and instead of handing it in to the kitchen, presses it into the palm of Freya's hand.

Freya looks down at the notepaper.

I've just slept with the girl I'm PTing and now she's asking me to dinner. Please don't let me sleep with my clients again.

Freya shakes her head slowly and smiles in spite of herself. No man or woman is sacred when it comes around to Khady's power of seduction; she's just one of those goddesses that breezes through life, leaving men swooning and women crushing on her wherever she goes. Trying to rein her in would be like trying to hold back the tide and there's no way Freya is even going to pretend to try. She stifles a smirk as Khady saunters over to the bar, hips sashaying, arms swaying, her tiny waist emphasised by her apron tie, and remembers the time they lugged a Peloton bike back from Sneinton, stopping every few feet across The Green to swap sides and alleviate the weight. Khady accumulated two phone numbers on the way: one from a girl with aggressive red lipstick, and another from a guy with a parrot perched upon his shoulder whilst the only thing Freya picked up was backache and a bruised toe. That's the thing about Khady; she's just got that *je ne sais quoi*.

Turning her attention to the carte du jour, Freya combs through the italic font of the desserts section, her stomach dropping at *Courtney Gayle's Cherry Cheesecake*. A high-pitched ringing sounds in her ears. There must be some sort of mistake. *Courtney Gayle's* Cherry Cheesecake? Her face feels hot and clammy, and she has the out of body sensation that her skin is moving around in pixelated patches.

'Courtney Gayle's cherry cheesecake?' Hot lava rises within her.

Charlie reaches for her hands. 'I guess the most important thing is that your cheesecake made it onto the menu, and we all know it's yours really.'

A volcano of ire threatens to erupt from deep inside her. 'You're saying I should be grateful that someone else is taking credit for my work?'

He fiddles with his floppy fringe. 'I'm saying, what's the big deal? It's just a—'

'And you're just a ...' The word 'fuckwit' dies on her lips. He looks confused.

'Don't expect me to rise above it, Charlie! This is *my* cheesecake we're talking about!'

Charlie clicks his fingers in André's direction. Good. It's about time Charlie stuck up for her. A moment later and André appears at their table, standing as tall as he possibly can. Freya is reminded of the Queen's guards at Buckingham Palace, his gelled fringe adding height in place of a bearskin. 'Freya?' he says, as though reporting for duty.

Charlie clears his throat.

Excellent, Freya thinks. Let him have it both barrels.

'Urm, I think Freya wanted a word,' Charlie mumbles.

Freya rolls her eyes, wondering what Michelle Obama would do in this situation and decides that as a speaker of truth, no way would she let this go. 'Why is my cheesecake down as Courtney's?' She summons her inner Michelle.

André looks behind him and lowers his voice. 'Freya, sometimes you've got to take one for the team. We're not working to promote ourselves as individuals, we're working together for the greater good of the restaurant. Courtney is a bit of a crowd-puller. He has a fantastic reputation and if people see he's created something new, customers will come along in droves.'

'Droves?' She glances around the room at the empty tables.

André clears his throat. 'Word has yet to get out.'

Fire blazes through her breastbone. Sure, she has felt deep shame in her life (the way she dealt with her mum coming off her medication for the very first time is not something she is proud of and will probably feel guilty about for the rest of her life) and she's experienced plenty of injustice along the way too, but never a betrayal like this. It feels as though the bottom has dropped out of her stomach. She looks up at André. 'I quit.'

'I think you might be overreacting.' André straightens his collar, puffs out his chest and clip-clops back over to the counter.

Freya's pulse throbs in her ears until it's all she can hear. Her palms turn to liquid. Has she really just quit the job she loves over a cheesecake?

Charlie tries to grab her hand which isn't ready to be grabbed. He looks across at her. '*I* know it's your cheesecake. *You* know it's your cheesecake. *They* know it's your cheesecake, so let's stay and give your cheesecake the moment it deserves. Come on, there's no need to get all emotional over a slice of dessert!'

Freya's jaw feels as though it has been welded together. 'Charlie, we can't stay. It'd be like Dele Alli falling out with Jürgen Klopp in the changing room and then having to sit next to him on the bus home,' she whisper-shouts through clenched teeth.

Charlie's forehead creases. 'Dele Alli doesn't play for Liverpool.'

'OK! It was a shit analogy!' She pushes her chair back and stands up.

Charlie remains seated. 'Come on, Frey. It'll all blow over if you apologise now.'

Apologise? APOLOGISE? Freya fumes. Is she really expected to go back, un-quit, be a good little girl and 'take one for the team?' Should she really be putting the restaurant's reputation ahead of her own? Her head spins. What would Michelle Obama do in this situation? She swallows hard. If André is prepared to go *this* low, how can she be expected to go *that* high? One thing's for sure: if she allows this to happen, then she's not taking responsibility for creative integrity and justice in the workplace. Going back would be saying it's OK to steal other people's ideas and present them as your own; confirming that behind every weasel-turd, a good woman is forced to prostitute her ideas.

This is gastro-plagiarism of the highest order, and she cannot allow it.

'Come on, Frey.' Charlie nods to the seat opposite him.

Frustration froths under her skin, the fire inside her mushrooming with such ferocity it feels as though she's about to explode. How can he not see that this is a betrayal? Perhaps if he had listened to her last night instead of fixating on the football, he might understand the magnitude of this moment! Wouldn't *he* feel furious if the roles were reversed? It may not matter to him, but it certainly matters to her. This isn't just about cheesecake.

'Charlie?' She takes a deep breath. 'I quit you too.'

CHAPTER THREE

Cyprus

Dear Ms Freya Butterly

Pack your bag, you're going on the adventure of a lifetime!

Congratulations, you have been chosen to compete for The Golden Spoon at our family-run cookery retreat in Cyprus. We look forward to welcoming you and your six selected competitors to Lappo where you will learn the secrets and techniques of Golden Spoon recipes using organic, local and seasonal products. You will be invited to forage for wild herbs, sample rare wines and cheeses, visit the local market, enjoy beach picnics and explore fishing villages.

Your chef, Christos, will not only teach you how to

prepare exquisite local cuisine but will also guide you
through the next stages of your Golden Spoon journey:

Days 1–5
- Each contestant will complete at least one task per
  day which will be judged by our food experts and
  awarded points for taste, texture and presentation.

Day 6
- Contestants will work as a team to cater for the
  Psimeni Raki festival, producing local dishes en
  masse for visitors to the island at this fun and
  fabulous annual celebration.

Day 7
- Day off (in addition to the excursions undertaken as
  part of the course) for you to spend at leisure.

Day 8
- Guest judges, Alexandros Papastathopoulos and
  Penelope Onassis, will assess the final round of
  competition dishes and will choose two finalists to
  go through to the grand final hosted in Paphos.

Days 9-10
- Free days.

Day 11
- The winner will be declared at the Grand Final in
  Paphos. However, this does not guarantee winning
  the much-coveted Golden Spoon, which is only
  awarded in exceptional circumstances.

We look forward to welcoming you to the sandy shores of
Cyprus and sharing what we do best: cookery.
Get ready to live the Golden Spoon dream.
With sunshine and wine,

The Bazigou family
The Golden Spoon Experience

Freya sits in the arrivals café at Larnaca Airport, trying to
enjoy her coffee which tastes so strong and bitter she can
almost feel her brain being stripped of its cells with each gulp.
Her mind flashes back to the pep talk Khady gave her back
in the departure lounge of East Midlands Airport.

'Enjoy every single moment.' Khady clasped her hands
around Freya's shoulders and looked at her square on, her face
aglow with excitement, wonder and several shades of bronzing
powder. 'You've jumped through hoops to get here so don't
for one second think you're not as good as anyone else. You're
the best, and that's final. And besides, it'll do you good to
hang out with other people. Other people that aren't Charlie.'

'I'm not there to meet anyone significant, if that's what
you mean?'

Khady raised an eyebrow. 'No . . . but there's no harm in
window-shopping.'

Freya bit her lip and smiled. Window shopping. Now that
might be fun.

'Now go get 'em, tiger!'

Freya glances around the terminal for her fellow gastro-tourists, panicking for a moment that she's flown to the wrong airport in Cyprus before spotting a tall teenager with a frog umbrella waving a sign for 'The Golden Spoon'. Her stomach churns, its emptiness reminding her of the time she lost PJ, a teddy her mother made her out of old pyjamas back in the day when things were 'normal', and schizophrenia was a far-away condition preying on people unbeknown to her. Has she done the right thing?

Khady

> Of course you've done the right thing. And stop asking if Charlie's OK. He's already back on Tinder with the same profile he had when he met you!

Freya's chest tightens. It is commonly accepted that men move on faster than women even when they are the *dumpee* rather than the *dumper*, but surely everyone should respect a mutual cooling off period of at least a week?

Khady

> He'll have done it just to piss you off. Revenge dating. Revating. Everyone does it.

Freya

> Do they? About to meet my fellow cooks. Wish me luck!

Khady

> Careful . . . Those Greek boys sure know
> how to woo a woman!

One thing's for sure, Freya has not come to Cyprus to be wooed. This trip is strictly business and there is no space in her life for romance right now. Besides, if she was going on holiday to hook up with someone, she'd go to bloody Butlin's. That, or an 18-40s Ibizan foam party package holiday whilst she still can. No, romance is totally off limits, thank you very much. Look where her last relationship got her – bed-wrecked with a buttery biscuit base. These next two weeks are all about focusing on food and having her best shot at The Golden Spoon. Oomph. Her stomach lurches. Those three words alone are enough to bring on an anxiety attack. The Golden Spoon. An award she wants so desperately, it's all she can think about. In fact, it's all she's *ever* been able to think about. With her only parent out of the picture for most of her teenage life, cooking has been the surrogate mother that never let her down and The Golden Spoon a validation of the skills she has honed over the decades. A culinary badge of honour.

Gathering her belongings, she ditches her coffee and makes her way over to the group of people gathered around the frog umbrella. As she draws nearer, she makes out a woman in waterproofs engrossed in a paperback romance, a serious-looking guy with his hair tied up in a Nike silky, black dastār, and a girl with white-blonde hair extensions and skin so orange it clashes with her Louis Vuitton luggage.

'Hi, I'm Freya,' she says, feeling like she did on her first day at catering college where, desperate for companionship, she befriended Lucy Williams, a clingy narcissist with severe halitosis who she would spend the next few years trying to shake off.

'Hazel Stevenson.' The woman in waterproofs looks up from her Jackie Collins novel, her piggy little eyes narrowing to pinpricks as Freya goes to shake her hand which remains glued to the money belt strapped around her waist.

'Harj.' The guy with the Nike dastār overcompensates with a fist bump. Hmm. Maybe not so serious after all. She tries to put an age on him, the silver flecks in his silky beard contradicting the youthful elasticity of his baby face. He could be anywhere between twenty and forty, the blocky white trainers and garish sports vest at odds with the delicately inscribed iron bracelet hanging from his wrist.

'Leandra-Louise.' Fake-tan girl steps out of her circle of Louis Vuitton hold-alls, swishing her plaited tresses over one shoulder to air kiss Freya over each cheek. Her accent is a heavy Welsh and her breath smells of strawberry bubble gum.

'Kwame.' A tall man with neatly shaved hair and the physique of an athlete props his didgeridoo against the wall and reaches to shake Freya's hand. His accent is strong Glaswegian.

'Hi,' she says nervously.

Georgios (according to his name badge) lowers his frog umbrella and explains that they're all to board a minibus which will take them to the coast and then, depending on the tide, they will either complete the journey to Lappo overland, or cross over to the islet by motorboat. Either way, they will be on their paradise island within all but a few hours where two guests from France will join them, making them seven in total.

'Hope we get the motorboat,' Harj says to the group. 'Arrive in style, innit.'

Freya offers up a nervous chuckle. She and seasickness are all too familiar bedfellows.

The guy with the frog umbrella slings their luggage onto a trolley and leads them to the exit. Freya feels a rush of hot air smack against her face as she steps out of the terminal and into a Cypriot summer. The sun pinches at her skin as they walk beneath a clear blue sky towards the minibus, the sound of birds chirruping from the branches of a line of lemon trees planted along the roadside, and a strong sense of calm overcoming her. This adventure has been a long time coming.

The drive to the Akrotiri peninsula takes just over an hour, but it's amazing how much longer it feels when someone is honking tunelessly through an indigenous wind instrument for the entire journey. They get out of the minibus at a rocky vantage point, everyone giving Kwame and his didgeridoo a wide berth.

Freya makes her way over to the edge of the cliff. The first thing that hits her is the fragrance of wild herbs carrying on the warm breeze. Filling her lungs with salty air, she looks down at a red pebble cove formed from volcanic rock, its cliffs stained by iron ore. The sea is an endless expanse of rolling emerald, waves glittering like silver streamers under the

Mediterranean sun. She reaches for her sunhat, her face tingling in the heat. The landscape is much greener than she'd imagined, the rainfall back home obviously having hit here too. Almond blossoms shiver in the breeze and a warbler darts between the blades of long, luscious grass growing on the hillside. Freya smiles. Nothing could be further from the polluted streets of urban Nottingham if it tried.

'Wicked, they're getting the boat!' Harj transports her back to the here and now.

'Great,' Freya says quietly, rummaging in her bag for a motion sickness patch and hoping for the best.

They clamber down to the red pebble beach where a small motorboat waits at the water's edge. Seagulls squawk and squeal, scavenging for scraps as a fisherman drags his haul over thick clumps of seaweed and onto a rusty trailer. A lighthouse further up the coast juts out like a proud peacock, its brilliant white tower rising from the deep green sea, Freya feeling the almost overwhelming impulse to swim out to it. One by one they step into the boat as it rocks from side to side, Kwame's didgeridoo getting in the way of the motor. Eventually they, along with their luggage, are strategically spaced to even out the weight and everyone is ready to go.

Georgios retires his frog umbrella and assumes the position of boat captain, tugging at the pull starter and firing up the engine with a cough and a whir. Wafting away the smell of petrol, Freya knocks back a Kwells tablet and prays that the sea is less choppy than the contents of her stomach. The noise of the engine settles into a growl as they skim the water's surface, powering towards a dark shadow of land that lurks in the distance. She leans back and tries to suppress the nausea clawing at her throat. Only twenty minutes to go. Her fellow cooks jostle for position in the pecking order of culinary chit-chat, Kwame and Hazel going head-to-head in a disagreement about black beluga lentils and as she looks at the faces around the boat, Freya is reminded of *The Life of Pi*. Wasn't it the hyena that symbolised the cook? And if everyone's a cook, then which one of them is the Bengal tiger? She glances at Hazel and then at the small print on the Kwells packet, noting delirium as a possible side effect. Still, fevered confusion is preferable to throwing her guts up in front of a bunch of strangers.

'My dad's a chef. His dad was a chef. My uncle's a chef and me and my three brothers are chefs, so I didn't have a choice. It's baked in my DNA,' Harj bellows directly into her ear to make himself heard over the engine.

Freya stares at the blood orange sun that hangs over the horizon, the sky becoming a streak of marshmallow pink stretching over the darkening indigo sea as afternoon becomes evening. Taking a moment to channel her breath solely through her nose (something she saw one half of the Hairy Bikers do on a choppy crossing to Sardinia), she watches the silhouette of volcanoes fade into the distance as the boat powers away from the main island of Cyprus and buffets against the waves until the distant blot on the horizon takes the shape of a small island bequeathed with luscious green trees and a small wooden jetty.

Harj gazes at their destination, a look of wonder spreading over his face. 'Mint.'

'Idyllic,' Hazel agrees, *Hollywood Husbands* propped open on her stomach.

Freya looks over as a small, sleepy fishing village set against a backdrop of pine trees comes into view, a handful of colourful wooden boats bobbing in the harbour. It would be idyllic, were she not about to throw up.

'My dad says he'll have my guts for garters if I don't come back with The Golden Spoon.' Harj squints up at the sun. 'He's full-on in love with Talia Drakos, innit.'

'I don't think there's a chef that isn't!' Hazel chortles.

'You do realise all of us will probably go home without it, don't you?' Kwame flicks sea water out of his flip-flop. 'Nobody is guaranteed to go home with it.'

Freya grips tightly onto the edge of the boat and tries to imagine that it isn't rocking, watching as Harj peels the lid off a Tupperware box and hands out home-made baklava.

'Who's Talia Drakos?' Leandra-Louise rolls down the spaghetti straps of her vest top and tucks them into her bra.

'Talia Drakos is the reason we're all here!' Hazel shakes her head with exasperation.

'She's the founder of The Golden Spoon.'

Freya bites her lip. How the hell could any self-respecting chef allow Talia Drakos to pass them by? She may not be an international phenomenon but amongst anyone serious about being a chef, she is nothing short of a culinary goddess, her modern twist on traditional Mediterranean recipes synonymous with flair and flavour and her quirky food combinations second to none. If it wasn't for Talia Drakos, who would know that watermelon, mozzarella and reduced balsamic vinegar would taste so delicious together? Or scallops, lime and strawberry. Orange peel and black pepper. The list is endless. And then there's her trademark jumpsuits. Sequinned all-in-ones for Christmas. Strapless gingham for the summer. And a variety of ruched denim playsuits for everything in between. How is it vaguely possible that Leandra-Louise hasn't heard of her?

Leandra-Louise peels her hair out of her lip gloss. 'I wasn't even sure what The Golden Spoon was when I applied. My friend told me to go for it, so I thought, well, in for a penny. I didn't get what all the fuss was about until the *South Wales Echo* got in touch and wanted to run a centre spread on how a Cardiff girl with no qualifications passed, what was it again, "an exam of a lifetime". I'm just here for the ride. And the sun. Gotta love a bit of sun, haven't you?' She tilts her head to the sky and wrinkles up her nose.

Freya looks out to the horizon and swallows hard. Can this really be true? By the very nature of the competition rules, nobody could qualify for a place on this 'gastro-holiday' without sitting a ten-page exam, submitting a ten-thousand-word dissertation on meal choices and achieving a score of over ninety-eight per cent. Who would put themselves through that level of scrutiny just to be 'there for the ride'?

The baklava makes its way around the boat, Hazel waving it away with her tattered paperback. 'I've been sugar-free for two years now – well, *refined* sugar,' she remarks smugly. 'Who needs sugar when you've got beehives?'

'You're a beekeeper?' Kwame says from beneath his sunhat, his long, spidery legs sprawled out over his backpack.

'Restaurateur, but I also keep bees,' Hazel says with an air of nonchalance. 'You?'

'No.' Kwame sits up. 'I run a gastro-village up in Glasgow.'

Freya's stomach churns and this time it's not motion sickness but nerves. How is it possible that she is the only person on the boat who doesn't own a vineyard, a bistro, a honey farm, a gastro-village, a restaurant or a whole chain of them? This was supposed to be a level playing field, not two weeks of hardcore culinary competition with Europe's greatest gastronomical billionaires. Yes, she passed the test and is technically as qualified as everyone else, but in practice, how is this going to work? Her exam adjudicator may have hailed her essay impeccable and described her section on Sicilian-style sardines 'a masterclass in the ways in which frying, baking and canning fish can affect the omega-3 content,' but does that really count for anything now that she's sitting with a literal boatload of chefs with far superior knowledge and experience? In the absence of a paper bag to blow into, she plunges her hand into the bottomless sea, letting a stream of warm water rush over her fingers. She has never felt so out of her depth.

The motorboat rises and falls as the engine cuts out and they float towards the shore. Freya grasps the handrail as the boat tilts one way and then the other. Back and forth. To and fro. Up and down, her inner pendulum rising and falling like a yo-yo. If she can just hang in there for the next few moments, they'll have reached dry land.

'Yah!'

Her attention is diverted to a tall man in khaki shorts who stands on the jetty and beckons for the rope. His legs are those of a tennis player; tanned and athletic. His jaw is chiselled and his shoulders broad. The sea breeze lifts his white cotton shirt to reveal a taut stomach and Freya becomes acutely aware that she is openly gawping at him, butterflies dancing in her stomach. Turning away, she tries to get a grip, but her thoughts have gone haywire, short-circuiting from culinary inferiority to unashamed lust. What the fuck is the matter with her? This trip is about fresh air, fresh food and learning local culinary techniques. It is not about hiding Cypriot sausage in the sand dunes with someone you haven't even said hello to yet. Still, as Khady said, there's no harm in a bit of window-shopping.

'Freya?' Harj calls out from the jetty.

To her horror, she realises that she's the only one left in the boat. What a cliché she has become; falling in lust with the first man she meets and dreaming that the population of this island is made up of athletic, ripped Greek gods.

A toothless old man reaches for her luggage. Maybe not.

Khaki Shorts Man beckons her over.

She sneaks another look at him behind her steamed up sunglasses as she reaches for his outstretched hand.

His olive eyes meet hers. 'Welcome to Lappo.'

For some reason, she has lost the ability to speak.

Straining, he pulls her over the thick rope coiled at his feet and she's reminded of the time a boy at her school gave her a piggyback through a deep brook and promptly dropped her in it, falling against the riverbank and clutching his back in agony.

'I'm Dimitri,' he says, struggling for breath.

'Freya,' she replies. 'How do you do?'

How do you do? Who the fuck says, 'How do you do?'

these days and why is she all of a sudden assuming the tone of Mary Poppins? She reaches for her phone to text Khady.

Freya

> Window-shopping firmly underway.

Khady

> Boom! Start as you mean to go on . . .
> Send pic!

Freya lifts her phone and turns to the group huddled on the shore, trying her best to style out a landscape photo featuring Dimitri that Khady can zoom in on, but it's just too cringe – she doesn't really know anyone well enough to take their picture yet and the only part of Dimitri she has managed to capture is his left elbow.

Freya

> Can't really send pic without it
> being obvious and have already
> made a tit out of myself by
> talking like Mary Poppins.

Khady

> Pish posh! Jigetty Jog! Spit Spot!
> Found your umbrella yet?

Dimitri groups them together further along the shore, the sea gently rolling over a rainbow of black, red and white lava pebbles that rush over each other to create a gentle percussion. He claps his hands together. 'Welcome to the island of Lappo. We have just a small walk to paradise.' He gestures to a conga-line of donkeys saddled with suitcases and backpacks; Leandra-Louise's Louis Vuitton luggage suspended precariously from a leather holster. 'Let's go!'

It's the sort of balmy evening unimaginable on a cold, dark night back home in Nottingham. The sun dips behind the mountains and a breeze teases the branches of the lemon trees lining the promenade. Freya feels a whole lot better on dry land, her mouth watering at the smell of grilled octopus mixed with citrus sea spray. Piano music carries from the window of an old taverna nestled amongst a small terrace of shops and restaurants lining the seafront. Filing behind the line of donkeys, they make their way along the promenade and towards the hill looming in front of them. Further along, a small, weathered man squats down next to several piles of fresh fruit. Figs, pomegranates, lemons, limes, apricots, peaches, grapefruits and cantaloupe melons – everything looking plumper, riper and more colourful than it does on the shelves of a UK supermarket. Freya can almost taste the sweet aroma of freshly sliced watermelon. She'll be happy here.

Church bells ring as the group ambles up the narrow path and although it feels slightly antisocial to walk in single file, Freya enjoys the peace of her own thoughts which ricochet between Cypriot cuisine and Dimitri's bottom which is having the same effect on her as Djokovic in his Wimbledon whites as he jiggles in anticipation of receiving a serve. Seriously, where have these hormones come from?

The evening is alive with the ticking of cicadas and the rustling of eucalyptus leaves. Two kittens fight over a fish bone at the side of the footpath, scarpering beneath the canopy of an orange tree laden with giant globes of sun-ripened fruit as the group approaches. Further up the hill on an abandoned agricultural terrace, a mountain goat ambles over the rocks, her udders so pendulous they nearly touch the ground. The footpath steepens, the donkeys slowing as they climb higher and higher. Out of breath, Freya wonders how much further they have to go when Dimitri signals their arrival at Villa Katarina, a stone building set back behind a row of olive trees.

'Welcome to our home.' He grins. 'You are all here to experience the beauty of Greek cuisine as one big family. As they say here in Greece, "a jackdaw is always found near another jackdaw." Those who love cooking, stick together.' The top buttons of his shirt are undone, his skin beneath dewy with perspiration. 'I say this because only last year, we had guests so competitive for The Golden Spoon that there was a big fight and four people had to be transported to Paphos in a helicopter and taken to the main hospital. Fighting will not help. It is like trying to grab an egg and shave it. Please be peaceful. Respect the island and respect each other. Thank you. And now, we must undress the donkeys.'

Freya smiles to herself.

Jackdaws. Golden spoons. Shaving eggs. Undressing donkeys. Cypriot gods . . .

What's not to love about this island?

CHAPTER FOUR

The Rat

Inside, Villa Katarina is beautifully un-fancy. Freya's room looks out onto a small courtyard dotted with geraniums and boasts nothing more than a simple bed, bedside table, wardrobe and chest of drawers. The floor is a patchwork of flagstones designed to take the sting out of the heat on a hot summer's day and the walls are whitewashed with the odd bit of nautical-themed artwork dotted around: a colourful lighthouse next to the window; a dried starfish on the chest of drawers; a seascape in acrylics hanging over the bed. With fresh towels laid out on the bedside table and a shared shower and toilet down the corridor, she has everything she needs.

Dumping her bag on the floor, she unpacks the handful of books Khady threw in before she left and rearranges them next to her bed according to size; cookery books at the bottom, paperback novels in the middle, and the odd novelty book on top – *The GI Diet*, a pocket Greek phrasebook, an island hopper guide to Greece – everything finding its place until she reaches for *Mediterranean Cookery*, a slim hardback book which smells of cinnamon, its pages crisp and turmeric-stained. The cover boasts a photograph of slow-cooked lamb *kleftiko* sprinkled with oregano and surrounded by oven-roasted tomatoes, peppers and potatoes. She peels open the pages, a warmth spreading over her at the sight of Mrs K's handwriting.

Dear Freya,

Congratulations on completing your apprenticeship at Aristotle & Pignon. May your future be full of flavour and your passion for food forever nourished. I'm very proud of everything you've achieved and look forward to reading all about your future successes – I'd love for you to get in touch!

Enjoy the process,
Konstantina/Mrs K x

She runs her fingers over her Home Economics school teacher's name and thinks about Mrs Kyriakedes ('please, call me Mrs K') and the stories she'd recount about Greece. About olives so plump and flavoursome that they inspired poetry. Grapes as big as tomatoes. Tomatoes as big as grapefruits. Grapefruits as big as footballs. About the sea, the sun, the sand. Bless Mrs K; it's not everyone who sticks their neck out for a child in need, especially when they have a young family of their own and yet there she was, mentor and confidante, offering both an ear and a hand when Freya needed it the most. Her support and supporter. Her backer and champion. When the chips were down, as they often were for the daughter of a mentally unwell single parent, she could always count on Mrs K.

It was, after all, Mrs K who noticed her decline in school attendance. It was Mrs K who took it upon herself to ask questions, recognising her self-isolation behaviours. It was Mrs K who noticed her increased weariness and failure to finish tasks she previously enjoyed (cooking, for example). And it was Mrs K's friendship and compassion that encouraged her to open up and talk about home life which in turn led to her enrolment with the 'Kids as Carers' scheme. Here, she could be a child once again, focusing on fun over domesticity, choice over duty, and at long last exercise free will over fulfilling obligational burden. It was here that Freya had learned the rules of Monopoly, Cluedo and chess, as board-games were an absent guest in the Butterly caravan home. If only there was a Konstantina Kyriakedes for every Freya Butterly in this world.

Deep in thought, she catches sight of movement out of the corner of her eye. Was that something darting out from under the bed?

'*Aaargh!*' She shrieks, vaulting onto the bedside table.

Lo and behold, a rat pokes its head out of the skirting board before scurrying back under the bed, dragging its wormy tail in its wake. Claws scamper across the stone floor. The sound of scratching. The gnawing of wood. A wave of horror travels down Freya's spine. Spiders, snakes, the dark; Freya isn't afraid of most things but if there is one thing she can't abide, it's rats. Musophobia may be illogical, but reason departed the moment she laid eyes on its conical face and wiry whiskers. Her mind flashes back to the very first kitchen she worked in; a rat-infested Whitbread pub with vermin freely roving the floorboards, the kitchen eventually condemned by a Health and Safety officer who'd gone in for cheeseburger and chips and come out with a nibbled laptop cable and a warrant to close them down.

It's not so much the droppings or the spread of disease, but more the thought that the rat might scurry across her face as she sleeps. And who knows, it may well be accompanied by a string of brothers and sisters, or worse – babies. She looks around the room and shudders. It's all very well blocking up the hole in the skirting board but what with all the cracks and gaps, it would be a fruitless exercise. The sound of gnawing again. Wood splintering between tiny teeth. Ewgh. What should she do? If she plays the damsel in distress card and cries for help, she'll look like a princess and everyone will think she's ridiculous. Or worse, Dimitri could come to her rescue and then it'll look as though she's fabricated the whole—

'Hello?' The door creaks open to reveal a man dressed in overalls, his hands smeared with what looks like dried blood. 'Are you OK?'

Freya teeters on the edge of the bedside table, wondering whether the bed will break if she jumps onto it.

'Is there a problem?' He scratches at the stubble on his chin and stares at the footprints her dirty sandals have made on the furniture.

'I think you'll find most people have a problem with rats,' she says snippily.

He makes his way into her room, rotating the khaki cap on his head until the peak faces backwards. His green eyes twinkle. Beneath his unbuttoned overalls, he wears a faded grey T-shirt that pulls across his chest where a tiny triangle of sweat has formed. He rolls up his cuffs to reveal the suggestion of a sleeve tattoo, the edge culminating in a band of brilliant reds, greens and blacks. 'A rat or a mouse?'

She can't seem to breathe quickly enough. 'A rat. I saw its tail, its conical head, its—'

'Conical head?' He frowns.

'Pointed.' She grabs at her nose and mimes stretching it out into a beak.

'A bird?' His emerald eyes shimmer against his olive skin.

'No! Definitely a rat!'

He takes his phone from his back pocket and turns on its torch, illuminating the area alongside the wall.

'Can you see droppings?' She tries to control her breathing.

He shines the light back in her face. 'Have you been smoking?'

'No! I . . . look, I'm not sure I can sleep in here. Not if there are rats.'

'Hmm,' he says slowly, pulling the chest of drawers away from the wall and raising an eyebrow.

'I just meant . . . look, I know you might not be able to

see one now what with the light on and all the noise, but I swear to God . . .' The muscles in her legs feel as though they've gone into spasm and the bedside table starts to shake. 'Is it, I mean, are they . . . Could you maybe block the hole in the skirting board for starters?'

'The problem with the rat is sex.' His piercing green eyes meet hers.

Her skin starts to itch.

'When they are only five weeks old, they have sex and then continue to have lots of sex. Lots and lots of sex.' His eyes remain fixed on hers and she is unsure where to look.

'That does sound like a lot of sex,' she concedes.

'The rat is only pregnant for three weeks and she'll have ten, maybe twenty babies. Lots and lots of babies.'

She goes to speak but the words get stuck in her throat.

He holds out his hand and gestures for her to jump down. Her eyes travel across his bloodied skin. 'It's wine,' he says, clocking her look of anguish. 'I make wine. I'm Xanthos, Dimitri's twin brother.'

She studies at him, struck by how different the brothers look; Dimitri tall with light skin and golden hair whilst Xanthos has more of a sprinter's physique, his legs sturdy and muscly and his long, shaggy hair a few shades darker than that of his brother. But now that she's looking for it, there is a similarity in the shape of their faces; they share the same low, narrow forehead, high cheekbones, and Greek nose – perfectly straight with narrow nostrils. Smiling apologetically, she reaches for his outstretched hand and jumps down.

His skin feels scratchy against hers, his palms a dot-to-dot of tiny cuts with jagged edges.

'I'm Freya,' she says, finding herself eye to eye with him.

'Pleased to meet you, Free-ya.' His English is not as fluent as Dimitri's and his vowels less pronounced. 'Wait.' He holds up a finger, his attention drawn to something behind the chest of drawers. Then, crouching down and smiling, he whispers in Greek, gathering something in cupped hands and then opening them to reveal a small, brown gerbil.

'Conical head?' His eyes dance.

'I'm sorry, I just thought . . . I don't know. Maybe I imagined . . .'

He smiles. 'This is Adonis, my brother's gerbil.'

Freya takes a step towards the bundle of fur and sees two shiny black eyes staring back at her, its tail fluffy rather than wormlike, its whiskers neither wiry nor coarse, its nose more heart-shaped than conical. She chews the inside of her cheek, feeling foolish, ignorant and above all else outrageously melodramatic. 'He has a gerbil?' Her voice wavers. She didn't have Dimitri down as a gerbil kind of a guy.

'It belonged to his wife, but she left it behind when she left him, and now they are close; Dimitri and Adonis. The gerbil is the one thing he has to remember her by. He'll be happy that you found him . . . Here, you want to hold him?' Xanthos creates a gerbil treadmill, Adonis scampering faster and faster over his wine-stained hands.

Freya doesn't want to go anywhere near the gerbil, but she feels so guilty for thinking it was a rat, insulting both property and pet, that she feels she can shun neither him nor Adonis.

'Sure!' She thrusts her hands towards him and tries not to gag as tiny paws scamper across her skin, but when Adonis jumps out of her hands and scurries across her chest, his claws gripping onto the edge of her top and the unbearable sensation of a rodent's whiskers tickling her torso, it's too much.

'Get off!' she screams involuntarily.

Xanthos reaches out to grab the gerbil, his hand sliding down her top as Adonis makes his descent between her breasts.

'Xanthos?' Dimitri's head appears around the door. He looks at Freya, then back at Xanthos, his eyes travelling to his brother's hand which is halfway down Freya's vest, and lets out a torrent of Greek, his face scrunched up in anger, his arms jutting out like windmill sails.

Freya feels her cheeks flush. She looks at Dimitri. 'I'm sorry. I thought your hamster was a rat and totally freaked and Xanthos was just showing me . . .'

Dimitri stares at them both.

'Gerbil.' Xanthos clarifies, looking at Freya.

Dimitri sucks his bottom lip and reaches out for the small furry creature.

'It's not what it looks like,' Freya says, mortified. She glances at Xanthos for help, but Xanthos, it appears, is a man of few words and just stands there, one arm held up in mock surrender, the other clasped around Adonis, the smile flickering across his face suggesting he is getting mileage out of his brother's outburst.

'I'll wait outside,' Dimitri says, cradling the gerbil to his chest and shutting the door behind him.

Freya's stomach drops. She grabs her phone and follows him out.

'Nice to meet you, Free-ya,' Xanthos calls after her.

She turns back to see his grape-stained hands running over the chest of drawers. What on earth must Dimitri think of her? She's been in Cyprus for all of a few hours and has already been caught with his brother's hand down her top. Her cheeks feel as though they've caught fire. The last time she felt this ashamed was when her mum came home early and caught her masturbating on the caravan banquette in broad daylight.

Skin burning with humiliation, she makes her way out of the room, wishing it had been Dimitri's hand that had found its way down her top. And under much sexier circumstances.

CHAPTER FIVE

Sleepless in Lappo

Freya can't sleep. It's not so much about being in a foreign country, in a bed she has never slept in before, nor is it the apprehension of their first cookery task, but something else is gnawing away at her and this time it isn't a gerbil. Or is it? Was that the whisper of the wind outside or could that have been the scurrying of claws?

She slams on the light and glances around the room, but everything is as it should be and even when she holds her breath until she can hear her heartbeat pulsating in her ears, there is no sign of anything scampering where it shouldn't. Gingerly, she pivots her shoulders over the edge of the bed, her eyes sweeping the floor, but still nothing. Pfft. She lets out a rush of breath, the neon numbers on her phone confirming that it's already midnight but it feels a whole heap earlier, what with the time difference.

Khady

> Hang on, hang on. His brother 'innocently' put his hand down your top? That's more than window-shopping!

Freya

> He was trying to get a gerbil.

Khady

> Is that prison lingo? You realise you could have him done for assault?

Freya

> Would it be un-feminist of me to say I enjoyed it?

Herein lies the problem. It's not about the mouse, or the rat, or the gerbil. Or any furry creature for that matter. It's not about the impending competition or The Golden Spoon, but try as she might, Freya can't stop reliving the moment where Xanthos's piercing green eyes locked with hers as his hand slipped beneath her top, his rough skin rubbing against her breast. Worker's hands. How ridiculous that she is fixating on this moment with Xanthos when it's his brother she has a thing for. It just goes to show how starved of attention she has been over the last year or so. Sex deprivation is a slippery slope and if she's not careful, she might soon find herself fantasising about shagging that toothless man with the donkeys. Well, not *with* the donkeys per se . . .

Being a modern woman is confusing. Whilst it's totally unacceptable to depend on a man, be it financially, emotionally or practically, there are certain things a woman can't provide for herself. She glances at the zucchini which is taking up the centre spread in *Talia's Tagines*. Does a sex drive make her any less intellectual, independent or valid? Can a woman have the raging horn and still be a credible, dependable and intelligent human being? Does sexual desire compromise feminism? For fuck's sake, why is she thinking about this in the middle of the night?

The temperature has plummeted. Wrapping a jumper around her shoulders, she pads over to the window and gazes up at the moon, her thoughts wandering to her mother who will probably be going to bed right now, the warden dimming the communal corridors to indicate lights out. She might be reading a book or watching the television – every room in Stocksbridge nursing home is equipped with a twenty-four-inch plasma screen these days. Either way, her mum will be filing her fingernails with an emery board so worn down it is virtually smooth. Having rasped her fingernails every day for the last two decades, today will be no different – right down to the cuticle until her fingers are red raw and bleeding. Freya bites the inside of her cheek, guilt curdling in her stomach. She should really have checked in on her mum before she left, even if it was just for an hour. It's all very well blaming public transport and bemoaning how awful her last trip to Stocksbridge was, but she knows deep down that she should have made the effort.

The scar on her hand catches the moonlight. Like the work of a seamstress who has embroidered a river, it carries a stark and alluring beauty. She brings it to her lips, rubbing the bumpy tissue against her mouth and forgiving her mother all over again. Everything's OK, she tells herself, the scar only painful when she's exceptionally cold, and although it may still hurt in many other ways, it was a one-off. Her mother didn't mean to do it. Of course she didn't. It was merely the illness. Hallucinations. Delusions. Chaotic thoughts. Who knows who or what her mother thought Freya was at that precise moment in time – a werewolf, a rapist, a vampire, an alien about to abduct her? One thing's for sure, she clearly didn't think she was in the company of her own daughter.

Freya exhales sharply, condensation creeping across the windowpane. The cruel thing about schizophrenia is that nobody knows what the person is seeing or thinking. Perceived reality can be merciless and understanding it, as Freya has spent her whole adult life trying to do, is like trying to catch water with bare hands. Cognitive behavioural therapy (CBT) might be the answer to some people, but it barely scratches the surface for her mother who, all these years later, is still in firm denial of her illness and therefore prone to throwing away her medication, claiming she doesn't need it and swearing it's all in the mind of other people who have misjudged her, the whole sorry cycle repeating itself.

If only things could be different. For years, Freya has yearned for a nice, 'normal' mum she could chat to, depend upon and involve in day-to-day life, rather than someone she tries to love from a distance. And then she feels guilty all over again. Guilty for feeling afraid. Guilty for giving up hope that her mum will ever get better and be able to live a full and meaningful life. Guilty for leaving her mother in a nursing home whilst coming out to Cyprus to pursue her own dreams.

With her fingertip, she traces a circle around the moon in the condensation, finding comfort in the knowledge that she and her mum are united under the same silver sphere, but it's Mrs K's voice that comes to her rather than her mother's. *You are allowed to be happy. Your mum would want you to be happy. You deserve to be happy.* Freya bites hard on her lip. Her mum may be in the best place right now, but it would be better if she could live freely and see the moon from this angle where it glows a milky cream in the velvet night sky surrounded by stars so bright, they really do twinkle like diamonds. *You deserve to be happy.* She takes a deep breath. 'Good night, Mum,' she says aloud.

Leaving the shutters open and the curtains pulled apart, she goes back to bed, moving her pillow to the other end, and repositioning it this way and that until the glow of the moon falls across her face like a mother's touch. Clutching her beloved empty perfume bottle she keeps in her bag at all times, and rubbing her finger over the smooth, solid glass, she eventually falls asleep.

CHAPTER SIX

The Rules

In the morning, Freya feels surprisingly fresh. Breakfast takes place on Villa Katarina's south-facing terrace, a large table set for seven in the shade of an old eucalyptus tree. Baskets of fresh sesame-seed bread sit alongside wooden bowls spilling over with fresh fruit. Peaches, figs, pears, plums. The smell of rosemary infuses the air and the view from the veranda is something Freya could only dream of waking to every morning for the rest of her life; turquoise sea framed by cypress trees, wild tulips and a vibrant yellow flower she doesn't recognise. Birds chirp, insects hum and a small, orange gecko scurries out from a potted geranium and darts up the stone wall into a tangle of honeysuckle.

'Mint, innit?' Harj says, passing Freya a glass of water.

Freya takes a sip, crunching on ice as the warm summer air coils around her bare legs; the Mediterranean balm is certainly a different kind of heat to the kitchen inferno she is used to. Feeling pleasantly aglow rather than uncomfortably hot, she wanders over to a tray of coffee brewed on hot sand and wonders what André and Courtney will be up to now and whether they've even noticed her absence. Probably not.

'A word of advice . . .' A well-dressed man with a strong French accent approaches her, lowering his voice conspiratorially. 'Do not drink the last bit.'

Freya stands there like a lemon, trying to work out whether his advice is actual or metaphorical. *Do not drink the last bit.* Is this code for something?

'I'm Stéphane.' He extends his hand.

'Freya.' She smiles.

'We arrived late last night so we haven't had the chance to meet everyone. This is my partner, Michel.' He beckons over a short man with a square jaw who stands next to the villa, studying the leaves of a small green herb in one of the window boxes.

'*Bonjour.*' Michel wanders over, shifting Dolce & Gabbana framed sunglasses onto the bridge of his nose. He wears a pristine chef jacket with gold embroidery and chequered trousers.

'Nice to meet you.' Freya goes to shake his hand, but he is already helping himself to freshly baked bread. Her eyes shift to his monogrammed lapel. *M.V. Chef d'Or.* Should she know him? Is he a popular brand amongst French cuisine?

Stéphane shakes his head apologetically. 'I'm sorry. He's always like this on a competition day. He has to be alone.'

Freya reaches for a bread roll. 'Do you do a lot of competitions?'

'For me, no. For Michel, many. He's the serious one and I am the support chef.'

'But you qualified too, right? It's both of you cooking?'

'Yes.' Stéphane takes a seat at the table.

'Hardly a support act then!' Freya lets out a nervous laugh. 'Most people don't get to sit the written exam, let alone pass it!'

Stéphane smiles bashfully. 'I didn't mean to be . . .'

'Flippant!' Hazel bustles between them with a full plate of spicy sausage. 'You didn't mean to be *flippant*.'

Freya raises an apologetic eyebrow in Stéphane's direction and sits down next to Kwame whilst Hazel assumes her position at the head of the table and helps herself to tea.

'Where are you from then, Freya?' Hazel says in a way that probably isn't meant to sound snooty but undeniably does.

'Nottingham,' Freya says, softening her voice to try to make it sound glamorous, but the potency of the treacly coffee catches her off guard evoking a sharp cough in her throat.

'Notting 'ill?' Michel tucks the label back into Stéphane's shirt collar and sits down.

'*Notting Hill* is Michel's favourite film.' Stéphane reaches for the marmalade. 'He loves Hugh Grant.'

'Not as much as I love Hugh Bonneville,' Michel says, helping himself to butter.

'I've always loved Notting Hill,' Hazel says. 'My father

once owned an apartment overlooking Portobello Road. One of the colourful Battenberg ones. I can't remember whether it was lemon yellow or baby blue, but it was smashing. We enjoyed a wonderful Christmas there one year and I believe the prime minister himself was there to turn on the lights.'

Freya wonders at what point she should clarify that she doesn't live in one of the Brit flick-worthy pastel-shaded mansions of Notting Hill but instead inhabits a crumb-ridden sofa in Khady's high-rise flat, situated in a suburb of Nottingham synonymous with gun crime where they're lucky if they get one of the minor characters from the *Coronation Street* of ten years ago to turn on the lights. However, the moment has passed and Harj is now holding court at the other end of the table, accompanied by Leandra-Louise who has crammed herself into a strapless dress and stiletto-heeled sandals for the impending day of cookery.

'It's like *Love Island*, innit?' Harj says, trying not to look at Leandra-Louise's chest.

'I hope not,' Freya mutters under her breath.

'*Love Island* meets *MasterChef*,' Leandra-Louise giggles.

'Is that the one where they have to eat bugs?' Hazel says, the corners of her mouth curling up in disgust.

'That's *I'm a Celebrity*.' Harj says. 'You've got to get down with the kids, innit Hazel?'

A smile spreads across Freya's face. Every ragtag group of strangers needs someone like Harj to break the ice and keep the conversation flowing.

'*Love Island*'s more of a hook-up show.' Harj explains and

with smiling eyes, nudges Hazel's arm. 'So, what are you doing later, Hazel?'

Hazel's eyes sparkle with mischief and for a moment Harj looks worried.

'Only joking,' he says hurriedly, looking to Leandra-Louise for assistance. 'My dad loves all those shows. My mum says he's wasting his life away, but he can't get enough of them. Especially anything with food. He'd die if *Bake Off* didn't get recommissioned.'

Freya coats her bread with the creamiest of butter and wonders what TV shows her father would like and whether he too has a flair for food. Her love of gastronomy certainly hasn't come from her mother who raised her on jacket potatoes and baked beans before she was left to fend for herself, aged eleven. Then again, her diet was probably dictated by economic constraints rather than any lack of culinary creativity, her mother unable to hold down a job once her health took a dive.

At times, it would be good to know a little bit about her father, her mother unable to recall whether he was tall or short, stocky or slight, or even what nationality he was. Is he still alive? Where does he live? Would he choose sweet or salty popcorn? Could he identify cheese by its taste alone? The only thing her mother does remember is that he was in the armed forces. Just that. Air Force? Navy? Artillery? Who knows, the uniform and medals were apparently memorable but little else, save that she thought she was a sex-worker called Esmerelda when she met him.

The conversation returns to food, Kwame mentioning

anecdotally that Gordon Ramsay swung by 'one of his restaurants' for lunch, leaving a rave review of his melt-in-the-mouth moussaka.

Freya feels her stomach churn.

'Have you met Chef Ramsay?' Kwame asks her.

She tightens her grip around her coffee cup and shakes her head apologetically.

Hazel's eyes light up. 'He's great, isn't he?'

''e was rude about my meatballs,' Michel says, dropping a large grape into his mouth.

'There's nothing the matter with your meatballs.' Stéphane slings an arm around Michel's shoulder.

'I once met Mary Berry,' Leandra-Louise says. 'She looked a lot smaller in real life.'

Freya's mouth goes dry. Is she the only one who isn't on first name terms with a celebrity chef and had her food sampled by someone in-the-know? She knocks back the last bit of her drink, coughing and spluttering as coffee grains cling to the roof of her mouth, the insides of her cheeks gritty and the gaps between her teeth full of sediment.

Stéphane laughs. 'I did warn you!'

The bitter taste and gritty texture are unbearable. She takes a gulp of water and rushes to the door of the villa which turns out to be locked. Running to the other side of the building, she swills the water around her mouth and as there is nobody around, goes to spit the residue into the branches of a rhododendron bush just as Dimitri appears around the corner, copping the whole mouthful on his flip-flopped foot.

'Ewggh!' He recoils, looking down at his coffee-flecked toes.

'Oh shit, I'm so sorry!' Freya says, her face burning with shame.

'What's the matter with you?' he says angrily.

'I – I – I'm so sorry. It was the coffee. And the grains. And I just . . .' she splutters, watching his retreating back as he heads to an ornate fountain sculpted into the shape of a mermaid and washes his feet under a jet of water.

How the hell did that just happen? Out of all the people, at all the times . . . Is fate conspiring against her? First the gerbil. Now the coffee. What the hell must he think of her? Mortified, she clasps her hands around her mouth. 'I'm honestly so sorry.'

'It's OK,' he says, plastering a 'the customer is always right' smile on his face. 'Maybe you could give me a hand with the board.' He nods to a wooden scoreboard on casters.

'Sure,' she says, her eyes drawn to the fresh white T-shirt that clings to his chest.

He drags one side of the wooden scoreboard whilst she pushes the other, her pulse quickening as his strong arms expand and flex as they navigate the corner of the building and it strikes her as odd that someone with his pin-up looks and Olympian athleticism should spend his extra-curricular time doting on a small rodent. Seriously, could she really ever date a guy with a gerbil? And why is she now fantasising about dating him? Window-shopping only, remember. Get a grip!

'Thank you,' he says as they reach the terrace.

She sits back down with the others and stares at the board. The names of each guest are neatly etched in chalk down the left-hand side whilst a variety of dishes are listed horizontally:

koupepia, pasticcio koupes with tzatziki, kolokythokeftedes, pantzaria gazpacho, kotopoulo me kolokassi, sheftalies and other unpronounceable words that on Freya's tongue sound as though they originated in the Jurassic period.

'Good morning!' Dimitri positions himself in front of them all, Freya swallowing hard as he removes his shades, his eyes glittering like polished jade.

'I hope you all slept well. Today is going to be great but before the fun begins, a few ground rules.' Dimitri smiles at the dragonfly that has just landed on his arm, its iridescent blue body twitching as its intricate lace wings unfold. 'You will have a task to complete every day. Sometimes one dish, sometimes more. Each dish carries a number of points. Five for first place, three for second, two for third and one for anyone who generally did a great job but didn't make the top three. Zero for anything substandard. You will be judged on taste, texture and presentation.'

Harj raises his hand. 'Shouldn't winning with a main course be worth more than winning with a starter?'

Dimitri pinches his jaw between his thumb and fingers, a small dimple forming in the centre of his chin. 'Is a cow more valuable than a dog?'

Harj's brow puckers.

Dimitri runs his fingers over his full lips. 'It's not about size; "Flavour and savour," my auntie always taught me. All dishes are equal in value. Never underestimate the complexity of a starter.' He kicks the gravel beneath his feet, his eyes flickering across the group. 'At the end of the week you will prepare your take on a traditional Cypriot meal for our judges.

Only the top two chefs on the scoreboard will go through to the final in Paphos.' Freya feels her chest tighten. 'I think you all understand the grand final: Three courses. An audience. A television crew. Screened for a small British television channel. You all speak English, so it'll be fine. It's a big deal though. Got it?'

Nobody says a word. The moment is too big, the stakes too high and the wind has been knocked out of their combined fleet of sails.

'And just to make things clear . . .' Dimitri's eyes flicker from one person to the next. 'There is no guarantee that The Golden Spoon will be issued at all. The food must be especially special – the best of the best – to merit The Golden Spoon.'

'Statistically, you have a one point nine eight recurring chance of securing The Golden Spoon.' Harj grins. 'My dad did the maths.'

'And that's what makes it so exciting!' Dimitri claps his hands together.

Freya's eyelid twitches. Does she really have less than a two per cent chance of attaining her life's dream? She cannot go home empty-handed. She has wanted The Golden Spoon since she was nine years old and spent her entire teenage life girl-crushing on Talia Drakos, her all-time hero whose magazine photo she tacked to the wafer-thin caravan wall of her bedroom. Wishing she could cook like Talia, talk like Talia, dress like Talia. Be Talia. Hell, she even tried to diet her way into a jumpsuit two-sizes too small plucked from a charity shop bargain bin, deluding herself that she, too, could be a high-energy, happy-go-lucky award-winning chef whilst all the other girls in her class favoured Britney and were clueless as to who Talia Drakos was. It's not just some fly-by-night fixation either. Freya has always meant business. She has studied, experimented, improvised and worked hard to improve her recipes and has the burns to prove it – cooking three-course meals out of a single pan on a caravan stove. Christ, she wants this so badly she could out-and-out combust.

'I'd honestly do anything for The Golden Spoon,' Leandra-Louise says, licking her lips and looking up at Dimitri.

'I think we all would,' Kwame says. 'This is my third time and I've yet to get through to the final.'

Dimitri clears his throat. 'There are no shortcuts. The only way is to cook to the best of your ability. Focus, focus, focus.'

Freya weighs up her competition. Kwame seems like the real deal and obviously has Michelin star quality what with his celebrity chef dealings and Glaswegian restaurant village. Having been here before, he knows what to expect and won't be anywhere near as terrified as Freya is. Hazel clearly has high expectations and seems to have done a whole load of research Freya hasn't. Then there's Michel and Stéphane who have rescheduled their wedding for this opportunity, Michel clearly taking it very seriously. And let's not forget Leandra-Louise who certainly has the potential to be a dark horse – as Mrs K used to say, 'Never judge a cake by its icing.' And finally, Harj who has already proven he can make a mean baklava and is as equally devoted to the quest. She chews her fingernails. It's too early to predict a winner, but it's clear that nobody is here for shits and giggles.

'The odds may be against you but it's certainly possible.

Others have proven it can be done but one thing is for sure: The Golden Spoon is only awarded in rare circumstances. It is not for the faint-hearted.' Dimitri wows them with a glittering smile, his eyes ablaze with effervescence. 'Now it's time for me to leave you in the expert hands of Christos, who is an excellent cook from mainland Greece. Raised in Athens, he comes with a wealth of culinary know-how, and my brother and I are delighted that he recently agreed to join our team. He will teach you how to make some of the finest Cypriot dishes around.' He reaches for the sunglasses on his head and drops them onto the bridge of his nose. 'Please, come this way and I will escort you to the Bazigou Taverna.'

Freya takes stock. The odds may not be in her favour, the competition is fierce, but The Golden Spoon is finally within her reach.

CHAPTER SEVEN

Bazigou Taverna

Khady

> Googled Bazigou Taverna and NOTHING.
> No digital footprint at all. Also when I type
> in Golden Spoon, it comes up with an
> octogenarian dating website. Is any of this
> legit?

Khady

> PS Yeah, the spitting coffee on his bare
> feet thing sounds deeply uncool and
> borderline foot fetishy, but you've done way
> un-cooler things.

Freya

Like what?

Khady

Having a crush on Stalin.

Freya

Young Stalin! And how was I supposed to know it was him? I thought they'd just got a model in for the book cover. Besides, retro crushes don't count. You thought Biden looked hot when he was in his twenties.

Khady

Touché, bitch.

Bazigou Taverna may not have a digital footprint, but it certainly has the most breathtakingly beautiful physical footprint imaginable. Hugging one of the sweetest spots of the island, it sits atop the craggy clifftop and looks out across an expanse of pristine, emerald water – the perfect place to dine whilst watching the sun set over the sea, and the moon rise behind the mountains. Dimitri leads them through a terraced dining area dotted with planters tumbling with vibrant flowers and over to the cookery school.

Inside, the taverna has neither the skylights of *MasterChef* nor the al fresco ventilation of *Bake Off*'s catering tent, but what it lacks in sunlight, it makes up for in character, the room dark and cool, its walls a mishmash of fishing nets and antique doors. Once her eyes have adjusted to the dark, Freya can make out an old sewing machine, a giant map of the island, a rope swing, and a vintage camera on a tripod; not a single bit of space is unclaimed, but it's not until Dimitri slides open the entire far wall, hinged wooden panels concertinaing back on themselves with a clackety-clack, and blinding daylight pouring in, that Freya can see the taverna in its full glory. Sunshine injects colour into the mosaic floor. Yellow golds offsetting vibrant turquoises. Plants climb out of baskets and into wine bottles, their leaves curling around framed photos, transistor radios, and over painted chairs that have been nailed halfway up the wall. From the ceiling hangs a cluster of plastic funnels, copper pitchers and metal colanders which jangle against each other in the sea breeze.

'Have fun, guys!' Dimitri says, grabbing his motorbike helmet and heading out. He turns back to them. 'I'll be back later to taste your goods.'

She smiles, deciding that gerbil or no gerbil, she'd quite like her goods tasted by Dimitri Bazigou.

'Come see the view!' A man in chef's whites appears from the kitchen, perspiration bubbling on his brow. His eyes are glassy and sunken, and the dark circles below them speak of heartache and sleepless nights. Thick, white whiskers jut out of his chin like potato sprouts born from neglect rather than by design. With cherry-red cheeks and wire-framed spectacles

perched on the end of his nose, he'd make a great Father
Christmas were it not for his thin body and the smell of his
hangover breath – a musty smell laced with the aftermath of
last night's liquor. Sherry? Whisky? Rum? Whatever it was, it
can't have been an isolated incident – the broken blood vessels
around his nose attest to that.

He shuffles over to the edge of the room, his swollen feet
stuffed into soft leather slippers which slap against the patchwork of intricately patterned floor tiles. The others follow,
Freya fighting her way to the front until she too can see what
everyone is oohing and aahing about. Teetering on the edge
of the cliff, the taverna is what the infinity pool is to the
bathing pond, its south-facing terrace giving way to a sheer
drop into the turquoise sea behind glass panelling. She takes
a picture of it with her phone but it's impossible to capture
either the magic of the view or the heady feeling of vertigo as
she looks down at the waves crashing against the rocks below.

'OK, everybody. Come, sit down, sit down, please.' With
movements befitting a man a few decades older than he looks,
he leads them back inside the taverna, clutching onto furniture
as he goes, and finally points to a set of high stools nestled
under a long trestle table.

Freya takes the seat between Harj and Kwame who proves
to be quite territorial about his kitchen utensils, moving his
chopping board and knives out of her reach and wrapping his
arms around his allocated stack of vine leaves. Paranoia,
mind-destroyer. She shudders, remembering that's what the
guy in the neighbouring caravan used to say about her mum.
She pushes the thought out of her mind, glancing at the various

saucers of pre-weighed ingredients set out for each contestant, making it more or less cookery paint by numbers.

'My name is Christos.' Their chef sharpens a large knife against a steel rod, the scrape of metal against metal sending a shiver down Freya's spine. 'Christos, King of the Kitchen.' He belly-laughs, stretching out his arms and beating his chest Tarzan-like. 'This morning we will prepare a traditional Cypriot dish, *koupepia*. Some of you may know this as *dolmades* but in Cyprus we do not add *avgolemono* sauce – instead, we season with a blend of cinnamon, tomato and seasonal herbs. And then this afternoon, we will prepare *pasticcio koupes* with *tzatziki*.' He enunciates each vowel, Freya realising she's been pronouncing both wrong for the best part of a decade.

Christos shuffles over to the head of the table and takes a gulp from a mug, featuring a semi-naked swimwear model whose bikini has faded away in the dishwasher.

'OK, *koupepia*. First, we will need vine leaves from the grape which we wash, blanch and drain.' He holds up a fresh, green leaf so thin it's almost translucent. His hand trembles, the leaf with it. 'Soon, we will explore the vineyards and show you how to find the most soft and tender leaves, but today we will focus on the filling.' He takes another gulp from his mug and swallows loudly, reminding Freya of the way her granddad used to drink tea.

'I suppose if the vine leaves are fresh out of a jar, they'll already be brined and it's just a matter of rinsing?' Hazel's expression carries the haughtiness of a camel.

'Fresh out of a jar?' Christos frowns. 'Nothing is fresh if it is out of a jar.'

'I'm talking about when we're back at home and don't have the luxury of a vineyard on our doorstep,' Hazel says curtly.

Christos massages his jaw as though deep in thought, then finally looks up. 'If you have no vine leaves, you use silverbeet. If you have no silverbeet, cabbage leaves or zucchini flowers, but if it's in a tin, it's straight in the bin.'

Freya smiles with satisfaction, enjoying his little rhymes and the way he is able to put know-it-all Hazel back in her box.

'Then the most important thing,' he says gruffly, his trembling hand reaching for a saucer of ground meat. 'Why do we eat so much lamb in Greece?'

'Because you have a lot of sheep?' Harj grins.

'Because you don't have any cows?' Kwame joins in.

'Because it tastes the best.' Christos roars. 'Lamb is tender. Lamb is succulent. Lamb is mouth-watering, versatile and rich in zinc and vitamin B and for this reason, I am a lambassador!' He smiles broadly as though waiting for applause.

'It's very fatty though.' Hazel fusses with her apron.

Christos cocks his head to one side and looks up at her. 'What's your name?'

'Hazel Stevenson,' she says proudly.

'Hazel Stevenson, I see the feet got up to hit the head. Yes, of course lamb has fat, but this is good fat. It is what makes it moist and taste so good!'

Christos spends the next ten minutes reeling off a dozen or so lamb delicacies whilst intermittently gulping from his mug. Taking a large bowl, he demonstrates how to mix all the ingredients which make up the stuffing, Freya observing his every move as he takes a frying pan and sautés diced onion until transluscent and then browns off minced lamb, mixing in wild rice, dill, mint and chopped celery. The smell of oregano fills the room as he folds herbs and freshly made tomato purée into the mix until it becomes a thick paste.

'Many people, they are thinking "why celery?"' he says, pouring in a litre of lamb stock and reducing the heat. 'Why use a food that burns more calories eating it than it gives? And I tell them this . . .' His eyes widen. 'The rainbow is not just made of red, yellow, blue. It takes all colours to create the full spectrum just as it takes all flavours to make a meal. Celery gives us texture. It adds depth. It gives us crunch.' He thrusts a stick of celery in Hazel's direction. 'A man without a stick is only half a man.'

Hazel's eyes widen until, with tufted eyebrows and a beak-like nose, she takes on the look of a tawny owl.

Christos plucks a leaf out of the bowl set in the centre of the worktop. 'Always shiny side down,' he says, embarking on a lecture about vine leaves and the importance of selecting a good light-green colour, four to five inches wide, and avoiding fuzzy thick leaves with holes. 'Small leaves will tear. Large leaves are tough and chewy. You want medium-sized, shiny smooth leaves.'

Once the filling has simmered for ten minutes, he tastes a little off the tip of his teaspoon, smacking his lips together with satisfaction and adding an extra handful of chopped mint for good measure. Then, spooning the mixture onto the stem of the leaf, he folds both sides towards the middle. Like centipede legs, his fingers gallop at pace, sprinkling, rolling, pinching and squeezing. He could clearly do this in his sleep.

'Roll up. Roll up. From bottom to top.' He demonstrates. 'And make sure there are no holes. Very important. Holy grail. Holy cow. Holy Moses. But not holey *koupepia*. OK? If you have holes, the parcels will open whilst cooking.' He sprinkles in lemon juice and a dash of olive oil, pours more stock over the small leafy bundles and covers the pot on the stove.

'OK, over to you,' he says, downing the dregs of his mug and rubbing his hands together with glee.

Freya starts to panic. Did he season with salt and pepper at the beginning or halfway through and has he used the lemon juice yet? She glances at her fellow cooks who give off an air of casual intrigue. *Koupepia* may be child's play to everyone else, but it certainly isn't to her. Her pulse quickens as she looks at the vine leaves set out on each plate, vein side up, but then a feeling of calm sets in. She knows to taste test throughout. She knows how and when to season. She knows that texture and touch on the tongue override anything you can learn in a textbook. She has all the tools for the job and if she's to go home with The Golden Spoon, she needs to trust her instinct and keep her nerve.

Taking on board everything Christos said, she makes her way over to her allocated stove and reaching over Kwame's pan, accidentally dangles her sleeve in his water.

'Tch.' He swats her out of the way with his tea towel.

'Sorry,' she says, trying to get a grip and calm the fuck down.

The trick is not to panic. Just as animals smell fear and play on it, food also needs a strong, confident hand. And love. She learned from Mrs K that you are always rewarded by the love you put into food. Stir lovingly. Kneed lovingly.

Grate lovingly, and do not rush. The moment you take a shortcut and deprive your food of the love that it deserves, it tastes just that one bit less delicious. People can screw you over – you can devote your life to loving someone and still not be loved in return, but food will always return your emotional investment.

Face tingling in the steam of the boiling water, she drops the vine leaves in, letting them swoosh around in the bubbles before plucking them out and dunking them into a bowl of iced water, watching as their deep green pigmentation comes to life. Then it's on to the lamb. The kitchen is alive with the shimmying of pan handles and the buzz of timers. She browns off the meat, adding in chopped celery, sautéed onion and a dash of sea salt, then stops to taste test, checking for depth of flavour, acidity and fat content. It's a little salty. Acidity will help neutralise the salt flavour. She reaches for the white wine vinegar and sees that she's already lagging behind. How is everyone else so lightning fast? Mixing in dill and fresh mint, she races to fold in her remaining ingredients and looks down at the sloppy sludge. Disaster. How did she manage to overdo it with the tomato purée? She glances over at Michel's beautiful blend of rice, lamb, vegetables, herbs and seasoning. How the hell can his look so perfect when hers looks like it's been vomited up? Breathe. Breathe. Breathe. She spoons the gloop into the centre of her leaf, but no matter how many times she tucks in the edges of the vine leaf, it springs back open.

'Not too tight, not too loose.' Christos walks between them, steadying himself on the furniture as he goes. 'Roll it like a small cigar.'

Mrs K's advice rings in her ears. *You can't hurry food like you can't hurry love. Shortcuts produce shortcomings. Enjoy the process.* But it's difficult when you're up against the clock.

'Looking good,' she says, glancing at Harj's row of perfect bundles.

'Plenty of practice from rolling all those joints!' he says, setting up his own mini production line and generating one leafy package after another.

Freya tries to resurrect her first roll, but every time she goes to tuck in the stem end, rice prolapses from the sides.

'You used too much filling,' Harj says loudly, inviting the others to rubberneck at her abomination.

One at a time they turn to watch as she attempts to patch the leaves together, all fingers and thumbs, her heart beating like the clappers.

'Fat fingers.' She smiles apologetically.

'All finished?' Christos picks up an enormous tomato and slices it so fast his fingers are a blur. Placing the wafer-thin segments to one side, he lines the base with a few leftover vine leaves and looks up. 'The leaves will prevent sticking and burning.'

Freya glances at the neat rows of equally sized *koupepia* stretching out in front of her fellow cooks and then looks back to her own, dread pooling in her stomach.

'Having a problem?' Christos watches as she tries to resurrect another bundle which has fallen open.

'Urm.' If only she could take a running jump out of the open window and into the sea.

Harj eventually takes hold of the leaf for her. 'It's because you're left-handed. You're trying to copy the King of the Kitchen but he's doing everything the other way around.'

Freya smiles weakly. Bless Harj, what a lovely way of rescuing her. Buoyed by solidarity, she finishes the dish, dripping oil onto a sheet of baking foil and wrapping it over the bowl as demonstrated by Christos who is now half-asleep at the end of the table.

'Forty-five minutes in the oven,' he slurs, but before they can ask him which oven, he has dozed off.

An hour later, Dimitri's motorbike judders over the gravel, the whine of its engine stopping abruptly outside the taverna. He removes his helmet and runs his fingers over his chin. Freya imagines what it would be like to sit on the back of his bike, her arms wrapped around his trim, taut waist, wind in her hair, her body pressed against his. She still has the image in her head when he is standing amongst them, fork in hand, steam rising from the plates arrayed in front of him, only snapping out of it when he nears her collapsed *koupepia* – the vine leaves splayed open and their innards spewed all over the dish like blown-out brains. If only they weren't hers, but there's no mistaking her turquoise sticker.

Dimitri goes to the first tray with the red sticker and spears the nearest food parcel with his fork, dropping it onto the small plate next to him and glancing around the group. Judging by the proud smirk on her face, this first batch belongs to Hazel.

'To begin, I am looking for presentation because we always eat with our eyes first. Then I am looking for texture. But most importantly, I am looking for taste,' Dimitri says.

Biting into the first of the *koupepia*, he chews softly. 'Beautiful fragrance in the rice.'

Hazel's smile broadens.

'A good blend of herbs and tomato. The meat though is a little dry.'

Hazel hastily rearranges the grin on her face into one of stoic acceptance as Dimitri pushes the plate away and moves on to the tray with the yellow sticker. 'This one, not too dry, the meat is tender. The mint and fennel are tasty. Very good. Whose is this?' His eyes dart from face to face.

Harj beams like a faithful lighthouse.

'Well done, very good job.' Dimitri smiles.

Hazel leans forward. 'Although shouldn't he have ideally made them look a lot better?'

Freya shares a wide-eyed look with Harj, her churning stomach ramping up to full spin as Dimitri draws nearer to her dish. Can he not just put her out of her misery?

'Good morning!' Xanthos appears at the door with a crate of wine bottles, his thick, dark hair escaping the confines of a baseball cap.

Dimitri beckons him over. 'Come and taste.'

Xanthos slides the wine bottles into a cupboard and joins the rest of the group. Plucking a fork from the table and turning it on its side, he digs into a *koupepia* wrap from the tray with the pink sticker that Dimitri has lined up and takes a mouthful.

Kwame watches eagerly.

'Not overcooked. Not undercooked. The rice is light and fluffy, the meat is tender, the flavours fresh and fragrant. Delicious.' Xanthos nods, still chewing. 'Congratulations to the chef.'

Kwame nods his gratitude.

The judging continues, Dimitri and Xanthos letting out a stream of complimentary grunts peppered with suggestions for small improvements. 'Don't overdo it with the fennel.' 'Wild rice is a tough seed, so it needs time to absorb the water.' 'Don't fold too tight as the rice will expand during cooking.'

'And finally, this one.' Dimitri nudges Xanthos over to Freya's dish.

Freya's toes curl inside her shoes as Xanthos peers into the meat dish and lowers his fork into the congealed mess. But before he can sample her dish, Dimitri grabs his arm.

'This one is a waste of time.' Dimitri frowns. 'It is neither *koupepia* nor *dolmades*. If the chef cannot be bothered to make this into a parcel, we cannot be bothered to taste it. Disqualified!'

Freya's face burns with humiliation as stolen glances shift across the table. At least on *Bake Off*, they're respectful and always manage to pluck at least one redeeming quality out of thin air but this is like being back at infant school, the only child unable to spell her name.

Xanthos lowers his fork once more. 'Maybe the taste will make up for it.'

'No.' Dimitri folds his arms with finality. '*Koupepia* means little cigars and yet here there is no roll of tobacco leaves, only mixture.' A sharp pain shoots through Freya's chest. To think that only yesterday she was crushing on this man and now he is crushing her to bits. Publicly. Loudly. Excruciatingly. 'This is not contained in the wrap and is therefore not a filling.'

Xanthos glares at him. 'Not everything is about looks, Dimitri.'

'Winner!' Dimitri points to Kwame's creations. 'Runner-up.' His finger travels to the dish that belongs to Harj. 'And this one, third place.' He points to Leandra-Louise's creation.

Michel turns the shade of grenadine and storms out of the room.

'*Chéri?*' Stéphane calls after him, then turns to shrug at them apologetically. 'He's very competitive.'

'Aren't we all!' Hazel quips.

'I'm afraid it's zero points for you, Freya,' Dimitri says, his tone now sympathetic.

Freya can't look at anyone on the way out. No matter how much she reasons that it's one small mistake and that she can recover on the next task, she feels sub-human and unworthy. Watching through the window as Dimitri chalks their names on the leader board, she feels the weight of failure bearing down on her shoulders. She has earned a great big fat zero points whilst her fellow cooks have all leaped ahead of her. How can she claw this back?

She must not let The Golden Spoon slide out of her grasp.

CHAPTER EIGHT

Tzatziki

Kwame	5
Harj	3
Leandra-Louise	2
Michel	1
Hazel	1
Stéphane	1
Freya	0

'Don't worry.' Harj holds up a wooden spoon as though it's a microphone and bursts into song, channelling his inner D:Ream. 'Things can only get better!'

Freya isn't so sure. This afternoon's task is to prepare beef and pork *koupes* with a side of *tzatziki*, something she must have made a hundred times over with Mrs K but performing under pressure is an altogether different proposition as this morning demonstrated. *Happy is the heart that cooks with all its soul.* Dear Mrs K.

She calls to mind her first taste of *tzatziki*, an experience she'll never forget. She was at school, Year 7, when unbeknown to her, Mrs K had peeped in her lunchbox and replaced her stale sandwich with a home-made brownie, a juicy apple, lamb in fresh pita and a creamy dip in a small pot. At first, she thought she'd taken somebody else's packed lunch by mistake, but when Mrs K's twinkly eyes met hers, she knew it was orchestrated. A special secret. The taste of the lamb was sublime, but it was the cool and refreshing *tzatziki* offset against the soft bread that really sated her taste buds, the sensation heavenly, and those minutes spent devouring it were some of the best of her life. Mrs K watched, smiling contentedly from the shade of an outbuilding, but before Freya could thank her, she was gone.

Back on the terrace, the afternoon sun beats down, a light breeze lifting the corners of the gingham tea towels covering the ingredients, reminding Freya of the annual summer party Stocksbridge nursing home holds, and sending a shudder of unease down her spine. She really should have told her mother she was coming out here. Wracked with guilt, she watches as Christos, back on his feet, winds down an awning that casts just enough shadow to shield everyone from the sun's rays. Music plays in the bar and as though choreographed, a butterfly dances over the pepper pot before retreating to a nearby geranium. Her mum would love this place. Oh, to be free to fly like that butterfly without the downward pull of guilt upon her wings.

Christos positions himself at the end of the table. 'And now, my friends, *pasticcio koupes* with a side of *tzatziki*.'

Making her way to the other side of the table, Freya finds a space between Leandra-Louise and Harj.

'OK, who knows what makes *tzatziki*?' Christos anchors his fists against the table.

'Tesco?' Leandra-Louise giggles.

Christos frowns. 'I'm sorry, I have lost my eggs and my baskets.'

'Just ignore her,' Harj says playfully. 'She knows not what she's on'eth about.'

'Ah, shut your face!' Leandra-Louise swats him away with what comes across as post-coital familiarity.

Christos clears his throat. 'Let me start again. What ingredients do we need for *tzatziki*?'

'Cucumber,' Leandra-Louise says, trying to regain favour.

'Cucumber.' Christos slams a cucumber down, making the table shake.

'Lemon juice,' Freya says, thinking back to Mrs K's recipe.

'Not just the juice of a lemon, but also the zest.' Christos pinches together his fingers and shakes them passionately before producing a lemon so large it doesn't look real.

Hazel steps forward. 'Fresh mint, garlic, dill and yoghurt.'

'What sort of yoghurt?' Christos reaches for one of the dusty bottles of wine from the shelf behind him.

'Strained.' A condescending smile lingers on Hazel's face.

'Greek!' Christos slams his hands down on the table, making the cutlery clink. 'It must be Greek!'

Hazel's eyes widen like saucers. 'But you said earlier—'

'Do not trust that the apple always falls in the same place, Hazel.' Christos pops the cork of a dusty wine bottle and refills his mug. 'The Greeks invented many things. The water-wheel. The Olympic Games. Democracy.'

A look of puzzlement descends across Harj's face. 'The Greeks invented democracy?'

'*Demokratia. Kratos* meaning power. *Demos* meaning people. Power of the people,' Christos says, Freya making a mental note to check this out on Wikipedia on their next break whilst Harj nods in awe. 'Now on to the *koupes*. Maybe you think you know them as croquettes, but they are different. With *koupes* we do not dust with breadcrumbs but panko crumbs to give that wonderful crunch.' He moves over to the hob, places a saucepan over a medium heat, adds a splash of olive oil and, once the pan is hot, dollops two great handfuls of minced pork and beef in the middle, breaking down lumps with a wooden spoon until the consistency is perfect. Freya watches transfixed as the meat browns and onion, roasted garlic and fresh tomato purée are thrown into the mix along with a jug of white wine. Thoughts evaporating along with the wine, she finds herself staring at a bubbling pan of stock and cinnamon sticks, consumed by fear. If she's to stand a chance in this competition, she cannot afford to fuck this up.

Putting aside the pan, Christos sets about making a Cypriot version of Béchamel sauce whilst the boiled bulgur wheat is cooling, and then it's on to the *koupes*. Dunking his fingers in a bowl of water, he takes a ball of bulgur wheat the size of an apricot and rolls it back and forth until it becomes the shape of a flattened disc. Freya studies his technique. In spite of his shaky hands, his movements are deliberate and precise – everything a chef should be. Moulding each one into a neat meat parcel and coating in egg wash, he then dusts with panko crumbs and grated *kaskavalli*. Freya shuffles her weight from foot to foot, the soles of her trainers squelching against the hot floor tiles. How does he make it look so effortless?

The temperature rises as the *koupes* hit the fryer and the smell of Mediterranean pork infuses the room, Harj sniffing the air and letting out a playful, 'mmm.' Then they all watch in silent appreciation as Christos serves up the final dish with a slice of lemon and a parsley and coriander garnish, inviting each contestant to sample it along with the *tzatziki*. To say it tastes delicious is an understatement – the crunchy, spicy coating dissolving into tender, aromatic pork and beef which melts in your mouth, offset by the cool, refreshing *tzatziki*. A hollow feeling of intimidation creeps over Freya. How can she match that, and all against the clock?

'OK. Over to you!' The table rattles as Christos sets down an egg timer the size of a small dog. 'I would like everyone to start with the *tzatziki*. You have half an hour and then we will restart the clock for the *koupes*. Ready? Your time for the *tzatziki* starts . . .' He grabs the timer by the base and flips it upside down, its lurid pink sand descending in a rush, sending a sharp shot of adrenaline through Freya. 'Now!'

The atmosphere is tense. Whether it's the pressure of the egg timer or scoring some actual points, she cannot relax. It's not like it is in the television shows where a stand-up comedian or food-loving celebrity swings by for some light-hearted chit-chat and everyone shares pleasantries about their pets. Instead, the atmosphere feels so tense that, like eggshell, you could tap it with a spoon, and it would fragment and shatter. She grates the cucumber into a bowl and adds a sprinkling of sea salt. Mrs K would insist on draining it overnight in a sieve but without the luxury of time, Freya will just have to hand-squeeze the liquid out.

The next bit is the tricky bit. Although the recipe doesn't tell her to wait five minutes, she knows it's key to getting more liquid out of the cucumber, which will make for a thick, creamy consistency rather than a thin, watery one. She looks around. Everyone else is already squeezing cucumber pulp through the muslin cloths provided to drain away the excess water and she hasn't even started yet. The egg timer sand continues its descent, Freya unsure whether she can hold her nerve for much longer. If she waits the full five minutes, will she have enough time?

'Eight minutes remaining,' Christos announces.

Kwame looks over to her. 'Are you missing something?'

'No,' she says. 'I'm just waiting.'

'What for? Enlightenment?' Harj laughs.

The temptation to dip her hands in and get squeezing is overwhelming but going against Mrs K's advice would be sacrilege. *You can't hurry love. Shortcuts produce shortcomings.* She drums her fingers on the table. Another minute goes by. This had better be worth it. Kwame is finessing his *tzatziki* with dill and is seconds away from completing. Can she really wait a further two minutes?

'Five minutes.' Christos motions to the timer.

Eventually the wait is over, and Freya is wrist-deep in pulpy flesh, pressing and pumping with all her might, slime sliding between her fingers until she has squeezed as much of the liquid out as possible with her bare hands – Mrs K always maintained that wringing the water out manually is far more effective than using a sieve or a muslin cloth. Adding the flesh to the yoghurt, she mixes in the remaining ingredients until it takes on a creamy consistency. She dips her finger into the *tzatziki*, closes her eyes and taste tests. Something is clearly missing. She tastes again. Dill. It needs a smattering of dill. *Dill can kill.* Mrs K's voice rings in her ears. *Always add last so it does not overwhelm the other flavours.*

'Sixty seconds.' Christos booms, and her heart leaps.

Finally, she adds dill and tastes again. Perfect.

The ding-a-ling of a small brass bell signals the end of their allocated time as the last grain of sand joins the rest, the group disbanding and scattering across the terrace to sip home-made lemonade in the shade of the old eucalyptus tree. A post-mortem of the task gets underway, Michel wondering whether he overdid it with the garlic and Leandra-Louise worrying that she squeezed her cucumber too hard.

'You can never squeeze a cucumber too hard.' Stéphane quips.

'*Tais-toi!*' Michel slaps at Stéphane's hand playfully.

Christos appears at the edge of the terrace. 'OK, round two. *Koupes!*'

Everyone files back inside and, after a hot and sticky half an hour in the kitchen, mixing and blending, chopping and simmering, reconvene back outside, a whole lot sweatier and a hell of a lot more nervous than they were an hour ago.

Freya keeps herself to herself and looks up at the endless blue sky. A sense of calm sweeps over them all, comfortable silences drawn out for the first time since they've been together, some of them disappearing to make phone calls to their loved ones. A few moments later, the Bazigou brothers appear side by side, Dimitri sporting the look of a *Grease* T-bird what with his shades, white T-shirt and black leather jacket whilst Xanthos, by the look of his wet hair and the swirls of dried salt on his shirt, is fresh out of the sea. Freya imagines them curled up in the womb, Xanthos arched around his brother, his yin to Dimitri's yang. Polar opposites united.

'And now for the moment of truth!' Christos appears at the door and waves the brothers over to the contestants' dishes.

Freya feels her stomach contract. She can't handle another defeat. The atmosphere becomes tense as Dimitri edges his way around the table, picking up a warm *koupe* and lowering it into its accompanying pot of *tzatziki*. He takes a mouthful. 'Good aromatic blend of meats, the cinnamon and roast garlic really flavoursome. The coating is a little oily, and the *tzatziki* . . . well, this cucumber has not been grated finely enough.'

He moves on to the second dish. 'A beautiful balance of succulent pork and melt-in-the mouth beef but the *tzatziki* is too creamy. Nobody wants death by yoghurt.'

Gradually, he makes his way around all seven dishes, licking his lips and remarking along the way. *Too oily. Too much lemon. Not enough lemon. Has this one even got any lemon? Love the strength of the coriander. Not so keen on the bittiness of the meat. I had a whole lump there. Wonderfully neat and precise. Beautifully creamy. Not creamy enough. The perfect blend of garlic and dill. Well done. Too runny. Gorgeous. Cool but tangy, fresh and just the right amount of garlic – not too overpowering but just that little kick. Did you roast the garlic first? It's got too much of an astringent flavour to it. Nobody wants to reek of garlic the day after. Far too runny.* 'Whose is this one?' He hovers next to Freya's bowl.

'Mine,' she says sheepishly.

He says nothing, circling back to make his judgement whilst Freya's stomach yo-yos into her shoes and back. The energy in the room shifts, trepidation almost palpable. Michel has had to go off for a cigarette to calm his nerves and Harj has taken to polishing his fingernails with a tea towel.

'OK,' Dimitri says, edging towards Leandra-Louise's dish and then overlooking it for the next dish along. 'Third place!' he declares pointing at Hazel's dish.

Hazel claps her hands with joy and breaks out into a huge smile.

'This one second.' Dimitri's finger travels to Michel's masterpiece.

'Chéri?' Stéphane calls out of the window. 'Deuxième place!'

Freya's stomach lurches further as Dimitri wanders up and down, scratching his chin in staged quandary. Given that he's awarded second and third place already, he must have already decided upon the winner but seems to be milking the moment for all it's worth. Harj looks at him hopefully whilst Kwame bites his lip with quiet determination.

'This one is the winner!' He points at Freya's plate. 'A beautiful mix that reminds me of my grandmother's, which is the best I've ever tasted.'

Freya's heart swells with pride.

'Well, well, well, just goes to show that she's not a total write-off.' Hazel snorts.

Xanthos shoots Hazel a death-stare and turns to Freya. 'Congratulations, Free-ya.'

Kwame squeezes her shoulder whilst Stéphane reaches over to shake her hand. 'Congratulations, *mon amie*.'

'Thank you,' she says, aware that Hazel is glowering at her from the other side of the table. Miserable toad.

Dimitri shuffles their names around on the leader board, Freya leapfrogging all but Kwame. A deep sense of joy spreads through Freya's core and although her mother always taught her to think the best of people, she'd be lying if she said she didn't feel a slight sense of smug satisfaction at wiping the smile off Hazel's face.

'Nice work,' Leandra-Louise says brusquely, unable to make eye contact.

Harj meets her with a toothy grin. 'Good one, Frey.'

Freya swells with pride.

A murmur spreads across the room and her fellow contestants line up to pat her on the back with praise. Buoyed by victory and lifted by sweet relief, Freya feels a few inches taller.

Not only has she redeemed herself in front of the others, she's also proven herself a culinary contender and is one step closer to The Golden Spoon.

Kwame	6
Freya	5
Harj	4
Michel	4
Leandra-Louise	3
Hazel	3
Stéphane	2

It may have been a sloppy start, but she's hoping she's found her groove now.

CHAPTER NINE

Going Bananas

'Anyone for a swim?' Dimitri says as they amble back down the hill to Villa Katarina.

Freya would love to go for a swim but feels too self-conscious to hang out in a bathing suit in the company of a man with Hollywood looks and the six-pack of a superhero. Just like her *koupepia*, she has lumps and bumps spilling out all over the place, and low-cut Lycra is not a friend of anyone with excess anything. But then again, why the hell shouldn't she go for a swim? Society does enough body shaming without her beating up on herself and let's face it, will Dimitri even notice what she looks like when she's standing in the shadow of Leandra-Louise and her gravity-defying chest? Besides, her *tzatziki* has just won first place and a victorious leap into the clear, warm waters of the Mediterranean would be just the thing.

High on adrenaline, Freya shoves a baggy dress over her swimsuit and applies lipstick (because lipstick is of course an essential prerequisite for a dip in the sea) only to find upon reaching the rocky Cypriot shore that the promise of a swim has been side-lined for an afternoon of 'water sports'. Unpleasant memories of a capsized canoe on a filthy, shivering lake in Sherwood Forest, courtesy of a Kids as Carers fun day, remind Freya that water sports are not her thing, so instead she cuts loose from the others, walking further along the coastline until she comes across a craggy cove backed by limestone cliffs. The sand is almost blindingly white, and the lapping waters have the turquoise hue of postcard appeal. To Freya's delight, there is no sign of anyone or anything within sight. No beach bar. No toilets. No bins. No rubbish. No nothing. Perfect.

Descending towards the beach, she picks her way through the rocks, her dress catching on the rugged limestone, her eye drawn to a small brown warbler taking flight over swaying buds of white sea campion. She breathes in the salty air, enjoying the way it feels against her face. Fresh. Wild. Exhilarating. Everything that Nottingham isn't. Gorse bushes squat between the rocks, their flowering branches buffeted by the warm breeze, releasing a sweet scent of vanilla that carries on the wind. Further down, the yellows of golden samphire mingle with the pinks and purples of sea bindweed. Picking up her pace as the path broadens, the label on her swimsuit starts to itch.

Ignoring it, she watches two seagulls fight over an oyster shell down on the beach, dragging it back and forth in their beaks until it shatters on the stones, the largest bird flying off with his prize. The discomfort of her swimming costume ramps up a notch – it can't be the label as she's itching in other places too. Hitching up her dress to inspect her skin, she sees that she is covered in big red blotches and realises she probably has an insect trapped inside her bathing suit. She could really do with taking it off. Fuck it. There's nobody for miles. She whips off her swimsuit beneath her dress and throws it into her bag, delighting in the summer breeze whooshing beneath her dress and caressing her naked body.

Upon reaching the beach, she gazes back at the imposing limestone cliffs, noticing a small wooden shack perched on the rocks, its doors painted in thick, vertical red and yellow stripes – lifeguard colours. She wonders who it belongs to and what's inside. A lifeguard's lookout? A surf shack? A bird-watching hut? A writing retreat? She takes off her shoes and presses her toes into the soft powdery sand, feeling the sun's warmth on the soles of her feet. How sweet the view must be from up there in that hut, looking down on all this natural beauty. Picking her way over a ridge of washed-up shells, she makes her way over to the water's edge and allows the sea to wash over her feet. It's invitingly warm. The perfect place for a skinny dip.

Pulling her dress over her head and throwing it onto a rock, she feels liberated and alive. Energised and reinvigorated. Free of clothes and the shackles of life; at one with nature. Striding naked into the water, the sun pinching at her skin, the breeze fluttering against her back and breasts, she wades out until the sea is thigh deep and so crystal clear that she can see her toes. Digging her heels into the sandy seabed, she ventures further until the water reaches her waist, soothing the sting of her insect bites. Gliding into the flow, she takes a few breaststrokes until her body relaxes and she becomes free to tread water, her long red hair unfurling in the cool brine. She tilts her head back, allowing the water to run over her face until everything fades away and the only sound that she can hear is the glugging and rushing of the surf. Soothing. Calming. Tranquil. Gazing at the endless blue sky, she floats on her back, relishing the peace and serenity that comes with drifting naked in the warm, shallow waters of the Mediterranean when to her horror, peace and tranquillity are rudely ripped apart by the deafening roar of an engine. Her ears fill with water and her wet hair sticks to her back as she looks up to see Dimitri at the helm of a jet ski zipping towards her with what looks like a giant yellow blow-up banana being dragged in its wake. The growl of the engine intensifies as he draws nearer, her fellow guests whooping and screeching with delight from atop his inflatable fruit craft. Freya takes stock. Here they are hurtling towards her at speed whilst . . . she looks down and curses the water for being so clear – oh fuck; she is butt naked and her swimming costume lies on the shore.

The air fills with the pungent smell of petrol. Over man-made waves Team Golden Spoon zig and zag, holding on for dear life. Dimitri pulls on the handle, making the tail of the jet ski flick sharp left and forcing the banana to flip sharp right, propelling Harj into the air, Kwame and Leandra-Louise following with a yelp and a squeal. Freya looks over to the rock on which her clothes are draped, but it's too far away to make a dash for it from the shore. Better that she stays submerged.

The engine cuts out. Dimitri grins. 'What are you doing on this beach?' He calls out from the bobbing jet ski. 'There's nothing to do here.'

'That's what I like about it!' Freya arranges her long mane of wet hair over her breasts and tries to tuck her knees up into a ball without sinking.

'Come and have a go! There's plenty of room for you.' He waves an arm at his large inflatable and then peers down at her with a chuckle. 'The sea is best enjoyed naked, right?'

Freya wants to die. She grits her teeth, willing his banana to snag on a rock and deflate. Seriously, if someone had told her when she booked this trip that she'd be considering the attentions of a man with an inflatable piece of fruit, she wouldn't have believed it in a million years.

'Come on, it's fun! Let me show you Aphrodite's rock.' He yanks the motor starter, the engine bursting to life once more.

Sea sickness.

Air pollution.

Water contamination.

Twenty feet of pure synthetic fruit craft.

Freya can't think of anything worse, and although Aphrodite's rock might sound romantic under other circumstances, it certainly doesn't now.

'I'm sorry for what I said about your dish,' he shouts over the persistent growl of the engine.

'It's OK.' Freya watches the others haul themselves back onto the banana.

'Come on, have a go!' he shouts. 'No hard feelings.'

'I've got enough hard feelings for both of us, mate!' Harj yells from the back of the inflatable, glancing at Leandra-Louise and grinning.

Freya is considering how to respond when a sharp whistle turns their heads towards the shore where a man is trying to get their attention, crossing his arms back and forth in the air. Is there a shark? Jellyfish? A rip tide current that's about to suck them deep into the sea? It takes a few seconds for Freya to recognise the broad shoulders and the outline of a toolbelt that belong to Xanthos.

'You promised you'd leave this beach alone. You're polluting the sea. You're polluting the air. You're polluting my ears!' Xanthos screams from the shore, bursting forth with a torrent of unintelligible words and concluding, 'Get the hell out of here!'

Freya treads water. She wants to explain that she has had no part in the banana excursion and that she only came to swim. She wants to tell him she's an active member of Nottingham Friends of the Earth and has hosted countless cake sales to raise awareness and funds to double tree cover, clean up air pollution and shift pension investments in fossil fuels to sustainable alternatives. She wants to tell him that she saw that photo of the seahorse coiled around a cotton bud on the front page of the *National Geographic* and the centre spread they did on the ninety pounds of plastic waste that researchers pulled out of a whale in the Philippines. But trapped naked between twin brothers and the deep blue sea, she can do nothing but watch as Xanthos eyes her discarded clothes, shakes his head and turns back to glare at Dimitri before retreating down a small path she hadn't noticed on her way down.

Dimitri zooms off, his fully-boarded banana zipping along behind him and at last, she is alone again. Free to float in the crystalline water and gaze up at the eternal blue sky. Free to let her mind unwind as the sunshine pinches at her cheeks and shoulders, and yet all she can think about is catching Xanthos up; something she can only do once he is clearly out of sight, allowing her to get reunited with her clothes. She watches until he disappears around the edge of the cliff and, satisfied that she is no longer within his sightline, makes a dash for it.

Rising out of the sea, alive with the thrill of the sun piquing her naked, wet skin, she tiptoes across the shore and bends down to pluck her dress off the rock when the ear-splitting roar of Dimitri's great yellow monstrosity returns, tearing the calm waters into choppy surf.

Mortified, she shoves her dress over her head and doesn't look back, but by the time she is decent, Xanthos has gone.

CHAPTER TEN

Foul Play

Freya is the first to arrive at cookery school the next day, the morning sun seeping through a thin layer of cloud and the hillside alive with the ticking of crickets and the chirruping of birds. Up at the taverna, *Radio Cyprus* is on full blast, Greek song slowly morphing into what sounds like the news. The day has a welcoming feel to it, the smell of warm pastry wafting through the open window and tantalising her nostrils. She pokes her head inside to see the room already set up, utensils and ingredients laid out for eight people, the blackboard menu announcing *galaktoboureko* as dessert of the day. Her heart sinks. Greek custard pie with syrup may be one man's idea of golden crispy perfection, but the thought of separating sheets of filo pastry against the clock brings her out in a cold sweat.

It's an activity that requires dexterity in both hands – something she hasn't had since her mother's pen incident.

'Ah.' Christos wanders out of the kitchen in shorts and flip-flops, his belly wobbling like a jelly on a power plate. He waves a croissant at the menu board. 'We have no semolina so instead we will make Greek cheesecake.' Freya feels her shoulders relax. She is, after all, the Cheesecake Queen. 'Please, delete *galaktoboureko* and replace with *Greek cheesecake*.' He orders between mouthfuls of pastry.

Freya picks up the dirty cloth he is nodding to and does as she's told, chalking up *Greek cheesecake* and is just thinking of the gravity-defying three-tier cheesecake Talia Drakos once made in the deep, dark depths of a cave-dwelling in Rhodes, baking it on hot rocks and cooling it underground when Harj, Leandra-Louise and Hazel burst through the door, chattering away excitedly. Gradually, the remainder of the group files in, Christos reappearing in chef's whites. He nods to a stash of pamphlets on the table whilst doing up the large buttons of his short-sleeved jacket. 'Please, take one.'

Freya picks up a leaflet and studies the glossy photos of mouth-watering food platters interspersed with sparkling glasses of crisp white wine. Splashed across the centre spread is a troupe of dancers in colourful costumes posing under fairy lights, promoting Lappo's Psimeni Raki festival which, according to the text below, will be hosted this weekend.

Shaping the island's reputation for culinary excellence is Lappo's annual Psimeni Raki festival; a weekend extravaganza of music, food and dance, bringing together local restaurants and food producers to deliver the best of the island's gastronomy, complementing the traditional Greek drink, Psimeni raki. If you're a foodie, don't miss this!

Christos clears his throat until it rattles with phlegm, exits the door behind him, hocks a mouthful of catarrh onto the ground outside and returns to his work area. 'We will cook something for the festival.'

'I'll do the menu.' Hazel volunteers before anyone else can. 'Though may I suggest that we don't make *koupepia*? I think we've established that it's not everyone's forte!' She looks down her nose in Freya's direction.

'Bring it on, I say. Let's show these locals how to cook!' Harj's eyes shine with excitement.

Christos slams a metal bowl down on the table. '*Plakountopoiikon suggramma!*'

Freya jumps, half expecting him to have brandished a wand from under his apron and be casting some sort of spell on them all. Maybe she's read too much Harry Potter.

'You may know *plakountopoiikon suggramma* as cheesecake' Christos reaches for his faithful mug and lowers a dusty bottle of what Freya now knows to be Commandaria from the shelf above him. 'You know who invented the cheesecake?'

'The Romans?' Harj rolls his sleeves up and grins.

'The Greeks.' Christos pops the cork and fills his mug.

Freya glances at her watch. It is 9 a.m. and Christos is already on the sauce.

'The first cheesecake was made on the Greek island of Samos. You know Samos?' Christos says.

All faces turn towards Hazel who smiles smugly and doesn't disappoint. 'The birthplace of Pythagoras.'

'Pythagoras is a person?' Harj wiggles his eyebrows until they undulate like caterpillars.

Christos wipes his mouth on his sleeve. 'Cheesecake is very important here in Greece not only because it tastes delicious, but also because it provides good energy. You know it was cheesecake that was served to athletes at the very first Olympic Games in 776 BC? A very important part of our history.'

'No disrespect, but how can you prove this?' Kwame says.

'Archae . . . archaeo . . .' Christos takes another slug of wine.

'Archaeology?' Hazel suggests.

He nods. 'And then the people . . . the archae . . . archaeo . . .'

'Archaeologists?' Hazel suggests.

He nods again. 'They found many carbon-dated cheese moulds proving that they were made all that time ago. The ancient Greek way is to pound the cheese until it is smooth.' He demonstrates with his knuckles. 'Then mix it with honey and wheat flour in a brass pan and heat it on the fire in one mass. Of course, the Romans stole our cheesecake along with our land.'

'Those darned Romans!' Harj says, rearranging the ingredients in front of him.

A smile flickers across Christos's face. 'Indeed.'

Leandra-Louise raises her hand. 'I've heard the Greek sometimes choose cheesecake as their wedding cake.'

Christos nods. 'My son was one of them. He picked a three-tier wedding cheesecake. It was wonderful, but it didn't last long – a little like his marriage . . . but still, it was a delicious cheesecake.'

This is one of the reasons Freya will never get married. Falling in and out of love is painful enough as it is without being joined in holy matrimony. Imagine going through an emotional break-up and having a ton of additional life admin because of it. Love can be deceptive. In the early days, she really thought she was in love with Charlie. A smile plays on her lips at the memory of how nice his mum was, a deep sigh finding its way out of her lungs. She can't carry on dating people because they have nice mothers.

'You have one hour to prepare your cheesecakes.' Christos flips over the giant timer, causing a rush of sand to descend.

Forced to focus, Freya grabs her rolling pin as Christos disappears outside.

The next forty minutes fly by. Freya is in the zone, smashing biscuits (how is it that Charlie is already on Tinder?) with a rolling pin and crushing them (why has he regrown his beard when he refused to do it for her?) until they become a sheet of fine crumbs (has he remembered Arteta's medication?). Adding melted butter, she presses the biscuit base into the corners of her cake tin with more force than is necessary (did he really have to make a thing of changing his relationship status so publicly on social media?) and wedges it inside the Bazigous's industrial freezer (and was it really necessary to cut her smiling face out of the photo of them at her last birthday party and use it as his dating profile picture?). She slams the freezer door shut (why is she even thinking about Charlie? She doesn't even miss him for fuck's sake). Maybe she's premenstrual. Grrr. Or maybe making cheesecake is a reminder of that fateful failed food-porn night. She cringes just thinking about it.

An aroma of wild herbs floats in through the window and slowly, her rising anger dissipates and an overwhelming sense of serenity she hasn't felt since she got high behind the bike sheds at catering college takes over. She feels rubbery and relaxed and wonders whether this is how Buddhists feel when they claim to have reached enlightenment. Inhabiting her subconscious mind, she floats around her work area in culinary nirvana, tapping into parts of her brain she didn't know existed, blending and buttering, sieving and stirring in a mystical daze. It's not until she glances out of the window and sees Christos comatose in a deckchair with a giant spliff in his hand that she realises it may not be esoteric culinary cosmology that has elevated her to a higher spiritual plane, but the passive inhalation of weed. Still, stoned or enlightened she feels connected to food in a way she's never felt before and pleasingly arrives at the point where all the ingredients have been meticulously measured and are ready to go. After a quick toilet break, she returns for the best bit: the mix.

Back at her workspace, she tends to the coulis, pitting and halving a mound of sweet-smelling plump, ripe cherries and placing them in a saucepan of water, sugar and lemon juice. The skill comes with boiling the mixture over a medium heat until the cherries are soft but not squidgy, before transferring it to the food processor. Once it has been blended into a purée, she strains out all the lumps and bumps through a small sieve and dips her finger into the full and flavoursome coulis to taste. The sweet cherry flavour infuses her mouth, reminding her of the sherbet lollies her school used to hand out on Sports Day, and it's all she can do to restrain herself from freebasing it directly out of the jug. Delicious.

She returns to the cheesecake, whipping and whirling until the creamy froth becomes light and fluffy, and adds a swirl of cherry coulis to flavour the mixture before pouring it onto the biscuit base which has solidified fast thanks to the strength of their industrial freezer. Once the surface is as smooth as she can get it with a spatula (she'll crown the topping with a ring of cherries once it's cooked), she stands back to admire her work. Swelling with satisfaction (or maybe the laissez-faire effects of inhaling Christos's giant spliff), she places her pride and joy in the oven and makes her way to the veranda. It feels liberating not to be constantly comparing herself to her fellow competitors – something she spent far too much time doing yesterday and detracted from the task at hand. As Mrs K would say, 'Focus only on the things you can control. At the end of the day, the only person you are in competition with is the best version of yourself.'

She wanders outside to find Christos asleep next to an empty wine bottle, the butt of a joint still alight in the ashtray. Sitting down next to him, she studies the thick white whiskers sprouting from his chin and the dark circles beneath his heavy eyes. Small tufts of silvery hair spring from his ears and nose, and the skin around his nose and cheeks has a purple tinge to it. She wonders whether he enjoys his life – each day being the same; a morning of cooking, drinking and smoking his way into the oblivion that constitutes his afternoon and evening. What reality is he subconsciously avoiding? Does he still love cooking or did his passion evaporate as soon as he was forced to teach it daily, dissecting and expounding until spontaneity is dead and the joy of creativity is replaced by burden? In some respects, he reminds her of her mother, talented but self-sabotaged. She thinks about her mother's poetry. Beautiful words laid out in notebooks which will never be read. Unpublished and forgotten. A three-book deal unfulfilled and neglected. Opportunity pissed up the wall and all because one minute she was a brilliant poet and the next she was Jesus on steroids and the whole world was ending. That fine line between genius and insanity crossed several times over. She runs her finger over the scar on her hand and removes the mug of wine from Christos's lap to let him sleep.

An hour later judging has commenced. In the absence of Christos (who, only a few minutes ago was slung over the back of a donkey and led away by an aggressive woman with laddered tights) Xanthos and Dimitri are both in the driving seat as far as tasting is concerned. They have so far rubbished Kwame's strawberry cheesecake for being too gloopy, Hazel's pistachio cheesecake for being too heavy (ha!) and Harj's honey cheesecake for being too sloppy. Freya meanwhile can't help but feel confident. This is, after all, her area of expertise.

'This one, the presentation is top-notch.' Xanthos eyes her cheesecake.

'Let's see if the proof is in the pudding!' Dimitri joshes, Freya wondering how she could ever have doubted that they were twins, the two of them performing like some well-rehearsed duo.

Dimitri digs his spoon into her cheesecake and lifts it to his lips, yet no sooner has the food entered his mouth, he is spitting it out and gasping for water, his whole face twisted in disgust. Spluttering, he wipes his tongue on a tea towel as though trying to strip it of its skin. 'What the fuck is this! Are you trying to poison someone?'

All eyes fall on Freya who has no idea what's happening. If only this stoned haze would depart her brain and she could think clearly.

'Try it!' Dimitri says angrily, handing her the spoon.

Tentatively, she brings the cheesecake to her lips. The taste of salt is immediate. Not just a pinch to season but the whole thing is like a salt lick. 'I'm so sorry, I—' She spits it into a piece of kitchen roll offered by Xanthos.

'You used salt instead of sugar!' Dimitri cries.

Xanthos dips his finger into the topping and gives it a tentative lick. 'It is definitely salt.'

Freya freezes, her senses returning. 'I distinctly remember measuring out the sugar. I remember the little blue bag. I didn't even use salt. I—'

'The granules do look pretty similar.' Harj offers up a sympathetic smile.

'No, they don't!' Freya says, defensively.

'They're both white grain.' Harj shrugs. 'It's an easy mistake to make.'

'No,' Freya says. 'I've been cooking all my life – I know the difference between sugar and salt.'

The energy in the room shifts from one of good-natured camaraderie to an atmosphere of charged tension. Freya's cheeks sting with heat. She feels humiliated. Belittled. Cheated. And yet nobody else appears to give a shit. Can't they see something has gone on here? GAH! For fuck's sake! She should probably walk out before she says something she'll regret but that will only make her look like a diva. Her heart beats faster. She definitely used sugar; she knows she did. She measured it out. She had her eyes on it the whole time. Or did she? She was pretty stoned, and her head is still mush even now. The more she thinks about it, maybe she did fuck up after all.

'Third place.' Dimitri points to Leandra-Louise's cheesecake. Leandra-Louise smiles gratefully.

'Second place.' Dimitri's finger hovers over the cheesecake with the purple tag. 'Who is purple?'

'Oh my God, that's me!' Stéphane says, a look of surprise spreading across his face as he turns to Michel who reaches for his cigarettes and stiffens.

Freya simmers with rage. How is it that everyone else is still acting completely normal whilst she is inwardly falling apart? Cheesecake is her area of expertise, her go-to, her signature dish. This cannot be happening.

'And first place goes to this one!' Dimitri holds up the mango cheesecake belonging to Michel. 'Bravo, sir. An absolute melt-in-the-mouth triumph!'

Unable to contain his delight, Michel jumps up and down like an overly sprung wind-up toy, holding his hands in prayer position before turning to Stéphane and kissing him.

'I'm afraid it's a zero for you again, Freya.' Dimitri adjusts the scores on the leader board.

Michel	9
Kwame	7
Leandra-Louise	5
Harj	5
Freya	5
Stéphane	5
Hazel	4

Fighting back tears, Freya glances around the table. Is she going mad or could her fellow competitors really be capable of foul play?

The afternoon is not what Freya would call fun – she may be going through the motions of preparing *kolokythokeftedes* but her mind couldn't be further from courgette balls if she tried. Paralysed by distrust, she scrutinises the body language of her fellow cooks. Did Michel just sneak a sideways glance at her? Did Kwame shuffle away from her too quickly at the sink? Is it guilt that has made Leandra-Louise trade places with Stéphane so that she is no longer sharing the same baking tray as Freya?

'Don't worry, it's only one task.' Stéphane realigns their ingredients, shimmying his cup of grated courgette alongside her cup of crumbled feta. Is he about to swap out the chopped garlic for the sliced onions like a light-fingered magician?

Adding a splash of ouzo to her mixture, she turns in flour and breadcrumbs until the consistency changes to a springy dough from which she can shape spheres the size of golf balls. She looks up at the leader board. Michel steals the lead with Kwame at his heels only two points behind. In spite of her *tzatziki* triumph, Freya is now trailing with the rest of the pack.

Kolokythokeftedes sizzle as they hit the hot oil, Freya's brain along with them. Why would someone do this to her? Why would someone sabotage her cheesecake? It's not as though it's even possible to mistake salt for sugar what with everything in the Bagizou kitchen neatly labelled, and she distinctly remembers the sticker reading *caster sugar*. So how the fuck didn't she notice? Salt is visibly so much different to sugar, its granules smaller, denser and whiter. Now she comes to think of it, she also remembers weighing it and leaving it out in a bowl before nipping to the loo. Could somebody have switched her sugar for salt whilst she was absent for only a few minutes?

At the end of judging, Harj is declared the winner which moves him into joint pole position alongside Michel, Kwame nipping at their heels in third place. And by some fluke, Freya is awarded three points for coming second place though she doesn't remember half of it. Whatever happens next, she will get to the bottom of this.

CHAPTER ELEVEN

The Shadow
of a Man

The beach shines with a silvery blue hue, its sand, pebbles and rocks dappled with the glow of moonlight. It took Freya a good twenty minutes to find the proper path and a further twenty to amble down to the shore, but it was worth it. Beneath the shimmer of the stars, she huddles her knees to her chest and listens to the whisper of the sea. Lulled by the hypnotic ripple of silver ribbons as they flicker and fade across the black water, she digs the heels of her bare feet into the hard, wet sand. Like a sedated animal, the sea has lost its growl to the darkness of the night, its tranquil waters crawling towards her toes, soft foam fizzing and frothing as it reaches the sandy shore.

'Hey!'

She jumps, her heart pounding as a dark, shadowy figure trudges over the seaweed. Slowly but surely, Xanthos emerges out of the night, a bottle of something in one hand and a beach towel in the other.

'Hi.' Freya returns her attention to the sea. She really needs to be alone to brood right now.

'You found my beach.' He trudges over the pebbles towards her.

Freya says nothing. Making small talk with someone is not top of her list right now.

'I'm ruining your vibe?' he says, as though reading her mind.

She laughs in spite of herself. 'Where did you learn that phrase?'

'I grew up watching a lot of American TV shows.' His voice is low and husky.

A gentle breeze blows through his thick, dark hair as he offers her a drink from his water bottle.

She smiles. 'Do you have anything stronger?'

'Stronger?' He looks at her as though she has broken the law. 'No.'

'Sorry, I didn't mean to offend, I . . .'

He sits down next to her with a thud, releasing an aroma of motor oil, citrus and something of himself which messes with her pheromones. A shiver runs down her spine and her whole body tingles. Balling a pebble in one hand, she steals a look at him out of the corner of her eye and then steadies her sightline on the sea, her heart racing. He looks up at the moon, his face part irradiated, part shadow, and although she wants to turn towards him and look at him properly, she knows she shouldn't for fear she'll never be able to turn away, for here, under the moonlight, she sees Xanthos for what he truly is: a beautiful man. Her stomach tightens and a surge of desire overwhelms her, goose bumps appearing on her arms and legs, and the hairs on the back of her neck standing to attention. In her peripheral vision, his hands run over the strip of shells lining the foreshore with matchless symmetry, sieving crushed coral through his fingers and picking out anything of interest – a hinged razor shell, a crab's claw, pink-red urchin spines, a sea anemone, mermaid's toenails – until he finds a clam. Establishing that the shell is empty, he clamps it between his thumb and forefinger and sets about scooping sand out of the soles of his boots.

'I know it wasn't your mistake,' he says in a low whisper.

She throws back her shoulders and looks up at the starry sky, the feeling of sweet relief washing over her at the realisation that he knows she wasn't to blame for the salt *mishap*. 'I just don't understand who'd do it. I mean it's not like I've been mean to anyone or spoiled anyone else's dishes, so I don't see that it's revenge.'

Xanthos rolls up his shirtsleeves and stares at the calm sea. 'Jealousy.'

'Jealousy?' Freya frowns, her index finger involuntarily drawing a question mark in the sand.

'Jealousy is like salt,' he says, digging his finger into the top of her question mark, mirroring its shape and giving it another side until it becomes a lightbulb with a further two dots beneath her original full stop to form the rings of a screw top. 'A little can enhance the flavour, too much and you are out of favour. A season of seasoning makes for good reasoning. No more than an inch, stick to a pinch.'

Freya smiles. 'Very poetic.'

'Sophocles.' His eyes twinkle with mischief.

She laughs, sneaking a look at his sleeve tattoo and feeling a hot flush of arousal at the way the intricate patterns swirl around the contours of his shapely arms. 'But why would anyone be jealous of me?'

He looks at her with an intensity that makes her stomach squirm. 'Because you are the best chef.'

Overcome by his words, she can't find any of her own, choosing instead to draw a circle around the lightbulb so that it takes on the shape of an animal's nose, adding eyes and ears until it becomes the face of a cat. 'I am so not!' she says finally. 'What about Michel? He's like an uber-chef already. Have you seen his qualifications?'

'You cannot argue with the belly,' he says softly.

Brushing his words aside, she continues. 'You know I only won the *tzatziki* task because I have a Greek friend who taught me how to make it properly? I must have prepared it a hundred times over.'

Xanthos reaches for a pebble and hurls it into the sea. 'What is his name?'

'Who?'

'Your Greek friend.' He picks up another pebble.

'Oh, it was my Home Economics teacher at school. Konstantina Kyriakedes.'

He drops his hands into his lap, his face relaxing.

'You don't know her, do you? She's got cousins in Cyprus and—'

'No.' He chuckles. 'I'm just happy it is a woman. As I said, jealousy is like salt.'

She turns towards him, the breadth of his shoulders catching her off guard. Moonlight reflects in the twinkle of his piercing green eyes and the sea breeze catches his hair. He clears his throat with a deep growl that does something to her deep inside. It's not his love for poetry nor the way his nimble fingers pick out shells from the sand, but there is something about his gentle but pronounced movements that hold Freya powerless. Their eyes connect and although she should probably look away, his gaze is magnetic and draws her in deeper until she feels as though she has become unearthed and is floating around in orbit, weightless and disorientated. Her stomach squirms and all she wants to do is kiss him.

'You want to swim?' he says.

She watches as he picks open the laces of his left boot and tries to work out the significance of the body art on his arms.

'Come on.' He reaches out to her. 'Your cheesecake is wounded. Your heart is saddened. The salt water is the perfect antidote to hurt and pain.' He kicks off his boots, flicks off his socks and pulls his shirt over his head. 'The sea is best enjoyed like this. In the dark, under the moonlight.'

Freya takes stock of herself, refusing to look at him. She is not here for a holiday romance and anyway wasn't that Dimitri's line? *The sea is best enjoyed naked. Come experience what it feels like to be Aphrodite.* The gall of those brothers!

Bloody Casanova and Casabanana wooing a new woman every time a new boatload of unsuspecting tourists reach the island and rolling out their Greatest Hits of hook-up lines in the hope of snaring fresh meat – well, she's not falling for that. She straightens herself out. 'You can spare me the bullshit about swimming naked to the Aphrodite rock. Your brother tried that with Leandra-Louise and all it got him was a jellyfish sting and a verbal dressing down.'

'Dressing gown?' Xanthos's eyes narrow.

'Dressing down! Telling off,' she says, catching sight of his shoulders and forgetting what she was going to say next. His chest is strong and sculpted, the contours of his abdomen unapologetically sprinkled with dark hair and Freya can't help but wonder what it would feel like to touch him. She bites her lip, her face flushed and her skin tingling.

'I apologise for the womanising ways of my brother, but I swear I was not going to talk about Aphrodite or getting naked. I meant only that the sea is best enjoyed when it's quiet and there is nobody else. This is why I come here, to be alone.' He drums his fingers against the hard, wet sand. 'As it happens, my vibe can get ruined too.'

Digging her fingernails into the sand, she is lost for words.

He picks up his shirt and reaches for his boots. 'Maybe it is better if I go, and you have the whole place to yourself. I have bathed here a thousand times and it never loses its magic. Have a good swim and I hope you feel better tomorrow.'

'Why is it so calm now?' she blurts out as he picks up his towel.

His dark brow puckers with confusion.

'Why is the sea so calm at night but has so much more fight during the day?' She goes on, desperate to stall him.

He pulls on his shirt and stares at the water. 'During the day, wind blows from the sea to the shore, warming the sand and creating a vacuum. At night, the land cools, pushing air to the sea.'

'Right,' she says.

She doesn't care about wind patterns or vacuums, land cooling or air currents. All she wants him to do is kiss her. She wants to run her hands over his moonlit chest. She wants to press her body against his and feel the vibration of his growl. Nothing has ever been clearer. She wants Xanthos. Now. Here on this beach.

'Good night.' He walks away over the stones. 'And please, no more jet skis.'

'Wait!' she calls to his retreating back, but he can't hear her; not with the arrival of Dimitri and her fellow cooks who have come down to check on her. 'Xanthos?'

She watches the shape of him diminish until he becomes the shadow of a man she should have kissed.

PART TWO

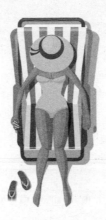

CHAPTER TWELVE

Steinbeck and Film Noir

Google search:

Can sexual chemistry be only one way?

Freya stares at the search results:

Report a Stalker

Stalking and Harassment – how to deal with unwanted attention

Fixated, obsessive, unwanted, repeated behaviour – are you a victim of stalking?

Is it possible that she has fabricated the whole mutual attraction thing in her head and projected feelings onto Xanthos who was purely trying to be nice in the aftermath of cheese-cake-gate? Was the simmering tension she interpreted as sexual longing merely frustration on his part that she was on *his* beach, ruining *his* swim, disturbing *his* peace? And is the crackling chemistry she has hitherto been obsessing over just a figment of her overactive imagination? No lightning bolts. No stirring of loins. Nothing?

No. It was real. *Surely*.

It takes two flints to make a fire. Two people to form a bond. Two to tango et cetera, et cetera. There's a truth in all those clichés, surely?

She replays last night in her mind's eye, picturing Xanthos's moonlit complexion and piercing green eyes. The smell of his skin. The resonance of his soft growl. The touch of his hand as it brushed against hers. There was an undeniable connection, wasn't there? An attraction. A spark. Wasn't there? WASN'T THERE?

Freya

Can sexual chemistry be UN-reciprocal?

Khady

You should have kissed him!

Freya

I know but . . .

Khady

> Cooking and getting laid are not
> mutually exclusive.

Freya rearranges her pillow and ponders. It's not so much the sex in general thing, it's the sex with Xanthos thing. Not that there is any sex thing with Xanthos, or that there will be, but if there were, hypothetically of course, it would certainly be looked upon unfavourably by her fellow cooks, and/or the judges, who would assume at best that she wasn't serious about The Golden Spoon and at worse that she was trying to sleep her way to the final. And regardless of what everyone else thinks, a summer fling might also distract her from her quest and there's no chance she's come all this way just to blow a lifetime dream for the sake of a sandy two-minute shag.

Freya

> Window-shopping only, remember?

Khady

> If something in the window catches your
> eye, surely you have to try it on?

Khady

> 51% of people experience a holiday
> romance at some point in their life. Why
> shouldn't you be one of them?

Freya's brain goes haywire. Firstly, she's not on holiday, this is serious business! Secondly, there's that guilty feminism thing again. *I am a feminist, BUT fifty per cent of my headspace is filled with fantasies of being seduced by Greek men.* There are a few problems with this fantasy. Primarily, that she has demeaned her intellect by spending most of the morning daydreaming about what *could* have happened with Xanthos, rather than spent it on something that would advance her mental agility – she glances at the pile of paperbacks on her bedside table and feels guilt-ridden that she hasn't read a single Booker Prize-winning page – but who needs Bernadine Evaristo's *Girl, Woman, Other* when you can relive Xanthos's moonlit growl? Then in addition, isn't it 'wrong' that in her fantasy she is submissive, allowing Xanthos to dominate her in what is almost predatory behaviour, him pushing her down on the sand and pulling at her dress urgently? Surely she's objectifying herself and deep down that means that some part of her yearns to be subservient? In which case, how on earth can these be the fantasies of a feminist?

But she is a feminist, right? She supports equal rights for women and refuses to be silenced by men. Take 'Courtney Gayle's cherry cheesecake' for instance. She's prepared to lose her job for her beliefs and is willing to die on the sword to right a wrong, but still, it's all so confusing. Pushing her thoughts aside, she presses her pillow to her groin and sets about masturbating her way through an alternative beach encounter with Xanthos, their sea-soaked bodies finding each other on the wet sand. Droplets of salty water dripping from his tousled hair onto her bare chest, her hips rising in anticipation as he moves breathlessly on top of her and is just about to take her then and there on fantasy love island when her phone bleeps with the pre-programmed ringtone reserved for her mother – a shrill jingle that turns her blood cold.

Mum

> Freya, they're here again. I've seen them in the building and although the security staff swear blind it's nothing to worry about, I know I haven't got long. Please know that I LOVE YOU x

She loosens her grip on the pillow and starts when the phone jingles again.

Mum

> They're armed! Nobody will believe me so it's important you keep this as evidence.

She tosses the pillow to one side and sighs with exasperation.

Mum

> Please donate my body to science – I have filled out all the forms.

FFS. If ever there was a mood killer . . .

Mum

> Don't forget I still have a building society
> account with approx. £500 in there. Help
> yourself. I love you and I'm sorry they got
> in the way of me bringing you up. Mum x

It's impossible to know how to respond. The trick is to acknowledge her mother's anxieties without getting sucked in. Keep things high-level. Offer love and compassion without indulging a world you know exists for her but that you yourself have never inhabited. Keep yourself afloat otherwise you too will sink.

Mum

> Frey, you there?

Freya shoots her breath out at the ceiling. When she was nine, her therapist, Dr Gaikaiwari, presented her with a box of felt-tip pens, telling her to draw what she was feeling instead of trying to put her emotions into words. Perhaps he was expecting her to sketch a rainbow, the clash of rain and sunshine symbolising inner conflict, or maybe a big rain cloud; angry, brooding and dark. In any event, Freya grabbed the first pen she could get her hands on and stabbed it through the paper, a macabre grin spreading across her face as the lurid red ink seeped into his whiter than white Scandinavian minimalist tulip table. Dr Gaikaiwari never did repeat his Pictionerapy technique but maybe now she should sketch how she feels and send the image to her mum? Something peaceful and calming. Serene, full of joy. Or maybe a sad, confused, frustrated horny face. Gah. Aware that she hasn't an artistic bone in her body, she falls back on words, drafting a message that pretty much resembles every other message she's sent over the last five years . . .

Freya

Sorry to hear that. Try not to freak.
Love you xx

. . . but each time she reads it back, her chest tightens, and she can't bring herself to press 'send'. Wouldn't it be great if she could *be* the person that wrote that text message? Sympathetic, unsentimental. Compassionate yet detached. Put her feelings in a box and move on. She may know how to take the emotional sting out of her written word, but she sure as hell hasn't mastered removing it from her heart. Try as she might to dredge up memories of moonlit beaches, the only image Freya can create in her mind is one of her mother crouched in the bottom of her wardrobe, hiding beneath the three tired outfits she rotates each week – a navy blue shirt dress and a floral print wrap dress she alternates on weekdays, saving the bold animal print robe for weekends and special occasions. Her mother has always been a creature of superstition – not in a black cat and voodoo doll kind of way, but that of an OCD mindset; beholden to rules that comfort and calm if followed, but taunt and torment if thwarted. Her poor, dear mum, alone and frightened.

A lump forms in Freya's throat. The phone screen looks blurry through tears. She thinks back to the person she used to be – someone who'd sigh, delete her mum's messages one at a time and move on with her life – but the more she ages, the tougher it gets. Compassion, it seems, grows deeper over time and it hurts to know her mother is constantly living in terror. And whilst her mother's tormentor may appear illusory to the outsider, it's all painfully real to her. Stab-your-daughter-with-a-fountain-pen real. Freya takes a sip of water from the glass next to her bed, closes her eyes and swallows, enjoying how the cool liquid feels in her throat.

It's important to focus on the positives and celebrate the woman her mother is when she's lucid and free of the demons that drag her down: a funny, intelligent, spirited individual, her stories captivating, her sense of humour enchanting, her *joie de vivre* beguiling. If it wasn't for her mother, Freya would never know the works of Vivaldi, Degas or Dickens. Without her mother's passion for the arts, she'd have no appreciation of *Sturm und Drang* poetry, grand opera, Steinbeck or film noir. And albeit indirectly, if it wasn't for her mother, she wouldn't have spent hours with Mrs K and subsequently learned how to cook. And therefore, were it not for her mother, she wouldn't be here now.

Freya

I love you x

She presses 'send'.

CHAPTER THIRTEEN

Ready, Steady, Cook!

Michel	10
Harj	10
Kwame	9
Freya	8
Leandra-Louise	6
Stéphane	6
Hazel	5

Today, is the dreaded 'make a meal from random ingredients in a ridiculously short space of time' task. Were it a freestyle activity, it would most certainly be easier, but all ingredients bar one have been chosen because together they make a traditional Cypriot dish. It's up to each chef to spot the red herring and discard the decoy – a food item which will only impede and obscure; something Talia Drakos excelled at when making a rare appearance as a guest chef on *Ready Steady Cook*, springing around in her jumpsuit like a sexy ping-pong ball and singling out the black sheep ingredient with such sultry pragmatism, it all seemed retrospectively so darned obvious. Freya tries to settle her nerves with coffee.

Dimitri and Xanthos have yet to arrive with the boxes of food and everyone has started to get restless at the taverna this morning. Kwame has been regaling them with stories about deep-fried Mars bars in urban Glasgow and Harj has been teaching Stéphane the dab. 'I'm Still Standing' comes on the radio, Leandra-Louise taking it upon herself to shimmy up and down, broom in hand, and by the time the chorus has kicked in, she's back-to-back with Stéphane belting out lyrics into a tablespoon.

'Come on, Freya!' Stéphane encourages her to join them.

Freya wishes she could be more gregarious. If she doesn't join in, they'll think she's no fun and she'll be left standing there like a dick. If she does join in, she'll die a tiny bit inside and hate every moment of it. Oh, fuck it . . . Taking hold of the tablespoon, she does her best to sing along, but it's difficult to properly cut loose without a drink inside her. Still, the ice seems to have broken and she's starting to get a proper sense of everyone. With the exception of Hazel who hovers like a hawk, ready to pounce on their misfortunes, everyone is pretty lovely and it's difficult to imagine any of them capable of food sabotage. Doesn't that in itself speak volumes? Is Hazel Stevenson the saboteur?

Hazel looks on with a stern grin. 'Today's task is basically *Ready Steady Cook* rehashed. Glorious, the original show was. Graham and I used to watch it religiously every Monday. I'm not ashamed to say that I used to have a bit of a thing for Ainsley Harriott.' She lets out a shrill laugh. 'Still do, truth be told.'

'Hazel, you saucy minx!' Harj jabs her with his teaspoon. 'I hope Graham doesn't mind.'

'Graham can't mind. He died last year.'

Freya's stomach knots with discomfort. The room falls silent and Harj retracts his teaspoon.

'Oh, I'm sorry, Hazel. Are you OK?' he says.

'Never been better,' she says in that sing-song voice of hers. 'Drove me crackers. Terrible cook. An interminable bore. I'm beginning to wonder why I ever married him.'

'Should've married Ainsley instead, hey?' Harj joshes whilst Freya makes a mental note to google 'murdered husband, Kettering' as soon as she gets the chance.

'Absolutely!' Hazel titters.

Stéphane pushes his empty coffee cup aside. 'Michel would prefer to marry Gino D'Acampo, *n'est-ce pas, chéri*?'

'He's beautiful,' Michel agrees. 'Don't you think?' He looks to Leandra-Louise.

'I'm more of a Gordon Ramsay fan myself,' Leandra-Louise says, taking a photo of them all with her phone and posting to Instagram (Siena filter, #cookery#TheGoldenSpoon#contestants-attheready) along with a wide-eyed, open-mouthed selfie captioned, 'Yikes!' She slips her phone back into her pocket. 'There's something about the way Chef Ramsay says, "take it away, please darling." Gets me hot just thinking about it!'

'Nooooo.' Freya grimaces.

'OK then, who do you fancy?' Leandra-Louise says, all eyes falling on Freya.

The door swings open to reveal Xanthos, a stack of food boxes in his arms and a beach towel over his shoulder. His hair is wet and his demeanour relaxed.

'Freya?' Leandra-Louise probes.

Freya becomes aware that she is openly gawping at Xanthos whilst the rest of them are still awaiting her response.

'Err. Probably Yotam Ottolenghi,' she says distractedly.

'Who?' Stéphane says.

A shiver runs down her spine as Xanthos passes behind her, the smell of sea salt and fresh air mingling with the musk of his skin and doing funny things to her. 'Yotam Ottolenghi. You know, the Israeli–English chef who loves Middle Eastern cuisine.'

'No.' Michel frowns.

Stéphane digs out his phone and types 'Yotam Ottolenghi' into Google search, a gallery of photos popping up. Ottolenghi in a black suit and open shirt posing on the South Bank with his boyfriend. Ottolenghi wrapped up in a swirl of scarves outside a restaurant in Tel Aviv. Ottolenghi in a designer stainless steel kitchen surrounded by bowls of superfood salads.

'Who is this?' Xanthos leans over Freya's shoulder to look at the screen, his warm breath on the back of her neck causing some sort of chemical reaction she struggles to hide.

'Freya's boyfriend,' Leandra-Louise quips. 'Handsome devil, isn't he?'

Xanthos raises an eyebrow, looks at Freya and disappears

into the kitchen without passing comment. Freya panics. He can't really think Yotam Ottolenghi is her boyfriend.

'OK.' Christos arrives on the scene, clapping his hands together. 'This is where the fun begins. You will have five minutes to consider your ingredients and decide what you will make with them, followed by fifteen minutes to createyour dish.'

Xanthos returns with four bags, passing them to Kwame, Hazel, Harj and Michel.

'Don't look in the bags until my word is final,' Christos says as Xanthos goes back into the kitchen and reappears with three more bags.

He passes one to Stéphane, the other to Leandra-Louise and drops the third one in front of Freya from such a height that it hits the worktop with a thud. 'Good luck,' he says flatly.

'OK, you may now open the bags,' Christos says with an air of authority.

Freya stifles a smirk. If she's to stand any chance at this task, she needs to manifest Xanthos out of her mind and concentrate. She inhales through her nostrils and gazes at the bag of grain in front of her, trying to ascertain what it is. *Kastano*? No, it is too seed-like to be brown rice, the kernels too large. *Trahana*? She picks up a piece of grain and digs her nails into it. *Kritharaki*? No, the grain is too hard to be any kind of bulgur wheat. She's definitely seen this somewhere before but can't for the life of her remember where. A hamster bowl? On her grandmother's bird table? Fuckety fuck. What the hell is it?

Other ingredients include crème fraiche, a lump of pork belly, two pomegranates, a lemon, sesame seeds, raisins, walnuts, caster sugar and a sprig of parsley. Hmmm. There's nothing to marinate the pork in . . . Do crème fraiche and pork really go together? She paces up and down. *Think, Freya, think.* She has five minutes to come up with an idea, and fifteen minutes to execute. FIFTEEN MINUTES! Palpitations start in her chest, subtle at first but quickly becoming rapid-fire bullets she cannot control. The immediate concern is the pork. If she's to have any hope of pulling this out of the bag on time, the pork needs to hit the frying pan ASAP. Actually, no. The grain needs to boil so that needs to go on first. Then the pork.

Christos glances around the table. 'Remember, there is one red herring ingredient that you should not use unless you want to ruin authentic Cypriot cuisine.'

Freya looks down at the food in front of her. Which ingredient is *her* red herring? The crème fraiche? Wouldn't the Greek way be to use yoghurt? Or is it the sesame seeds? Aren't sesame seeds from East Africa? She's sure she remembers Mrs K once telling her that ancient Egyptians ground them up and used them as grain flour. Or is it the grain itself? No, it has to be the sugar. Why would you use sugar in a savoury dish? Especially in a competition which goes out of its way to be as refined-sugar-free as possible.

'Hang on a minute. I've lost the garlic!' Hazel throws her arms up in panic, her chopping board clattering to the ground – she should really put a wet cloth under it; something Freya learned several years ago to avoid slippage. 'It was here a second ago.' She rifles through her ingredients, knocking over a pot of cinnamon and sending her lemon bouncing to the floor.

Christos rolls his eyes. 'Has anyone seen Hazel's garlic?'

Everyone goes through the motions of combing the kitchen for garlic, too consumed by the task at hand to search properly. Freya vows that the moment Christos says 'go', she'll grab a saucepan and race to the tap. Then once she's got the water on, it's over to the pork. But the sauce . . . The sauce is a bit of a problem. Will crème fraiche and garlic suffice?

'I had a whole bulb!' Hazel wails.

'Don't panic.' Christos disappears into the store cupboard and re-emerges a moment later with a string of garlic draped over his shoulder. He plucks off a bulb and hands it to Hazel. 'Good luck.'

Freya's heart races as Christos takes a stopwatch out of his pocket and glances from face to face. The nervous energy in the room swings from frenetic fever to desperate unease. Hazel sneezes, sending a trail of freshly ground nutmeg across the table. Harj and Leandra-Louise share a look of apprehension. The room falls silent and Freya can barely breathe.

'Ready, Steady . . . Go!' Christos clicks the stopwatch.

Freya's stomach lurches. Grabbing a saucepan, she charges towards the sink, bumping straight into Stéphane and sending his courgette flying.

'Sorry!' she says, igniting the hob and settling her saucepan of water on the ring as a queue forms at the sink.

Back at her workstation, she thinly slices the pork. It feels like sacrilege not to slow roast such a succulent cut of meat but with limited time, she has no choice but to fry it. Seasoning each sliver with salt, pepper and lemon juice, she looks over at Harj who stands motionless, a bag of tiny new potatoes in one hand and a beetroot in the other.

'You OK?' she says, manoeuvring each slice of pork into her greased frying pan.

'I've no fucking clue what I'm doing,' he says, throwing down the beetroot.

Freya gives her pan a shimmy shake. 'What have you got?'

'Black beans. Potatoes. Chives. Pumpkin seeds . . .'

'Beetroot?' she says, over the sizzle of pork.

He nods.

'They want you to make a salad. Boil the kettle. Chop the beetroot and go!'

She flips over the slices of pork and looks over her shoulder to see Harj completely freaking out, head in hands, and for a moment considers helping him, but a rush of adrenaline and a hot fleck of pork fat are enough to focus the mind and just as they say you should tend to your own life jacket before anyone else's, she knows she must save herself first.

She looks at the rapidly whitening meat. Ideally, she'd have pre-boiled the pork to make it more tender, giving it a crisp texture when fried but with only eight minutes remaining, that's not an option. She empties two large handfuls of grain into the bubbling water, burning her wrist on the side of the frying pan. And then it hits her – she shouldn't be cooking the freaking pork! The pork is the red herring. It has to be. There's nothing worse than undercooked pork – not just from a taste sensation but also from a health risk point of view – imagine if she were to poison the judging panel! Her blood runs cold and a high-pitched ringing invades her ears. Cursing herself for the five minutes she has wasted, she returns to her workstation. How could she have been so stupid?

Think, Freya, think! She stares at the ingredients in front of her. The room starts to shrink but then an idea starts to unfold: *koliva*. Isn't that what it's called? Rather than mix everything together in crème fraiche – the obvious choice given that it's the only ingredient from which she can create a sauce – she'll boil the wheat grain and mix it with all the other ingredients to create a salad packed with nuts, dried fruit and chopped parsley then sprinkle with sugar (yes, that's where the sugar comes in!), which she can serve with a blob of crème fraiche and a slice of lemon to flavour. *Koliva*, of course that's where she's seen this grain before: in a Taste the Difference Sainsbury's Mediterranean salad. But has she got enough time?

'Eight minutes remaining!' Christos announces.

It feels as though the walls are closing in on her and she's trapped inside a nightmare, everything shapeless and blurred. Judging by the way Harj stares into his mixing bowl, his shoulders rounded with despondence, he feels it too.

She glances at Leandra-Louise who slices a cucumber at lightning speed and then at Michel who is fully absorbed in crumbling feta over simmering garlic prawns with a meticulousness she's never before seen under competition conditions.

Stéphane has meanwhile lost both his cool and his chopped nuts following a collision with Hazel. But Hazel is unperturbed. She looks as though she's thriving off the pressure as she drives her knife through a block of halloumi. And as for Kwame? As always, he remains detached, busying himself with his Cypriot omelette. Cool, calm, collected Kwame.

Freya slips a tray of sesame seeds and walnuts into the

pre-heated oven to roast and returns to her workstation where she rolls two pomegranates, one with each hand, across the chopping board to loosen the seeds. Scoring around the middle of each piece of fruit with a sharp knife, she then tears them open one at a time to release the pinky droplets.

'Five minutes!'

Mixing in the raisins, sesame seeds and walnuts, she inhales, holding the air in her lungs until it burns. Three, two, one . . . and release. Ditching the pork is one of the boldest and riskiest decisions she has ever made in her culinary career and in a couple of minutes, she'll learn whether it was a stroke of genius or an act of madness. She chops the parsley and sprinkles it into the bowl.

'Three minutes!' Christos cries.

Freya rushes to the stove, removes her pan of boiled wheat grain, drains it over the sink and with steam rising from the sieve, mixes the small brown kernels in with the other ingredients, her face tingling in the hot vapour. She spoons the mixture into the serving bowl provided and . . . the sugar. Where's the sugar?

'Two minutes!'

Her mouth dries as she mixes and mixes. The sugar was just behind the pomegranates and isn't anymore.

'You don't think that looks a little dry?' Hazel squints at Freya's dish.

'One minute!'

'Did someone move my sugar?' Freya shouts. This cannot be happening.

'Behind you!' Harj says, nodding to the table where she

now remembers placing it. Paranoia, mind-destroyer. There she goes again . . .

'Thirty seconds!'

'Who took my coriander?' Hazel cries.

Freya plunges her spoon into the bag of sugar and sprinkles it over the mix, adding a sprig of parsley to garnish.

'Where the shitting hell's the honey?' Harj flaps.

'Ten!' Christos looks at his stopwatch.

Fuck. She still has the slice of lemon to add and the . . .

'Five.'

Shit.

'Four.'

She adds the slice of lemon.

'Three.'

She grabs the tub of crème fraiche.

'Two.'

She plunges her spoon into the carton.

'One.'

She dollops the crème fraiche next to the lemon.

'STOP!'

She closes her eyes and pleads with the universe to throw her a bone. Heart beating like the shake of a rattlesnake, legs like jellied eels, she clings onto the edge of the table and tries not to pass out. Was she supposed to cook the pork? Please somebody tell her she was not supposed to cook the pork. Pigging hell.

CHAPTER FOURTEEN

Who Done It?

'OK, let's bring in the judge,' Christos says, as the taverna door opens with a creak.

Freya looks up in anticipation of Dimitri, but it's Xanthos who strides into the room, his shirt salt-stained and his hair still damp from the sea but now drying in ringlets. She feels her stomach flutter. It's confusing – discombobulating – to be filled with terror one minute and lust the next. Like patting your head whilst circling your torso, it feels out of sorts. Desire and dread are a heady combination, and her hormones are all over the place. Isn't anxiety by its very nature supposed to make you retreat into a lustless, monastic cocoon? Anxiou-sexuality. Is that even a thing? Trying to get a grip of her emotions which have boarded a roller coaster and are hurtling up, down and all over the place, she presses the soles of her feet into the floor tiles in an attempt to earth herself and be present in the moment, but each time she looks at Xanthos, her internal organs feel tight and fizzy. What the hell is the matter with her?

He inches closer, claiming the space at the table between Leandra-Louise and Harj and she's forced to interlace her fingers to stop them from shaking. All she can see of him are his hands and about an inch of his sleeve tattoo which pokes out from beneath his cuffs. Secrets inked on forbidden skin. Hair tousled from a dip in the sea. Shirt buttons waiting to be undone. The symmetry of his hand movements. It feels as though she has turned to liquid, her power deserting her further when he moves to the head of the table where he can better address everyone, his emerald-green eyes meeting hers, then flickering away.

'Whose is the *louvi* with taro potatoes?' he says, inspecting a dish of black beans, courgettes and tomato slices with a fork and for a moment Freya is so taken aback that he can function normally whilst she is awash with hormones, that she wants to smash her fists on the tabletop and demand that he looks in her direction. How can he be so blissfully unaware of the effect he has on her?

'Mine.' Harj fidgets. 'Sorry if it's not what you were after. I just . . . I didn't think I'd got enough time to . . .'

'It looks good.' Xanthos smiles. 'Congratulations on leaving out the beetroot.'

Freya feels like a fraud. Hadn't she told Harj he should use the beetroot? Thank God he didn't take her advice.

Hopefully he realises she had good intentions and wasn't trying to stitch him up.

Harj grows an inch in height. 'Oh, man. Really? I was crapping myself that you'd . . . thanks.' His bottom lip starts to quiver. 'Thank you.' He lifts the bottom of his apron and wipes away tears of joy, his whole body shaking with relief.

Freya's skin starts to itch. If her instincts around Harj's dish are anything to go by, she's just shot herself in the foot by discounting the pork. Heart in throat, she watches as Xanthos takes a mouthful of Harj's *louvi*.

'Mouth-watering. The dressing is perfectly balanced, the sweetness of the plum juice really giving it a lift. Nice work, Harj,' Xanthos concludes before moving on to Kwame's Cypriot omelette. Freya stares at the table. 'Again, well done on spotting the red herring ingredient. The salmon. Although you could have ignored the egg and gone for a salmon salad, the Cypriot omelette is a lot more "Cypriot".' He leans over and cuts himself a slice, lifting a forkful to his mouth, Freya's eyes drawn to his strong, stubbled jaw and shapely, kissable lips. 'A little oily but delicious nonetheless.'

'Thank you.' Kwame nods gratefully.

Freya returns her gaze anxiously to the abandoned slices of pork on the plate next to her elbow. Did she make the right decision?

'What do we have here?' Xanthos leans over Stéphane's concoction – pan-fried sardines in a tomato sauce, flavoured with red onion, chilli and topped with feta cheese.

'I've forgotten the name,' Stéphane says sheepishly.

'Are we sure there is a name?' Xanthos winks, a playful

look in his eye. 'OK, let me give it a taste.' He takes a mouthful and raises an eyebrow. 'Nice try but if you'd left out the sardines and gone with the prawns instead, you'd have a wonderful seafood *saganaki*. The sardines were the red herring there. Sorry.'

Hands on hips, Stéphane puffs out his cheeks and blows his breath out in short, sharp bursts before collapsing in a heap on his stool.

Xanthos moves onto Leandra-Louise's cucumber yoghurt salad. 'Beautiful.' And then onto Hazel's *pilafi pourgouri* – Cypriot bulgur wheat cooked in a tomato and onion sauce, served on a bed of vermicelli and crowned with Greek yoghurt and a sprig of fresh mint. 'A triumph.' Before he reaches Michel's Greek-style garlicky shrimps with feta. 'Looks delicious.'

Freya steals a glance at the seafood platter, a wave of envy rippling through her. If only they would put her out of her misery and tell her if she was supposed to cook the damned pork.

Xanthos lifts a prawn to his mouth. That stubble. Those green eyes. That growl. That cough. Actually no, not that cough. Heads turn as Xanthos begins to choke, his hand wafting back and forth over his mouth. 'Water!' he croaks. It's not until tears start to run down his cheeks that Harj realises Xanthos is not playing a prank and passes him his drink. Michel looks on in horror.

Xanthos thumps his chest with his fist. 'Oh man, oh man,' he gasps.

Kwame offers him a serviette.

'What happened?' Michel says aghast.

Xanthos blots his lips on the serviette and wheezes. 'How much garlic did you use?'

'A clove.' Michel looks over to the remaining garlic bulb on his workstation.

Xanthos's eyes narrow. 'A clove or a bulb?'

'A clove.'

'Trust me, there is more than one clove of garlic in this dish. This dish is death by garlic.' Xanthos dabs at the corners of his eyes with his knuckles.

'Impossible.' Michel's eyebrows invert with frustration. 'Let me taste.' He gestures for the dish which Xanthos slides over, pops a prawn into his mouth and spits it out almost immediately. '*Putain, con! Mais qu'est-ce que c'est que ça?*'

Stéphane looks at him. 'How many—'

'I didn't do it!' Michel leaps around angrily, his face turning redder and redder. He picks up his fish slice and thrusts it at Hazel and then at Kwame. '*Il y'a un saboteur entre nous . . .*' Stéphane looks at him with an intensity that adds further weight to an atmosphere already charged with conspiracy and blame. He glances around the table. 'One of you did this. One of you spiked his prawns.'

Kwame dismisses him with a frown. 'How would anyone have been able to tamper with anyone else's ingredients? We were all concentrating on our own dishes.'

Michel's face turns the shade of a beetroot, his knuckles whitening as he grips the fish slice. '*Je vous assure . . .*' He raises his hand theatrically. 'I assure you that I did not use an entire garlic. Somebody added five maybe six cloves. Taste it!' He thrusts a prawn at Kwame. 'One hundred per cent garlic!'

'No, thanks.' Kwame bats it away.

'TASTE IT!' Michel thrusts the garlic prawn platter further towards Kwame who throws up his arms, the ceramic dish falling and smashing against the floor tiles, thick globs of melted feta oozing between the cracks.

'OK, OK. Let's calm down.' Christos reappears from the cellar with a purple stain on his teeth.

Leandra-Louise folds her arms over her chest. 'Hazel, didn't you request an extra bulb of garlic?'

'Only because mine went missing!' Hazel says defensively.

'Did it really, Hazel?' Harj steps in.

'Yes!' Hazel says, incredulous. 'One minute it was there and the next it was gone!'

'Because somebody stole it?' Michel eyes them all as though they are the devil's spawn. Slamming his fist into the palm of his hand and grinding his knuckles like a pestle against a mortar, he storms out onto the terrace.

'You can't take away his points when it's out of his control!' Stéphane pleads with Xanthos.

Freya can't help herself. 'Really? Because that's what happened to me when someone sabotaged my cheesecake!'

'Everybody out!' Xanthos motions to the door.

They all trudge out, still squabbling, leaving Xanthos to collude with Christos on the results of a task that hasn't so much drawn to a close but exploded into fire and is being fanned by the flames of competitive spirit.

'Congratulations.' Christos nods at Freya on his way out. 'You won the task. The best *koliva* Xanthos has ever tasted apparently.'

'Really?' Freya says, feeling a surge of relief although she can't help but think that feedback would have felt a whole lot more special coming from Xanthos himself.

'A great decision not to cook the pork,' Christos goes on. 'You know what they say here in Cyprus? Roast pork, all talk. Wham, bam, go for lamb!'

Freya does her best to laugh along but with all the bickering and gossiping going on around her, it's difficult to focus, let alone savour the moment. Her attention turns to the behaviour of her fellow contestants. Childhood games of Cluedo at the Kids as Carers summer activity days spring to mind as she assesses each suspect. A prime candidate for a heart attack, Michel clearly isn't faking it, which means it could be any one of the five others. Hazel is a contender; she has a hostile manner – colder and frostier than a January dawn – and likes to point out others' misdemeanours. ('Shouldn't you have lightly browned that first? Couldn't you have added a touch more nutmeg? Wouldn't you have ideally made that look a lot better?') but does she really have the vindictiveness or indeed the competence to pull off a full-blown act of sabotage? Then there's Kwame who is also a possibility. Autocratic. Aloof. A bit of an automaton. Is there more to Kwame than meets the eye? Quick to detach himself from the group, he's so far chosen to read on his own of an evening rather than join in the alcohol-infused camaraderie that's building amongst the rest of them. Then there's Leandra-Louise. If ever there was a case of misrepresentation, it would be Leandra-Louise: *Financial Times* content in a *Hello!* magazine cover. Judging by her consistent successes, she's clearly got hidden depths.

It's all very well pretending not to know who Talia Drakos is, but she can't have got this far on luck alone, so what else is she hiding?

Freya's head spins, her attention diverted to the French couple. Stéphane would have to have a serious death wish if he was going to sabotage his partner's dream. Knowing how much it means to Michel, it seems too brutal a betrayal for someone who loves their partner to screw them over like that. And although they may argue at times and are clearly both competitive, Stéphane set his stall out by declaring himself the side act to Michel's main event. Surely he couldn't possibly do this to the man he loves?

Then there's Harj, who was in Freya's line of sight the entire time and spent most of the allotted minutes in what looked like a lobotomised state, his panic attack impeding him from doing even the basics, let alone racing across the kitchen to lace somebody's dish with garlic. Having confessed to her over breakfast about killing a cockroach and not being able to sleep for guilt, she very much doubts Harj would be capable of such malicious behaviour.

Mr or Ms X in the kitchen with the garlic. But who the hell is it?

CHAPTER FIFTEEN

Tea with Mrs Anastasis

Freya	13
Harj	12
Michel	10
Kwame	10
Leandra-Louise	9
Stéphane	7
Hazel	6

Lights have appeared all over the village as preparations take place for the Psimeni Raki festival. Paper lanterns flutter in the sea breeze and the front façade of the community hall is illuminated in purple. Costume parades, processions, carnival floats and a village dance are advertised along with a feast of local food and a kite-flying competition. The honey-sweet smell of *flaounes* (a tart made with cheese and mint, served as a festival delicacy) wafts out of the bakery, sending Freya's taste buds into overdrive.

'I swear to God, he wanted my head on a spear.' Harj wipes a bead of sweat from his temple with the back of his hand. 'Coming out with all that bollocks about seeing me with a handful of garlic. I mean we all had garlic, right?'

'I'm sure he accused everyone,' Freya says, looking up at the overhanging balcony of geraniums and realising they have just gone full circle through the labyrinth of village backstreets.

'Did he accuse you?' Harj follows her down a narrow side street.

'No, but . . .' They reach a dead end.

'There you go then,' Harj says, shadowing her U-turn.

'Only because I've been a victim of sabotage too.' She ducks beneath a row of low-hanging washing and bites her tongue. Why is it that when her cheesecake got tampered with, nobody gave a rat's arse, choosing to ignore her protestations and believe the sugar/salt mix-up was simply her mistake and yet now that it has happened to Michel, everyone is up in arms?

'Thanks for coming with me,' Harj says as they continue to saunter through the cobbled backstreets of Lappo, seeking the shade of whitewashed walls and bougainvillea trees to avoid the midday sun.

'Pleasure,' she says, reaching for her water bottle. 'I know nothing about turbans, so you'll have to educate me.'

With a shopping list as long as a city electoral roll, the

pair of them have volunteered to wander down to the village in pursuit of a few extra ingredients for the meze platters they have been tasked with producing for the festival tonight. Harj's ulterior motive is to pick up a turban for the occasion which Freya can't help but think may be a challenge in such a small village. Collectively, they have fourteen dishes to prepare. Freya is starting on lamb moussaka whilst Harj must make a vegetarian equivalent. Having won the *koupepia* challenge, Kwame has been tasked with making them all over again much to Freya's relief – she'd be happy if she never had to set eyes on a vine leaf forever more. Meanwhile, Hazel is making *keftedes*, Michel *kolokythokeftedes* and Leandra-Louise has teamed up with Stéphane to take on several types of hummus – creamy avocado, smoky sweet potato, roasted red pepper, and a traditional black bean hummus which uses garbanzo beans in place of chickpeas.

The sun is blistering hot and although they are supposedly heading for the village square, the narrow alley has brought them out onto the beachfront where fishermen sell their catch of the day from wooden carts, stainless-steel trays bursting with fresh seafood. Following the smell of raw fish, they make their way over to a stall where giant shrimps are piled up next to a tangle of octopus tentacles, and mounds of mussels and seaweed-covered clams lie on crushed ice. Barracuda, tuna, dorado; the list is endless. The blancmange-like squid make Freya think of the Talia Drakos' blooper which went viral when she held up the giant mollusc by its bulbous body only for a jet of black ink to spurt all over her pressed white jumpsuit, a look of abject horror flashing across her face.

'I hate dead fish.' Harj pulls a face. 'All those glassy eyes looking at you.'

'Yeah,' Freya says, unable to stop thinking about the impromptu herbology lesson Xanthos gave them before they set off, his strong fingers handling feathery fronds of fennel with such a tender caress, she feels weak at the knees just thinking about it.

'My nana had a glass eye,' Harj says, discarding the mussels in his hand much to the displeasure of the fisherman behind the stall who makes a point of spitting onto the shale they are about to tread upon. 'You never knew whether she was talking to you or the person next to you.'

Freya chuckles. 'My mum's like that and she doesn't even have a glass eye!'

Harj proves to be easy company. Unafraid of saying or doing the wrong thing, his childlike openness and lack of inhibition is a breath of fresh air in this environment, and for the first time in a while Freya finds she can properly relax and be herself. Harj will definitely be someone she'll stay in contact with beyond her culinary quest for The Golden Spoon. She leaves him to peruse the octopuses and trudges over to the water's edge, kicking off her sandals and wading out until the sea creeps up as far as her knees. Looking across the bay, she decides she could live here forever. Fresh air. Fresh fish. Fresh fruit, vegetables and herbs, and a sea to bathe in morning, noon and night. Screw Nottingham and its noise pollution, air pollution, high street shops and heavy traffic. Why not live in a place you love? She glances behind her at the small stone church balanced precariously at the foot of the hillside, its smooth steps eroded by the sea, and smiles at the way the door has been doused in colourful powder – vibrant pinks and dazzling blues. The huge brass bell in the church tower has been polished to within an inch of its life, and the bottle banks and recycling bins that lined the car park only yesterday have been moved out of sight to improve the aesthetics. This festival must be a big deal.

'I suppose we'd better crack on.' Harj appears at her side.

Reluctantly, Freya strides out of the sea, a million tiny shell fragments exfoliating her toes as her feet press into the rainbow shale. She pictures herself owning a small apartment over the bakery and waking to a view of the bay every morning. Foraging for fruit and nuts, vegetables and herbs, she'd cook up a storm with each catch of the day.

'Ready?' Harj appears in her peripheral vision.

'Sure,' she says, putting on her sandals and retrieving the crumpled shopping list from a pocket full of grit.

Conscious of time, they stick to the main thoroughfare which has bunting fluttering from the street lights and arrangements of pressed flowers at every corner. A garland of marigolds has been slung around the neck of a statue of Terpsichore, the Greek goddess of dance, who has been planted in the village square to welcome visitors with a feather in her hair and an obligatory breast falling out of her ballgown.

'Pretty fit if you ask me.' Harj leers at the statue.

Freya rolls her eyes. Maybe she won't stay in touch with him after all.

'Not as fit as Leandra-Louise, mind.'

She smirks. 'Have you two got it on yet?'

Harj stops in the shade of a sycamore tree and reaches for his water bottle. 'Give me time, Freya. Give me time. Once she sees me in the new turban, she'll be all over me.'

Freya laughs as he wipes the opening of his water bottle with his sleeve and offers her a sip. 'What about you and the Greek god of love?' he says.

Freya's eyes widen. Is it that obvious? 'The Greek god of . . .'

'Dimitri!' he continues.

Freya relaxes. Were it obvious she had a thing for Xanthos, it would make the whole thing super-cringe. It's important nobody knows. That way, there is no expectation for anything to happen. Not that anything is going to happen of course. Just playing devil's advocate and all that.

Over in the village square, men in white shirts and polished shoes sip coffee from tiny cups whilst enjoying a game of backgammon, young children play hopscotch and a group of teenagers huddle around a game of bottle flip. There's a buzz about the market, elderly women haggling over a huge mound of walnuts and a long queue forming in front of a stall of pastries: *diples, loukoumades, bougatsa, baklava, galaktoboureko* . . . Freya's mouth waters. The patisserie options are endless.

'Sorry to throw a dampener on your pulling strategy, but do you really reckon you'll be able to buy a turban in this tiny village?' she says, eyeing up the aubergines and wondering how many they can afford with their allocated budget.

'You don't just buy a turban, Freya.'

'You don't?'

'You buy the material to make one. There's a fabric shop around the corner with a striking emerald silk in the window. Let me show you.'

An hour later, Freya and Harj find themselves standing inside The Fabric Emporium surrounded by roll upon roll of eye-catching prints – bold florals, paisley, tartan, gingham, tweeded herringbone, botanical ferns, sausage dogs repeated in diagonal rows, a series of Big Bens appearing intermittently between Eiffel Towers and Colosseums. Brushed cotton in every colour imaginable – dark charcoals, muted yellows, burned orange with scribbly black dots, emerald green with little white swans and a dark teal with dandelion seed heads. Freya runs her finger over the intricate gold embroidery of a turquoise silk and is just wondering how the shop manages to stay afloat when her eye is drawn to the back of the shop, where a woman with snow-white hair and jet-black eyebrows sits at a sewing machine, her unsteady hands feeding a length of denim beneath a large bobbing needle. Guiding the material this way and that, her fingers work deftly, flitting every now and again to one of the dressmaker pins affixed to her floral overcoat. A cluster of coral and pearl bestowed upon each earlobe catches the light which creeps in through a small window. Her skin is wrinkled with untold stories, a pinch of flesh hanging loose at each elbow, and the web of laughter lines around her eyes suggest that she has experienced much joy in her life. The electric fan propped up on the table behind propels cold air onto a pile of fabric samples which flap and flutter in the breeze.

'Hi! Hello! *Yamas!*' Harj calls over.

Freya grabs hold of his arm. 'I think *"yamas"* is for toasting,' she whispers.

'I'd like to buy fabric to make a turban,' Harj goes on.

The woman withdraws her sheepskin slipper from the foot pedal, the spool of cotton rumbling to a halt, and looks up through thick cataracts.

'Turban.' Freya smiles, wrapping her hands over her head in a circular motion which is not proving the best way to mime religious headwear, the lady clearly mistaking it for a choreographed dance move.

'I need a turban for the festival.' Tracing the edges of his silky black dastār, it's Harj's turn to circle *his* finger around the top of *his* head, which Freya interprets as requiring a halo and can't stop laughing.

Harj smiles. 'Something for my head.'

'Ah,' the woman says, raising a bony finger that suggests she is in the know. Grasping the edge of the table, she shuffles her weight to the front of her chair, and painstakingly slowly pulls herself up to standing, Freya feeling guilty for having disturbed her. The table wobbles, and hot brown liquid sloshes from side to side in her teacup while a reel of blue cotton bounces to the floor and rolls behind a length of fabric.

They watch as the small woman totters through a back door, her fingers twiddling a string of rosary beads as she negotiates the step into the next room. A good ten minutes pass, Harj and Freya sharing muted looks of concern, before she reappears out of breath with the sort of large felt black hat that might suit a snowman.

'Like this?' she says.

'Kind of,' Harj says, flicking through his phone and flashing up a photo of his younger self wearing a turban.

'Ah.' The woman smiles, holding up her finger once more and shuffling off to a shelf at the back of the shop.

'The one in the window looks great,' Harj shouts over to her but she carries on regardless. Freya and Harj share a look of concern when she reappears with three rolls of fabric under her arm, weighing surely as much as she does.

Heaving each roll onto the counter, she invites them to study the fabric: one ruby-red with a velvet feel, one sky-blue with a hint of a paisley pattern to add texture, and a shimmery gold one that catches the light each time it moves between her fingers.

'Oh my days, that one is amazing!' Harj reaches for the gold voile and runs a layer of the fabric between his fingertips in the way that you might rub butter and flour together to make short crust pastry. 'It's so much thinner than the Rubia shit we wear back home.'

The woman blinks at him through thick, misty eyes. 'Rubia shit?'

'You get different weaves.' He shuffles about awkwardly. 'Rubia's a lot heavier, it's a much thicker weave. This voile one is loads better considering the temperature outside.'

'You like it?' she says.

'Love it!' he says excitedly.

The lines around her eyes deepen. 'You will look like a king.'

Freya watches as the small woman unravels the roll of gold

fabric using the rubber thimble on her index finger to part the material before looking up at Harj and tapping the side of her nose. 'You are missing your spirituality. Mrs Anastasis knows this.'

Freya glances around the shop in anticipation of Mrs Anastasis before realising that the woman is referring to herself in the third person.

'No, I just wanna look good, innit.' Harj grins.

Mrs Anastasis nods. 'First though, you will need tea.'

A few moments later, and they are sitting in a dark room that smells of mothballs, waiting for Mrs Anastasis to reappear. Each item of furniture is lovingly covered with an intricately embroidered white throw – the teak dresser, the mahogany dining table, a set of nested coffee tables and an uncomfortable wooden sofa whose cushions have been sewn into another cotton cover that reminds Freya of her childhood bedspread and makes her think of Ribena stains. The whitewashed walls are dotted with oil paintings in dark wooden frames and the dresser is covered with a collection of curios – china teapots, a mandolin made from a dried-out gourd, a small white statue of a woman holding a child, a glass vase of dried flowers, a pack of faded playing cards, a composition of peacock feathers and an old-fashioned sewing machine.

The tinkling of china suggests that Mrs Anastasis is on her way, and Freya straightens herself up in the same way she does when she's forced to go to church. She tries not to get wound up by Harj who keeps fingering the porcelain figurines on the windowsill to inspect their handiwork, but it's difficult what with them being so delicate.

A moment later, a young woman around Freya's age with long braided hair and a septum nose ring appears with a tray of teacups and a plate of pastries sprinkled with icing sugar. The Betty Boop tattoo on her upper arm stretches as she lowers the plate, the garter on Betty Boop's thigh elongating as she does so. She smiles at them both, her eyes drifting to The Golden Spoon emblem on Harj's bag which makes her instantly recoil.

'My grandma didn't know if you'd already eaten or not,' she says in a tone that suggests she cares neither way. 'Avoid the burned ones. The filling is like glue and if you've got fillings, you won't have for long.'

'Wow, your English is like amaaaazing,' Harj effuses.

She remains stony-faced. 'International school. Athens.'

Mrs Anastasis emerges from the dark hallway with a pot of tea and mutters something to her granddaughter who rolls her eyes and shouts, 'Good luck!' as she bounds upstairs, her heavy footsteps thumping overhead.

'*Shiamishi.*' Mrs Anastasis lowers the tray onto the coffee table and places it on a frilly mat embroidered with primroses.

'*Shiamishi.*' Freya returns the salutation, adopting a prayer position with her hands and glancing at Harj with the suggestion that he should do the same.

'Ah sorry. *Shiamishi,*' Harj says, getting up from the sofa and performing a deep bow.

Mrs Anastasis chuckles. '*Shiamishi* is the name of the *panigyri* . . . the pastries. You don't know *shiamishi*?'

Freya looks at her blankly.

'Please . . .' Mrs Anastasis gestures to the neatly folded

jackets of filo pastry and hands them each a plate. 'Today, we celebrate St Martha.' She prods the corners of an imaginary crucifix into her chest with her bony finger and looks up at the ceiling. 'When it is the name day of a saint, we must always have *panigyri.*'

Freya bites into the pastry. It crumbles in her mouth, small flakes cascading onto her plate. The taste is an explosion of aromatic semolina and orange blossom offset by crisp, buttery layers of textured pastry, finished off with a hint of cinnamon.

'Delicious,' she murmurs.

'You are here for The Golden Spoon?' Mrs Anastasis takes the roll of golden voile that Harj has chosen and spreads it out over the dining table until the mark she has made with a black pen becomes visible.

'Yes. We're staying up the hill with the Bazigou brothers,' Freya says, her mind looping back to their foraging trip, Xanthos crouching beneath a grapevine to display the translucent qualities of a Xynisteri leaf, his emerald eyes ablaze with passion. His strong thighs. The way his fingers glided over the imbricate pattern of a pine cone lying at his feet. *A great source of fibre and vitamin C.* She does so love and admire his respect for nature. *One man's weed is another man's salad.* And his refusal to take a cutting of chicory as it was the last of its kind.

'The Bazigou brothers.' Mrs Anastasis shakes her head and tuts, lining up a huge wooden ruler against the pen mark on the fabric. 'I know all about the Bazigou brothers. Untrustworthy. Unreliable. Uncouth.' She tears the material along the ruler with a loud ziiiip.

Freya feels a tiny stab of hurt in her chest. 'Really?'

'Really.' Mrs Anastasis holds up the sheet of fabric by pinching at the corners, allowing the length of gold voile to float down to the floor. 'My granddaughter was married to Dimitri for all of fifteen days, and then paff! He finds interest in another woman.' She jabs a pin into the material as though sedating a wild animal, Freya misjudging her saucer and accidentally catapulting her teaspoon onto Harj's lap. 'And then there was the thing with Xanthos stealing Helena away. The two brothers are not to be trusted.'

Freya's mind goes into overdrive, wondering who Helena is and whether the Bazigou brothers are small-time crooks, big-time bandits or merely loveable rogues? Surely if they have raped or murdered, kidnapped or assaulted, they'd be behind bars?

'What did they do?' she says, trying her best to sound impartial.

Mrs Anastasis gives her a stern look, clears her throat with a rattling cough and busies herself with the fabric.

Realising that she's not going to get a response, Freya takes a sip of tea and goes back to her pastry whilst Harj compensates for the awkward silence with a monologue about turbans and the way in which they symbolise all of mankind being equal in sovereignty and purpose. A confused look falls across Mrs Anastasis's face. Their exchange switches to one of formality – payment, best wishes and thank yous, Freya never sure whether to place the emphasis on the 'ef,' the 'har' or the 'isto' – and they leave The Fabric Emporium with enough gold voile to wrap a whole family.

'What's up with you?' Harj says halfway up the dirt track to Villa Katarina.

'Nothing,' she says, splashing the last bit of water from her bottle down the back of her neck in an attempt to cool down. 'She really didn't like Dimitri and Xanthos, did she?'

'Petty village politics, you mark my words. Probably parked in her allocated spot or something, you know what rural life can be like. My mum once went to Solihull and it was the same.'

Freya wipes her forehead on the sleeve of her dress and wishes she hadn't forgotten her sunhat whilst Harj peels off his dastār and uses it to dab at his face.

'Do you think we should be worried?' Freya says.

'About the heat?'

'About them being "untrustworthy and dishonourable". Do you think they're part of some sort of Cypriot mafia? The Bazigou Sopranos?'

Harj laughs. 'Smacks of a sex crime if you ask me.'

Freya fixes him with a stern look. 'Then I'm definitely not asking you!'

They amble back in silence, save the heavy breathing that comes from climbing a cliff in the searing midday heat, Freya resolving to unlock the mystery of the Bazigou twins. Surely a man with a pet hamster – gerbil, sorry – and his herbologist brother aren't going to be on Cyprus's Most Wanted list? Still, if she's going to crush on one of them, she needs to know exactly what she's crushing on.

CHAPTER SIXTEEN

Yes, Chef!

Khady

> Why have I just fucked André?

For fuck's sake. Freya loves Khady with all her heart but gets infuriated with her at times. This is people's lives she's fucking with and meanwhile she doesn't mean any of it. She never means any of it. It's all about proving that she's still got it. Self-affirmation, which is ridiculous considering how many heads turn the moment Khady so much as walks into a room. André's poor wife! Freya blames it on Khady's mother, a catwalk model back in her prime, who puts way too much emphasis on looks and the influence of beauty.

To: Khady

Maybe you should stop sleeping
with everyone to fill your inner void.

Khady

At least my inner void is getting filled ;-)
I think I need to quit the waitress job.

Freya

It might be an idea.

Khady

I was only ever waitressing because of
André and the beautiful Indian girl who
comes in on Friday lunchtimes to write her
book over steak frites.

Freya

PUT YOUR OVARIES ON A LEASH!

Khady

TRY LIBERATING YOURS!

Freya

I'm after The Golden Spoon, not The Golden Truncheon! Seriously, Khads. I'm only just out of a long term relationship and I'm here to cook, not to get laid . . .

Khady

Seriously, Frey, live a little!

Freya

I know but . . .

But what? She stops typing. What exactly does she know? That an old lady in the village says the Bazigou brothers are a couple of wrong'uns? That she's holding back on her feelings because she's too fixated on The Golden Spoon? Khady's right; she should throw caution to the wind and give herself a break once in a while.

With another half an hour before she needs to be up at the taverna, Freya lies down on her bed and stares at the ceiling fan and as it rotates, so does her mind; a windmill of thoughts. She misses Khady. When push came to shove last week and she'd needed a roof over her head, it was Khady who'd taken her under her wing. Cohabiting was fun, their conversations reminiscent of those they shared when they lived together as students in a ramshackle apartment in St Ann's years ago where the water got cut off every time their neighbour took a shower and went from bad to worse when their flatmate started dealing pills.

Khady

> I read your tarots last night. Apparently, Freya Butterly, you are heading for love.

Freya Butterly may be heading for love, but she is also heading for disaster – she's only gone and nodded off and is now half an hour late for food prep, her phone showing umpteen missed calls from Harj and Leandra-Louise. How could she have fallen asleep on festival day? Serious points are at stake and here she is out sparko! Pulling on clothes and tying her hair back, she runs to the communal bathroom and splashes water over her face before racing out and up the hill.

When she reaches the taverna, she finds Kwame browning off her minced lamb and mixing in chopped onions, bay leaves and what should be cinnamon but could be paprika. A surge of horror rushes through her at the realisation that it may already be too late: he may have tampered with her ingredients to pull off his greatest act of sabotage yet. Snatching back the wooden spoon, she glares at him.

Kwame pulls a face. 'A thank you wouldn't go amiss!'

'Thanks,' Freya says tentatively before ladling a spoonful of the mixture into her mouth. It tastes beautifully aromatic, exactly as it should do. She should probably apologise.

'Can I have your attention?' Kwame holds up a wooden spoon and addresses everyone in the kitchen before she gets a chance to say sorry. 'I just want to clear the air and say, I know you all think I'm the food saboteur but I'm not, so if you could all stop treating me like a leper, that'd be much appreciated. Thank you, you can go back to your cooking now.'

'OK, OK.' Christos shuffles into the kitchen clutching his faithful mug and a bottle of Keo Cyprus brandy. 'We are not here to fight. We are here to cook. Everybody needs a clear head for this evening.' He fills his mug with a generous serving of brandy and takes a gulp, the irony not lost on Michel and Stéphane who share a look.

'I don't think we're ever going to get to the bottom of it,' Hazel says, moulding lamb around a kebab stick. 'But as we're all wise to it now, I'd be surprised if the perpetrator would strike again.'

Freya eyes Hazel with suspicion. Is she effectively suggesting that she is the saboteur but has taken it far enough and is going to put a stop to it now?

Hazel turns and glares. 'I hope you're not taking too much skin off those potatoes. They'll lose their flavour if you remove too much.'

Freya returns her attention to the chopping board and bites her tongue. Carnival music travels in through the open windows, the jingling of procession bells accompanied by the heavy thump of bass adding to the sounds of the kitchen, and although she's itching to be a part of the celebrations, she's not ready yet; not until she's made the meze of her life. After all, it's not every day that people come to town to partake of merriment and sample your food. Excitement and nervousness make for a heady atmosphere, everyone keen to impress.

A rota has been drawn up, allowing each chef two hours to spend time at the festival down in the village with the understanding that they should remain sober enough to cook upon their return. Dimitri has drafted a group of his friends to space themselves along the hillside track, offering meze at one hundred-yard intervals to entice revellers up to the cliff-top taverna. Today's task isn't about going head-to-head with each other over the same dish, it's about working together as a team; all seven of them unifying to become a well-oiled machine operating under the watchful eye of Christos. Each person has been tasked with the preparation of individual dishes, but they must take it in turns to wash the pots, take orders and work as a team throughout the course of the evening.

Freya stretches out her fingers and pulls at her knuckles. Peeling potatoes always gives her cramp in her bad hand and it's a relief when Christos swaps her onto lamb *kleftiko*. Running out of oregano, she smiles to herself. Back home, this would have meant a trip to Lidl, but here in Cyprus, it's a matter of wandering out onto the hillside and helping yourself. She ventures outside, the sound of music and laughter drawing her to the edge of the cliff where she peers down on the festivities below. Barbecues have sprung up all over the beach, glowing like lanterns. Women dance, men whistle, and children twirl and skip around the flames. A fleet of rowing boats full of party people paddles towards the shore, sequinned headdresses twinkling beneath the setting sun. Getting back to the job at hand, Freya plucks a few sprigs of oregano from the earth, relishing the feel of the soft, fuzzy leaves against her fingertips.

Just as she is running the oval leaves under the outside tap, she hears a yelp indoors. Hazel has managed to take half her thumb off with a kitchen knife and is being ushered onto the terrace by Christos where she collapses into a chair with her head between her knees, and although she claims she doesn't need an ambulance, the rapidly reddening dish cloth wrapped around her hand suggests otherwise.

'If I go to A & E, I'll miss the whole thing,' Hazel mumbles as Christos tosses a batch of bloodstained lamb into the bin. 'And if I miss the whole thing, I'm out of the competition.'

It's amazing what people will do for this competition, Freya thinks. They're prepared to sabotage their fellow contestants' dishes. Steal ingredients. Cheat. Lie. And now, it seems, lose body parts. Crushing a handful of garlic cloves with a mortar and pestle, she throws in cinnamon and black pepper, her hands cramping again. It's intimidating to think that everyone wants The Golden Spoon as much as she does.

'More speed!' Christos yells as she loosely chops a handful of oregano on a wooden board.

'Yes, chef!' She wills her fingers to work faster but chopping at pace has always been a challenge since the resetting of her wrist, what with a ruptured artery and long-term damage to her tendons.

'Much faster!' He roars, taking a swig directly from the brandy bottle.

Freya exhales with exasperation. Is she really supposed to peel, slice, chop and grate with such speed that her fingers bleed? She doesn't want to follow in Hazel's footsteps.

Having drunk dry the brandy, Christos refills his mug from

a dusty wine bottle, his hand jittering as droplets of Merlot splash over the kitchen counter. 'If you're to be a master chef you need to get a lot faster at food preparation. Your potato peeling for example is very poor.'

'Yes, chef,' Freya says with an air of defeat. If she explains her injury, it will only look like she's making excuses – the dog ate my homework, the sun was in my eyes, my shoelace was undone. Rubbing her scar, she takes the marinated lamb she prepared yesterday and bastes it in fresh paste, before adding a parchment pocket of potatoes to the mix and sliding it into the oven.

'Not like that!' Christos slurs. 'The lamb is supposed to go on top of the potatoes!'

Freya's mouth goes dry and her sweaty palms can't quite clasp the oven door handle. How is everyone else keeping a clear head whilst she is mentally unravelling? Hot air blasts out of the oven and swirls around her ears. How could she have forgotten to put the potatoes under the lamb? *Like a bird laying eggs.* She hears Mrs K's soft voice. *Relax and enjoy. Food, like animals, can smell fear.*

Trying to relax, Freya forces out a hum. No tune in particular but the mere sensation of vibrations in her mouth and throat are somehow soothing, her jaw loosening and her breath slowing but even so, there's no denying that the heat is getting to her. She takes another sip of 'refresher juice' (water, lemon juice, sugar and a pinch of sea salt to provide electrolytes) but still can't seem to cool down. It's thirty-three degrees outside so God knows what temperature it is here in the kitchen where steam is coming out of every orifice and still the heat rockets. Sweat pools at the base of her spine and trickles from her temples, her upper lip is dewy, and she can't wait to take her bra off.

At the next hob, Kwame whistles. Freya has come to understand that this is a cover for his anxiety whilst Harj shakes his legs in time to imaginary music and Leandra-Louise flits about like a cornered moth, unable to settle on one particular thing. There's no getting away from it; they're all under the cosh tonight.

Freya ignites the gas ring in front of her. There are four sets of stoves, each shared between two people. She has been partnered with Michel, who confides in her that he has smothered his genitals with cornflour to 'absorb moisture', a trick he learned from Jon Favreau's hit film, *Chef*. Unsure how she is supposed to respond to this nugget of information, she continues to stir her moussaka.

'OK, team!' Dimitri struts into the kitchen in enviably aerated flip-flops, dumping a cardboard box on the nearest table. 'You'll all need to look the part.' He dips his hand into the box and pulls out one apron after another, each one bottle-green and neatly embroidered with 'Golden Spoon holidays' in white font above their logo – which when replicated in cotton, looks neither golden nor like a spoon and bears more of a resemblance to a yellow magnifying glass.

They each grab an apron and line up as a team just long enough for Dimitri to take a photo and, although Freya is relieved that Xanthos is not here to distract her, she secretly wishes it was he who was fiddling with the strings of her apron to ensure 'Golden' hadn't got lost to her cleavage.

Christos leans against the doorpost in a way that suggests he'd fall over without it propping him up. 'Everybody ready for me to open service?'

'Yes, chef!' They chime.

'Have fun!' He says, grabbing frozen towels out of the freezer and slapping them on the back of each person's neck before reaching for more Merlot.

Pans clank. Spoons clink. The temperature rises further, ovens belching out heat that mingles with the steam from broccoli stems and intensifies with each pan that simmers on the hob until the kitchen is nothing short of a smouldering inferno. Despite the whirring fan and open windows, there's no ventilation, and the air is thick and choking. Sleeves are rolled up, foreheads mopped, water consumed by the gallon, but nothing seems to cool them down, and only a few moments later Leandra-Louise has fainted in the doorway whilst Stéphane is lying under the spray of the outdoor tap, gasping for air.

With Hazel on the side-lines clutching her bloodied thumb, Stéphane overheating, and Harj reviving Leandra-Louise with an ice pack outside, the kitchen is four chefs down. And still the temperature climbs, tempers fraying with it. Kwame and Michel embark on a full-on slanging match over a batch of hummus resulting in Michel taking time out to redress the wound on his toe since Kwame 'accidentally' stamped on it.

Freya feels light-headed. She takes another gulp of water from the tap. If she can just get through the next few minutes, she'll soon be down in the valley having some time to herself at the carnival. She slides her moussaka out of the oven – the cheese a nice golden brown and the potatoes the right side of crispy. A sense of satisfaction passes over her. This task is about volume over perfection and damage limitation over talent, something she learned from the dinner ladies at school. Burn a whole tray of brownies and you've lost twenty children their pudding. Bring carrots to the boil too late and the lamb chops will have gone cold. Take a break at the wrong time and your whole production line grinds to a halt. It's like preparing a Sunday roast on a very large scale. In a sauna. With no escape button. And she's still got five more trays to bake.

'Fuck this shit!' Kwame rips off his apron and hurls it to the ground.

'Kwame?' Michel calls after him.

'I wasn't good enough the first time around. I wasn't good enough the second. And I'm certainly not good enough the third!' He throws his head back and roars at the ceiling, fingers splayed wide, the whites of his eyes emanating fury.

'It's the heat.' Freya throws him an ice pack.

'It's *me*.' Kwame holds the ice pack against his head and then dabs it under each arm. 'I'm just not good enough.'

'We get the day off tomorrow and there's still everything to play for!' Freya reasons.

'There may have been, but it's over for me. Good luck!' Kwame says, grabbing his bag and yanking his phone charger out of the wall socket. 'I quit.'

And with that, he storms out of the kitchen, the rubber soles of his shoes squelching against the sticky floor. Freya holds her heart in her mouth as the door swings shut and the realisation dawns upon her that she is now single-handedly at the helm of the kitchen.

Christos appears from the store cupboard with another wine bottle in his hand. Swaying from side to side, he looks at her through sunken, bloodshot eyes. 'I need to take a walk. You got this?'

She glances around at the bubbling pans, the flashing hob lights and discarded chopping boards covered with capsicum seeds and aubergine stalks. Oven timers tick, sausage sizzles and the smell of smoky aubergine is just beginning to morph into the whiff of smoke.

'Yes, Chef,' she says quietly.

She turns back to look at Christos, but he has already disappeared.

CHAPTER SEVENTEEN

Al Fresco

'What do you mean he went for a walk?'

'He said, "I need to take a walk." And by the time I looked up he'd gone.'

'Gone where?'

'I dunno. He was quite wasted.'

'He was pie?' Dimitri drags two beers out of the fridge and passes one to Freya.

'Pie?' she says.

'More drunk than usual?'

'Yes.' Freya presses the cold can against her forehead and rolls it under her chin.

'Great!' Dimitri snaps open his can of Estrella with a fizz and struts off.

Freya presses the cold can of beer against her chest and returns to the stove where Stéphane prods at a pan of lamb, his clothes soaked to his skin. A post dinner-service shower will not suffice; they'll need to be hosed down every few minutes at this rate. She glances at her fellow contestants and, choking on the hot, soupy air, wonders who will pass out next. Sweat drips from Stéphane's forehead, his eyes are glazed and his movements slow. He looks through Freya as though she is a mirage; a sheet of water in a hot desert. Stumbling around, dehydrated, he smacks his head on a kitchen cupboard.

'You OK?' She passes him a glass of water.

He can barely get the drink to his mouth quick enough.

'Go easy,' she says, heading out onto the terrace where Hazel is chalking up the price list on a portable blackboard with her left hand, her ambidexterity sufficient to write, but not to cook, apparently.

The sharp metallic sound of a bouzouki accompanies a drumbeat, a group of revellers appearing at the top of the track, all feathers and glitter. Olive trees rustle, the music getting louder as the festival makes its way up the hillside, snaking between orange trees and apple blossoms. Freya feels a tightness in her chest. Leaning against the barbecue, she peers over the terrace wall and tries to work out how many mouths they have to feed – tens? Hundreds? Hot pink plumes flicker and fade through the foliage, costumes shimmering and shining between the dark-winged leaves of lemon trees. Trying to get a better look, she stubs her toe against something hard and solid. A gas bottle. And by the weight of it, it's full. Her eyes dart across the terrace to two other barbecues standing dormant: all of them gas. Eureka!

'Guys!' She runs back to the kitchen. 'Why don't we take the kitchen outside?'

Her voice is lost to the clanking of pans and the whir of kitchen appliances.

'Can anyone hear me?' she cries.

Hazel looks up from the blackboard and then looks down again.

Filled with frustration, Freya marches over to the electricity box in the broom cupboard and flicks the master switch to 'off', the kitchen powering down instantaneously – ovens, blenders, kettles, toasting grills – everything grinding to a whirring halt.

'Nooooooo!' Harj screams into his frying pan.

'*Putain!*' Michel tosses his sauce into the sink and smashes the cupboard kickboard with his foot. 'Ruined. Everything is ruined!'

'What the fuck?' Leandra-Louise flings her whisk across the floor.

The rotating blades of the ceiling fan slow to a sluggish creak and the sound of the crowd forming outside filters in.

'Freya?' Hazel turns to face her.

Their hyena-like eyes narrow, the pack closing in on her. Michel strides towards her with a ladle in one hand and a cheese grater in the other, but she must not cave in. Success is at stake here. 'We need to shut down the kitchen. We're dropping like flies and the heat in there will kill us.' She backs away before anyone can lynch her, retreating to the terrace.

They follow her like hungry wolves, Michel glowering.

'Close the kitchen?' he growls. 'Surely, that's suicide?'

Freya returns his glare with one of her own. 'Cooking in ninety-degree heat is suicide. I'm not suggesting we abort what we're doing; I'm just suggesting we move it outside. There are three working gas barbecues out here and if we fire them up, we can grill everything we were going to cook.'

'What makes you think you're in charge all of a sudden?' Hazel folds her doughy arms over her chest, reminding Freya of Yolanda Wooton, the school bully at Gamston Primary who'd think nothing of punching you in the gut if you didn't hand over your packed lunch.

Freya chooses to ignore her. 'If we go back in there, we'll be more than one man down again within minutes.'

'She's right,' Stéphane says to Michel and then turns to the others. 'I myself nearly fell in the apples.'

Freya frowns. 'Fell in the . . .'

'Fainted. He nearly fainted,' Michel clarifies.

Stéphane goes on. 'We may cook super food, but we are not superheroes. My underpants are wet, and I am totally out of cornflour.'

Freya walks over to the nearest barbecue on the terrace and lifts the lid. 'If we adapt our menu, there's no reason we can't cook out here. We've got three barbecues. Let's use them.'

'I'm not sure lamb *kleftiko* would work on a barbecue.' Hazel frowns.

'Then let's go for lamb kebabs!' Freya says.

Leandra-Louise takes a step forward and smiles. 'I'm in.'

Harj looks at her like she's lost the plot before he too steps forward to join her. 'I mean, it is like an inferno in there.'

'I do love barbecues,' Michel pronounces.

'And I vote we stay in the kitchen.' Hazel remains rooted to the spot, her fingers clasped together like sausages swollen in the heat. 'We have made a solemn promise to serve traditional Cypriot food and for that, we need a proper oven. Think about the moussaka.'

'Why don't we ditch the moussaka? It's too heavy for a hot day and five more trays seems a bit excessive,' Freya says.

'Over my dead body.' Hazel fronts up to her.

Freya takes a step back. 'OK, OK, we can keep the moussaka. It's all prepped anyway, but the rest we'll cook outside.'

'Yes, Chef!' Harj smiles, encouraging the others to join in.

As the others quickly set about transferring the food from the kitchen, Freya takes a moment to rest in the shadows, allowing herself a private smile and the satisfaction of rising to a challenge. Adaptable. Organised. Cool in a crisis. Talia Drakos, founder of The Golden Spoon, would be impressed – a strong supporter of new talent, she'd shoot Freya one of her sassy little 'go, get 'em, tiger' winks and give her a playful high-five to boot. At last Freya has proved herself to be a real contender.

Twenty minutes later, the smell of grilled lamb and oregano lingers in the air and the terrace is swarming with people. Dimitri holds court, cracking open bottle after bottle of Commandaria from the Bazigou wine cellar and inviting guests to sample delicacies from the three different food stations.

Delivering another tray of sliced sweet potatoes to Stéphane, Freya surveys her newly instated al fresco operation.

Closing the kitchen and adapting each dish to be barbecue-friendly was definitely the right thing to do. Hazel and Michel have a whole queue of people waiting for grilled lamb in *tzatziki* pita, Harj (now showered and sporting his gold turban) has teamed up with Leandra-Louise to make halloumi and vegetable skewers and Stéphane is churning out sweet potato chips like there's no tomorrow. The only thing that hasn't succeeded is Freya's attempt at shifting a ton of moussaka which is predictably proving too hot and too filling for a summer festival. Still, everything is under control, nobody is passing out, and although Kwame hasn't returned, the rest of them are working as a team and now that the masses have started to climb the hill in anticipation of the fireworks, the taverna is coining it in.

Dimitri reappears at Freya's side, his eyes shifting around the terrace. 'Looks like Hazel has got everything under control.'

'Hazel?' Freya feels a pique of annoyance.

'Good plan of hers to move everything outside,' he says, nodding and smiling at the busy stalls. 'And such a great idea of hers to abandon the lamb *kleftiko* and go for kebabs. She's clearly got an eye for a summer menu. You should have taken her advice and replaced that with something lighter.' He peers down at her tray of moussaka before wandering over to the scoreboard and shifting the names around.

Freya is speechless. Did he just . . . She follows him inside, her chest burning with fury and her skin so hot, she could barbecue halloumi on it. Is Hazel seriously claiming this evening as her own victory? Shaking with rage, she tries to calm down but finds herself caught between the need to vomit acid bile and the overwhelming urge to ram the barbecue fork she is clutching up Hazel's nostril and skewer her onto a kebab. This was her one chance to get ahead before people start leaving the competition at the next task, affectionately dubbed D-Day, and now she has been well and truly screwed over. This is dog eat dog. Adrenaline pumping, she looks up at Dimitri. 'It was actually my idea.' Her voice wavers mid-sentence.

Dimitri's face crumples with confusion and Freya is about to elaborate when Michel and Hazel swing by with a platter of meze. 'Lamb?'

Freya shoots Hazel an evil stare and presses on. This may be undignified, but she can't stop herself. 'To get everyone out of the kitchen and barbecue the food outside. It was my idea. Right, Hazel?'

Hazel looks down at the lamb and says nothing.

Freya's pulse quickens. 'Right, Michel?'

Michel looks at Hazel with engineered mystification and says nothing, which only makes matters worse – one woman's word against another.

Freya's face burns with rage. The backstabbing, double-crossing treachery of it all. She feels as though she's about to explode. If she stays here, she will say or do something she regrets.

Down the hill, she tramps. Past candyfloss stalls and coolers of beer. Past a group of men hammering Catherine wheels into a row of wooden stakes. Past jugglers and fire eaters. Past a group of folk dancers threading leather corsets over puff-sleeved blouses behind the remains of an old stone lookout tower. She flashes a furious smile and stomps on. Through an olive grove dotted with fairy lights and down towards the lighthouse, anger bubbling under her skin. It doesn't help that she really needs to pee. Further and further, she descends, all the way down to the narrow rocky path that leads to the sea. Spotting a patch of foliage next to an enormous slab of limestone rock, she leaves the beaten path of bottle tops and abandoned cardboard food trays to trudge through the overgrowth and over a grassy hillock giving shelter to a patch of sea anemone. Dipping behind the rock, she's just about to hitch her dress and squat for an al fresco wee when the shape of something further down the hillside catches her eye and the outline of a man, his arms and legs stretched out across the grass, comes into focus.

'Sorry, I didn't see you there!' She shuffles a little further around the rock to escape his eyeline and is about to empty her bladder when it strikes her that the man – is it a man – hasn't moved an inch. 'You OK?'

She peers over for a closer look and it's only then that she recognises the pattern of his shirt. Pale-blue with a diamond print. Her eyes travel to his chequered trousers and worn leather slippers.

'Christos?'

He doesn't move.

'Christos, it's Freya!' She ambles over the uneven land towards him.

His skin is an ethereal grey. A bottle of Mavro lies at his side, his mouth and chin blotted burgundy with wine stain.

Holding her breath, she circles his body, crouching to get a closer look at his face and when she does, she wishes she hadn't. His eyes are closed, the circles beneath them as dark as rain clouds and the tiny bit of flyaway hair that sprouts from his head is blowing in the breeze with a haphazardness that is almost cruel – the only part of his body that is moving. The sound of the festival becomes distant, and in its place her heart pounds as though it inhabits her ears. Holding her hand beneath his mouth in the hope of detecting the exhalation of breath and feeling nothing, she lowers her ear to his nose, but there is no sound either.

'Christos?'

The smell of urine lingers in the air. Glancing down at his abandoned limbs and sunken torso, she sees the damp patch around the crotch of his trousers.

Christos?' She shakes him by the shoulders. 'Wake up, wake up!'

But Christos does not wake up.

CHAPTER EIGHTEEN

Christos

'Xanthos!' She crosses her arms back and forth above her head in frenzied panic as she runs towards the terrace.

He turns around, waves, and moves to join a group of friends.

'Xanthos!' She screams.

He looks over again.

'Christos has collapsed! Quick!'

Xanthos does a double take. She watches, heart in mouth, as he shoves his water bottle into his back pocket, vaults the terrace wall and races down the hill towards her, hurdling an abandoned picnic as he flies through the air. She turns on her heels, grabbing at his sleeve, the relief of finding him palpable. Xanthos will know what to do; a safe pair of hands in a maelstrom of madness. Down the hill they run, ankles buckling over grassy tussocks and overturned soil, weaving their way around a group of teenagers smoking grass, holding onto each other as they lope past Catherine wheels and candyfloss, overflowing bins and mounds of empty beer bottles. At the gorse bush, she pulls him sharp left, through the fairy-lit olive grove, over the grassy hillock, behind the huge lump of limestone and . . .

'Papa!' Xanthos stares at the body lying in the small gulley, soiled and lifeless.

Freya's skin tightens. Christos is Xanthos's father?

Xanthos's face hardens with fear. Like a leopard stalking its prey, he approaches the body with caution, eyes on the prize before pouncing down beside it.

'Papa?' He slaps at Christos's face. 'Papa?'

Freya's head spins, everything playing out in slow motion.

'Papa!' Xanthos kneels down on the ground and studies his father, his eyes travelling from his wine-splotched chin to his urine-stained crotch.

She bites her lip, a metallic taste forming in her mouth.

'Papa?' His eyes, a misty jade under the moonlight, pool with desperation.

'Is he . . .'

'Papa!' He flings the empty wine bottle down the hillside where it lands with a thud.

'Your water bottle!' Freya cries. 'Shouldn't we try to . . .'

Xanthos takes the plastic flask out of his pocket and squirts his father's face with water but still nothing.

Twisting the hem of her dress around her fingers and

chewing at the inside of her mouth, Freya crouches down beside him. 'Does Lappo have a hospital?'

Xanthos feels for his dad's pulse and says nothing.

'I wanted to call an ambulance,' she says, unable to articulate why she hadn't, 999 not recognised as an emergency number in Cyprus and Freya not knowing what is, and then the small matter of not speaking Greek and understanding where exactly they are situated – it all feels a bit lame now.

Xanthos's forehead furrows. He draws his phone out of his pocket and taps three digits into the screen. Within seconds, there's a voice on the end of the line and he's gabbling loud and fast, urgency palpable in every syllable. Faster and faster he speaks, grabbing his father's wrist and trying once more to locate a pulse. Following the instructions being barked down the phone, he pinches at Christos's nose and sighs with frustration, eyes like dinner plates. He puts his phone on loudspeaker and sets it down on the grass, looking up at Freya with such an intensity it feels as though she is being vacuum packed, his stare sucking every particle of oxygen out of her body and sealing it shut. She wants to look away, but his gaze is magnetic. Apologetic. Imploring. And all the while, the woman on the other end of the phone blurts out a series of commands, none of them comprehensible to Freya.

'We need to lie him like this.' Xanthos demonstrates the recovery position with his arms. 'You take his legs and I'll turn him over.'

Freya feels a surge of panic.

'Ready? On three . . .'

She grabs hold of Christos's ankles, her heart skipping a beat at their lifelessness.

Xanthos's eyes remain faithful to hers; a connection made that can't be broken. 'One . . .'

Her stomach drops. She cannot let him down.

'Two . . .'

She senses a whirl of emotion in his pinprick pupils. Love. Fear. Faith. Dread.

'Three!' he growls.

They tiptoe along a tightrope of hope and uncertainty, both of them wavering as they try to navigate their way along an invisible wire, neither daring to look down to affirm there's no safety net. With all her might, she twists Christos over at the hip, wrapping his left thigh over his right as Xanthos rolls over his torso, which flops over onto the ground. The woman on the other end of the phone barks more instructions.

Head lolloping like a pumpkin skull, Christos falls onto his front. Wiping her hair out of her face, Freya watches as Xanthos lifts his dad's left arm so that it lies flush with his ribcage and sets his right arm level with his head. Then, rocking Christos's waist back and forth with one hand and slapping at his cheek with the other, Xanthos closes his eyes and mutters prayers only he can hear.

'Xan . . .' Freya's voice fails her.

She wants to throw her arms around his neck and tell him everything's going to be OK, but it clearly isn't and anyway, words are futile right now.

Tears form in his eyes. 'We have to get him into the sea.

Dimitri threw him in the bath and turned the shower on him last time. He needs the shock of water. Heavy water.'

He grabs his phone and ends the call, then reaches for Christos, dragging him under the arms into a sitting position, shoulders slouched, head lolling. 'Come on, come on.' He pats at his father's cheeks, but still nothing.

Freya threads her arm under Christos's and gestures for Xanthos to take the other side. Together, they drag him through the thinning grass and onto the sand dunes. Scarecrow. Ragdoll. Strawman. Father. Chef. Drunkard. Puffing and panting, they heave and strain, losing their grip every few yards and eventually collapsing beneath Christos's limp body only a few inches from the sea. Xanthos looks up, defeat etched on his face. He has taken the lion's share of the weight and slumps down with exhaustion.

'Come on!' Freya yells, taking Christos's right shoulder and forcing Xanthos's hand onto his left. 'On three!'

Xanthos nods silently.

'One, two, THREE!' She pulls as hard as she can and this time, such is the magic of the moon's pull on the sea, that the tide inches towards them, it too playing its part.

Together they haul Christos towards the water, rolling him across the wet sand, his worn leather slippers abandoned to the shore and at last the pull of the current joins forces with them and he is finally in the sea. Kicking off their shoes and flinging them to the shore, they drag Christos further into the dark water, trapped air ballooning inside his chef's shirt until he half floats, half sinks in Xanthos's arms. Water rushes over his face, his chequered chef trousers darkening, and his feet giving the impression that they are kicking. Illusion is a cruel beast at times. Propping up his back and taking hold of one of his hands, Freya feels the weight of the universe upon her shoulders. The coward in her would love nothing more than to bolt right now. Far, far away from the immensity of this situation and the ever-increasing prospect of death. Her eye is drawn to the lanterns spaced along the cliffside which twinkle to the hum of festival music and she's just wondering where Dimitri is now that she knows Christos to be his father too, when Christos's hand spasms in hers. Another cruel illusion? She looks down at Christos, his head jolting to one side, his eyes opening and his mouth gasping for air.

'Papa!' Xanthos's face fills with joy.

Freya feels as though her heart might burst. Is this nothing short of a miracle?

Christos shudders, his body momentarily folding in two before unleashing a torrent of red wine vomit into the surf. He gurgles and chokes, Xanthos cradling his head in his arms and swilling his face with sea water. He plants a kiss on Christos's forehead, tears of relief flowing from his eyes. Jubilant, they heave him to the shore where he vomits again.

Freya looks up as sirens wail and an electric blue flare illuminates the hillside. Xanthos waves his arms at a pair of paramedics who pick their way through the rocks down to the beach, one carrying a medical supply box and the other a stretcher. Like soldiers, they trudge across the beach.

Xanthos stands up, explaining in Greek what has happened as the male paramedic lays out a blanket and the female paramedic crouches down to shine a torch in Christos's eyes.

He pulls away, a good sign apparently. The male paramedic searches through his medical supply kit and brings out a foil bag of liquid. Removing the lid, he attaches a long tube and feeds it into Christos's mouth. Freya's hand finds Xanthos's as they huddle together, breath bated. Christos does as he's told and sucks on the tube, spluttering first and then finding his rhythm, taking in the liquid contents as a Velcro band gets wrapped around his upper arm. The digits flash on the paramedic's handheld device and like a roulette wheel, slow until they finally draw to a halt. The paramedic frowns for a second, Freya's stomach dropping, before he gives them the OK sign with a rounded finger and thumb. She feels her jaw loosen, a sense of relief passing over her as she looks up at Xanthos.

'Freeya?' His voice wavers with emotion as he squeezes her hand, his piercing eyes peering through dark tendrils of hair and there, in that moment, she forgets every thought she's ever had as he lowers his chin onto her hand, the bristles of his stubble scratching against her skin. Enveloping her shoulders with his arms, he hugs her tightly until they become one and it's no longer clear who is supporting whom.

CHAPTER NINETEEN

Kindred Spirits

'Why don't you call him dad or papa? Publicly, I mean.' Freya stares at the hospital sign – a simple H etched onto a blue square metal panel welded to a nearby lamp post.

'It was Dimitri's idea. He thought it would sound more professional if our chef was an outsider. The downside of a family business is that everything looks so small and amateur.'

Freya huddles her knees to her chest not because she's cold but because she doesn't quite know what to do with her hands. 'I think a family business has charm. Heritage. A sense of familiarity. You know, love and care being passed from generation to generation.'

His eyes meet hers, then dart away. 'If I'm honest, Dimitri

and I used to be ashamed and then we got so used to calling him Christos and it kind of stuck.'

'Ashamed of what?'

'His dependency on alcohol.' He scratches at his stubble. 'He's tried everything. Herbology. Cold turkey. Hypnotism. The alchemist down in the village. Alcoholics Anonymous in Paphos. Cutting down. Cutting out. Nothing works . . .'

Freya brushes her dress down over her knees and wonders how many people this 'hospital' can care for with only four beds, a consultation room and no actual waiting area – she's not seen a single person come or go in the hour that they've been there – no nursing staff, nobody sneaking out for a crafty fag. Nobody. She thinks of Christos lying there in that small, narrow bed on top of that wafer-thin blue blanket and looks over to Xanthos. 'Is that why you don't drink? Because you think you'll end up like him?'

Xanthos looks up at the starry sky, his face swathed in moonlight. 'Maybe.'

She scrunches up her nose. 'And yet you're a winemaker?'

'Pathetic, isn't it?'

A pair of pigeons strut across the village square in pursuit of kebab leftovers, the iridescent green and purple throat feathers around their necks expanding and retracting in perfect harmony. A loud crack. An almighty bang. The pigeons take flight as a firework torpedoes through the air with a fizz and a crackle, releasing a fountain of glorious gold stars that shimmer and fade through the midnight sky.

Freya feels guilty for envying those celebrating. 'How did you end up with vineyards?'

'They've belonged to my family for centuries. My father was a winemaker for years until his drinking became so bad that my mother made him change career. He got a job as a chef in mainland Greece when I turned eighteen and I took over. Of course, half of the land is Dimitri's, but we manage it together like we do the cookery school.'

His openness unsettles her, and she feels the need to kiss him, which might not be wildly appropriate given that they're waiting at a hospital for his half-dead father to revive. Instead, she pulls at her eyebrow and says nothing. A giant ball of silver sparks explodes in the night sky with a pop and a whizz, Freya just plucking up the courage to put her hand on Xanthos's thigh when Dimitri appears out of the darkness on the other side of the road.

'Hey!' Xanthos stands up and waves his brother over.

A gaggle of girls in sequinned bikinis and feathered head-dresses emerge behind Dimitri in the glow of the street light. He shouts something in Greek and wanders off in the opposite direction, his arms around the tallest two.

'He said he'll be back,' Xanthos says in response to the look of revulsion on her face, shaking his head and chuckling under his breath as his brother disappears out of sight.

She pulls a face. 'He's not even just a tiny bit worried about his dad?'

Xanthos looks down at the ground. 'He's a good man really, he just finds it really hard.'

Freya keeps her thoughts to herself.

'When we were eleven, our school made a trip to our vine-yards where my father promised to teach children how to plant grapes. How to grow grapes. How to pick grapes, tread them, ferment them. Everything. You know how long the trip lasted?'

Freya isn't sure whether his question is rhetorical. 'Go on,' she says.

'Five minutes! We got there. Sixty children, two teachers, four parents. All ready and excited to learn and then, paff! My dad stumbled out of the wine cellar, smelling of urine, and crashed into them all! A minute later he was asleep on the floor.'

Freya presses her lips together, feeling embarrassed on his behalf.

'It was so humiliating. Dimitri and I were outcasts from then on. Nobody let us play football. Nobody wanted to sit next to us in class. Nobody would come to our home. "*Vromos*," we were known as, and all because of dad.'

Freya frowns. '*Vromos*?'

'Stinkers, I guess you'd say.'

'*Vromos*,' Freya says, putting on her best Greek accent.

He throws his head back and laughs. 'You sound like my grandmother.'

'That's exactly what I was going for,' Freya says, her eye drawn to a bat swooping and diving beneath the street lamp and her thoughts turning to her mother. 'So, I might not understand what it's like to have an alcoholic parent, but I totally understand what it's like to have a parent who suffers with an illness that can humiliate you to the very core.' She swallows hard, her mind flooded with a million memories.

His eyes follow her line of sight. 'How do you mean?'

The bat flutters beneath the bunting further down the street, its flight path angular and inconsistent. No sooner has it darted one way, it swerves the other, its direction forever changing. Unpredictable. Beautiful. Free. Freya smiles. Certain creatures weren't born to fly in straight lines.

'My mother is schi . . . a schiz . . . a . . .' The words get stuck in her throat.

'Schizophrenic?'

'Yes.'

He frowns. 'I've said it correctly?'

'Perfectly.'

'Schiz-o-phren-ic.' He repeats.

A wave of nausea overcomes her. Must he really say it over and over again, stretching out each syllable until it's bent out of shape? Just the once was enough; the word alone so stark, its consonants so pointy and shouty, it sounds as though it should be dictated as a military command. Couldn't they have come up with something a little softer? More palatable? Easier on the tongue?

'It's a Greek word, you know. Schizophrenia.'

'It is?'

'*Schizo* is "split". *Phrene* is "the mind".'

A sense of calm flows over her. It doesn't sound so bad when you break it down like that. Logical. Explanatory. Descriptive. Not quite as sharp and pointy. Not so harsh and abrupt. Still, with her mother, it's complicated. She swallows hard, her good hand automatically shifting to the scar on her 'bad' one. 'OK, so you know how you were saying that your dad embarrassed you on your school trip . . . well I can probably do one better.'

'Yeah?'

'Not that I'm trying to trump your tragedy! It's just . . .' It feels as though her throat has been filled with cement – she's never divulged this story to anyone, not even Charlie or Khady. She goes to pick the skin on her knee and thinks better of it, holding her hands hostage by sitting on them. 'I don't know how much you know about schizophrenia, but there are a few different types. My mum has paranoid schizophrenia which means she suffers with hallucinations and delusions. When she's lucid, you wouldn't have a clue that she's got a person- ality disorder – fuck, I hate that term – but when she goes, she goes big time. Once, she turned up to a parents' evening dressed as a nun and went around telling all the staff to go home and pray for the parents to be forgiven of their sins.'

'She *what?*'

'She told the headmaster that the school was going to be firebombed and then started banging on about them installing all this fire safety kit she'd found on the internet.'

'Oh dear,' he says, wide-eyed.

'I wouldn't have put it past her to have blown up the place just to prove herself right. She was wild. Completely possessed. And I'm ashamed to say that I used to pretend she wasn't my mother. Through school, I pretended she wasn't my mother. I never introduced her to anyone.'

Xanthos's face fills with so much horror it's as though she's just admitted to selling her mum's kidneys on the black market. He blows out his lips. 'But your mother is your mother! You can't pretend she's not!'

Feeling rotten to the very core, Freya digs her thumbnail

into the scar tissue on her knee. 'Everybody understands alco-holism,' she says with an air of frustration. 'Everybody knows someone with an alcohol dependency, and nobody mocks it because they can relate to it – most people like a drink and can at least imagine what it feels like to want one too much, but this . . .'

'Schizophrenia?'

'Yes. Schizophrenia is different. The moment people know your mother is in a psychiatric nursing home, they imagine her frothing at the mouth and strapped into a straitjacket. You know, there was a boy in my class who doodled a sketch of her in shackles, entitled it Schiz-Bitch and gave her a speech bubble saying she was coming after everyone's blood.'

Xanthos looks at her earnestly. 'I'm sorry, Freeya. It must be very hard for you.'

'The hardest thing is seeing her robbed of her own life. She can't live independently. She can't hold down a job or a rela-tionship. She can't see the people she loves when she wants to. She can't get on a plane and travel. She couldn't come to The Golden Spoon finals even if she wanted to.'

'It's a cruel illness,' he says softly.

'I was lucky really. It didn't get really bad until I'd left home. I didn't have to get fostered or anything. She did the best she could for me.' Freya dare not look up. She knows she's said too much already, and he'll think of her as someone who needs fixing, or worse – pitying. That's always what happens. She could draw it as a diagram; the cycle of attrac-tion, sympathy, circumspection, detachment – broken on the inside and too much trouble to deal with. Baggage. Emotion catches in her throat, her nostrils filling with a pin cushion of spikes as the sharp metal nib of her mother's fountain pen appears in her mind's eye, oozing blood instead of ink, and although Freya tries to push it out of her memory, it refuses to disappear, stabbing its way through her flesh, fresh pain rocketing through her veins. She runs her fingers over the livid pink scar on her hand, remembering reaching for the panic button. The anger in her mother's eyes. Scratch marks on the wooden table. The unrelenting scream of the alarm, nursing staff arriving from all directions. *Let's clean you up, dear.* Her mother coming at her again and again with the pen, wielding it above her like a weapon and sinking it into Freya's skin, her face twisted with hurt. *You understand it's nothing personal. She's not seeing what you see now.* Arteries rupturing, skin shredding, agony screaming through Freya's body, the functioning of her brain suspended in disbelief. Blood. So much blood everywhere. At first, she thought it belonged to her mother, the pain on her mother's face suggestive of heavy bleeding, but then as shock turned into an agonising throb, she knew the blood was hers. There was a lot of it. *Put the pen down now, Madeline.* Blood trickling down her wrist, over the chair, onto the carpet. *It's your daughter, Madeline.* Blood everywhere. *Drop the pen, Madeline!* How was there so much blood?

It would be a whole year before Freya saw her mother after the fountain pen stabbing. Having had her hand operated on to repair damage to a major vein along with several wrist ligaments, and countless rounds of therapy for post-traumatic stress, it took a while before she was 'match fit' to face her mother again. The senior psychologist assigned to her case was at pains to point out that this was a classic case of the drama triangle, her mother making that subtle switch from persecutor to victim which meant a change of role for Freya too – she may have started as the victim of violence, but it only took a few weeks before she was the rescuer once more. But what did it really matter whether she was the rescuer, victim or the persecutor? Labels wouldn't solve anything. At the end of the day, she'd been hurt by her mother on so many levels and had to learn to trust her again.

Through the blur of tears, Freya gazes at the moon until the tightness in her throat has relented. Perhaps she does need fixing – or healing at least – after all. But just when she feels at her most wretched and that all is lost, Xanthos surprises her with the weight of his arm as it envelopes her shoulder. Breathing in his warm skin, she gives in to his embrace, allowing her head to fall against his broad chest. He smells so good, so reassuring. And although she can admit that part of her wants to crumple in his arms, she knows she doesn't need to be saved. Not by man, woman nor beast. She has managed to deal with her mother's illness her entire life and as ugly and twisted as it is, she will continue to do so, at her own pace and on her own terms. Resilience has become part of her armour.

'Mental illnesses are complicated,' Xanthos says softly. 'Schizophrenia, especially.'

'I prefer not to put a label on it,' she says snippily.

He shrugs his shoulders. 'Sometimes a label can be a good thing. The more diagnoses, the more funding, the more support.

The more these invisible things are talked about, the more they are understood, and the more open everyone is about it—'

'The more normalised it becomes . . .' Freya looks down at her feet.

A beguiling smile breaks out across his face. 'You are not alone, Freeya.'

A warm swell of happiness suffuses her body which dissipates as quickly as it arrived upon realising that he is staring at her big toes which are not only gargantuan but a tiny bit hairy. His face becomes an unconscious frown as she scrunches them up in an attempt to hide the sprouts of hair around her toe knuckles. There is no way out now. Tonight, he has seen everything. Feigning the need to stretch her legs, she springs up off the step and is about to bring the focus back to him when the door behind them slides open and a doctor appears, a stethoscope hanging around his neck.

He looks down at Xanthos. 'Bazigou?' he says with a frown.

'Yes,' Xanthos says in English, getting to his feet, his face clouded with worry.

Freya takes his hand and squeezes it gently, letting him know she's there for him.

The doctor looks at Freya and then returns his attention to Xanthos. 'Your wife?'

'No.' A smile plays on Xanthos's lips.

The doctor looks at Freya sympathetically. 'I'm sorry, family only.'

Xanthos presses her to his chest. 'Thank you,' he says, the force of his gaze sending a shudder down her spine.

Her skin tingles as his cheek brushes against hers, his hot

breath catching on her neck and for a moment she thinks he's going to kiss her. Were it not for the doctor's impatient clearing of his throat, who knows, maybe he would?

She watches as the hospital door slides shut behind him and it takes all her strength to walk away.

CHAPTER TWENTY

Cheese Porn

'Do you know the story of the Greek mermaid?'

'Isn't that the line Dimitri used on Leandra-Louise?'

'I take no responsibility for my brother.' Xanthos lets go of the oars to hold up his hands in surrender. 'How he makes his bed is how he is going to sleep.'

The boat rocks back and forth, Freya's insides with it. The Qwells tablet she took in anticipation of the trip is certainly working its magic at the moment, but who knows for how long its effects will last. Seasickness and sunburn – two stead-fast ways of killing the vibe on a Mediterranean boat trip for two. And although she has slathered herself in the highest factor sunscreen, her English rose complexion is already starting to burn under the powerful glare of the Greek sun.

Legs astride, feet anchored below a beam of wood that runs the width of the boat, Xanthos pivots the left oar in its holder and, skimming the paddle across the gentle waves, showers her with a fountain of water.

She shrieks, relishing the touch of the cool saltwater spray against her hot skin.

Tilting, the boat slowly makes a U-turn, its wooden helm rotating once more towards the shore. She takes hold of the oars, comforted by the way they feel in her hands. Heavy, solid and still warm from Xanthos's grip.

'Do you know the story of *The Owl and the Pussycat*?' she says, admiring the boat's pea-green paintwork.

He undresses her with his eyes. 'Is that a line too?'

'Touché!'

'You're very red,' he says flatly. 'Do you have sunscreen?'

Freya feels her cheeks burn. Maybe he wasn't mentally undressing her after all. When they'd spoken on the phone this morning, it had been business-like; she asked how Christos was and Xanthos confirmed his father was in a stable condition and then, knowing that they all have a scheduled day off today, offered to pick her up at 10 a.m. to show her the island. And that was pretty much it. No flirting. No loaded pauses or tongue-tripping awkwardness. No laughing, joking or even good-natured joshing. Short and sweet. Perfunctory. Transactional. Efficient. Last night's heavy events cutting through frivolity. Maybe she should have text messaged him instead. It's always easier to flirt via text. Throw in the odd emoji. Winky faces and thumbs up, keeping the bantz light-hearted and fun. But she felt the occasion called for a proper conversation – not only because she wanted to hear the soft huskiness of his voice, but because a text might seem too flippant given the circumstances – his dad being on a drip and fighting for his life and all that. Of course, she'd planned to say a lot more than she actually did and was hoping he'd be a bit more forthcoming but hey, whatever works. And worked it has because here they are now, halfway around the island, floating on a rolling, sapphire carpet, skin tingling in the morning sun.

'Go on then . . .' She plucks the translucent patches of her dress away from her chest. 'The Greek mermaid?'

He clears his throat with a growl, sending a shiver down her spine. 'You know you remind me of her.'

'Of the Little Mermaid?'

'Goddess Atargatis! She has your flaming red hair and snow-white skin.'

'You make me sound like a clown!' Freya says, looking down at her arms and inspecting them for new freckles. Can't he see that she's actually got a suntan? If he thinks she's white now, God forbid he should see her in her milky-translucent winter state. 'Albs' she used to get called at school – the kids at Gamston Comprehensive somewhat apathetic to the true definition of albino, and although there was one other girl in her class with red hair, Samantha MacMillan's tresses were distinctly more auburn than Freya's, meaning that only she got ginger-slammed. English rose by the kind-hearted. Ginger minger by the less charitable.

'You have beautiful hair,' he says earnestly.

She starts to feel self-conscious and not unlike a modern-day

Shirley Valentine; another English girl on a boat trip around a Greek island about to get sailed and nailed. Oh, the cliché. But then again, why ever the fuck not? Everything could come crashing down around her ears tomorrow and it could be the end of the competition for her so she may as well 'let her ovaries off their leash' to coin Khady's phrase. And besides, given the frosty atmosphere over breakfast this morning, it's not like she wants to hang around with her fellow cooks today. Kwame, it appears, has stayed true to his word and has not yet returned and whilst Hazel maintains that she's not dropping out of the competition, she's keen to milk her recent injury as much as she can, Michel having to cut her toast up for her this morning and Harj delivering it to her room. Everyone else is at loggerheads and although Michel and Stéphane had a romantic day trip planned, the pair of them were last heard screaming at each other in their villa. To say things are fractious is an understatement, and adding to the melting pot is Xanthos's insistence on downplaying the drama with Christos. The others must know that he's not just plain 'ill' and she feels guilty for going along with this narrative at breakfast this morning.

'The Greek mermaid?' She returns her attention to Xanthos.

He offers her water from his flask. 'You tourists are always in a rush.'

'Are we?'

He puts on his best British accent. '"What time is breakfast?" "What time do the shops shut?" "Do we have time to go to the supermarket?" "When does the launderette open?"'

Freya laughs. 'I guess . . .'

'OK, let me put you out of your mystery; the Greek mermaid.'

'Misery. Let me put you out of your *misery*.'

His brow furrows. 'Misery? That makes no sense. Mystery makes a lot more sense.'

She smiles, brushing aside the burning sensation in her shoulders. It actually does make a lot more sense.

'OK, the Greek mermaid . . . goddess Atargatis was worshipped by the gods for her beauty, but she didn't want to be adored for looks alone.' He takes the oars from her and steers the boat towards the shore, finding his groove as he powers the paddles through the surf. 'As a test to see if the gods would still devote themselves to her without her beauty, she transformed herself into a plain, grey fish. Nothing too colourful. Nothing too special. Nothing too "bling" as you'd say . . .'

'I would never say "bling".'

He raises an eyebrow. 'Unable to stay on dry land now that she was a fish, she dived into a lake and stayed there. The gods became angry. They didn't want her to surrender her beauty and wouldn't allow her to give up her face, her hair, her breasts . . . so she kept her top half in human form, and they allowed her to become a fish from the waist down.'

'How thoughtful of them.'

Xanthos laughs. 'As a mermaid, she swam to freedom. The moral of the story: a man can never tie down a woman. He can use his physicality, but he can never crush her spirit.'

'Riiight,' Freya says, questioning whether this is truly a story of female emancipation or moreover feminism told from a man's point of view. It may be that she's supposed to be impressed, moved and spiritually awakened, but all she has is an undying, groin-pulsing, ovary-clacking horniness that won't even go away when she thinks about the competition tomorrow. Truth be told, she'd be quite happy for Xanthos to use his physicality and crush her spirit right over the back of this boat. In fact, she wants nothing more than her spirit to be crushed in all manner of ways. Does that make her a bad person and an anti-feminist? What the fuck is the matter with her?

'I hope you find this story romantic.' His eyes sparkle.

'It's a solid gold aphrodisiac. My boat is officially floated.'

He frowns. 'Your boat is floated? That is romantic?'

'I just meant . . . It doesn't matter.'

His attention is drawn to her rapidly reddening shoulders. 'Do you have a shirt?'

Reaching into her bag for her sarong which doubles as a shawl, she rummages through sunscreen, lip balm, sunglasses case, phone, wallet, a paperback she has no intention of reading, and then remembers leaving it on the end of the bed. A rooky error.

Xanthos lets out a grunt of disapproval. 'You are burning.'

'Like a disco inferno.' She tries to laugh it off, but a quick glance at her shoulder tells her it's going to be painful and more than a tad humiliating when she turns up tomorrow with her skin burned to a crisp and sore with blisters. Ouch. His fingers travel to the neck of his blue linen shirt and then to both her surprise and delight, he unclothes himself, one button at a time, revealing soft olive skin she wants to touch so badly it feels as though she may inwardly combust, burning almost as much beneath her skin as she is on its surface. Torso taut, he peels the shirt sleeves away from his bulging arms and hands it to her like it's nothing.

'Very gallant.' She smiles playfully, every fibre of her body smouldering with desire.

'I just don't want you to burn.'

'What about you?' She tries not to stare at his chest.

He holds her gaze. 'I was born here. I'm used to it.'

Taking pleasure from the touch of the cotton as it brushes against her skin, she pulls the shirt over her shoulders and inhales the scent of his body's musk. She smiles, reminded of the lad three caravans down from her childhood home who, in a bid to secure her, insisted she wear his tracksuit top for a week. It felt oddly gratifying, being swaddled in someone else's clothes, knowing that they cared. Of course Darren What's-his-face had a multitude of tracksuit tops doing the rounds at Chiverly caravan park and it turned out he didn't care that much at all, but still, it felt good for a while.

Xanthos clears his throat. 'May I ask if there is a Mr Freeya?'

'A Mr Freya?' Freya giggles. Maybe he is interested after all.

'A husband. A partner . . .'

She flashes him a coy smile. 'I wouldn't be on this boat with you if there was a husband or partner!' she says, proud at herself for being so direct and making a mental note to tell Khady how flirtatious and un-Freya she was.

He says nothing though his eyes do all the talking with an

infectious sparkle of mischief and she finds herself unable to stifle her smile.

They follow the dazzling white rock formations of the craggy coastline, exploring hidden caves shaped by wind and water, the sea becoming an ever-changing palette of colour beneath the dancing sunlight. Xanthos rows the boat towards a huge limestone rock jutting out of the water, its stone sculpted and smoothed over time. Further along, tamarisk trees cling to the rocky shoreline leading to a row of whitewashed fishing houses, their doors painted an Aegean blue. Freya breathes in the scent of sea lavender, her eye drawn to a tattered Cypriot flag suspended from the bough of a deserted boat, flapping in the breeze. She drinks in the moment, a frisson of happiness travelling through her.

'You know who these caves belonged to?' Xanthos walks his hands across a chunk of rough bone-white rock to leverage the boat into the gulley. '*Kleftes.*'

Freya wrinkles her nose with ignorance.

'Thieves. Pirates. Guerrillas. Back in the days of the Greek Revolution, *kleftes* would hide in these caves and ambush incoming ships, then they'd stash their loot here. They'd pillage the land too, stealing goats, sheep, cattle. This is where the word "*kleftiko*" comes from. Stolen lamb. The *kleftes* would capture an animal as it grazed, then kill it and cook the meat over red-hot stones in a hole in the ground for hours and hours. Any hole in the stones they had to block with soil so that no steam could escape and give them away.'

Freya nods in appreciation. His island facts are fascinating and she's learning way more on this boat trip about Cypriot culture and history than she could possibly learn from a whole fortnight up at the taverna. He seems to know what makes her tick and from now on, she'll look at *kleftiko* in a whole new light. That said, she's also beginning to worry that Xanthos's guided tour around the coast is actually a legitimate educational excursion. Maybe the Mr Freya question was a test, and this isn't the flooze-cruise she'd assumed it would be, his intentions honourable after all. A wave of disappointment overcomes her. Has she been too flirty? Has she not been flirty enough? Maybe she hasn't expressed sufficient appreciation of his tales of Cypriot history and Greek mythology? Maybe she's as shallow as the waters beneath her and should stop obsessing about getting naked with him and start listening a bit more.

The boat glides between two walls of limestone, Xanthos patting his hands along the rugged rock on one side as they slide into a narrow strip of cool shade.

'We'll stop at the next beach for a picnic,' he says, steering the boat towards the crystal-clear waters of the next cove along – a small, horseshoe-shaped bay, deeper than it is wide. 'Achivadolimni,' he announces.

'Same to you!'

'The lake of shellfish.' He gazes into the water. 'Look down.'

Freya peers over the edge of the boat and can't quite believe what she's seeing. The whole seabed is made up of thousands of clams and conches, a montage of shells jutting angularly in every direction. Cockles and mussels, alive, alive-oh. A mosaic of seafood. 'Amazing.'

The boat drifts towards the shore, leaving the dark indigo

of deeper waters behind. Xanthos steps out and guides it onto the pebbles of a small, rainbow-coloured shale beach, reds becoming purples, purples becoming pinks, pinks becoming a slate grey which gradually morphs into a burned orange. A spectrum of shells entirely for them.

'Jump out!' he says.

Leaning on his shoulder and trying not to trip over the bottom of her dress as it gets caught around the oar, she climbs out of the boat and onto dry land. Together they pull the small wooden rowing boat up onto the shore, a rush of wild rosemary on salt air hitting her nostrils. Glancing back at the crystal-clear water, she takes stock of the moment and vows to never forget it. Rainbow shale. Turquoise sea. The smell of fresh herbs. Stories of Greek revolutionaries. Xanthos's twinkling eyes – they will all forever be etched in her memory.

Only a few feet away, an oystercatcher wades through the shallow water, its bright red bill dipping into the froth and re-emerging with a shell, then disturbed by their movement, it takes flight, flapping its dark feathers, a flash of white on its wing tip, and soars high above them, gliding over to the clifftop where it lands on a small ledge to deliver a beak of food to hidden chicks. A moment later, the bird is back again. Motherhood; it's relentless.

She wonders what her mother is doing now. Having lost track of time, it takes her a while to work out that it's a Monday, which means her mum will be stuck in a frayed armchair in the communal lounge of Stocksbridge nursing home, reading whatever crime thriller she's got on the go whilst her fellow residents indulge in a game of bingo in order that their bed linen can be changed. A chaperoned walk around the local park – three trees, a dilapidated children's play area and a designated dog-walking field, followed by microwaved steak and kidney pie with two different types of vegetable for lunch. What. A. Life.

'Are you OK?' Xanthos reaches for her knee.

'Fine,' she says, bouncing back from her daydream.

'Hungry?' he says, heaving a basket of food out of the boat and peeling back a gingham tea towel to reveal a variety of cheeses.

As she peers into the hamper, a swirl of emotions overcomes her – joy, rapture, hunger and lust. This Greek god has sailed her to the other side of this paradise island and is about to present her with cheese. She really is living the dream.

He lies back on his elbows, sprawls his legs out and squints up at the sky. Positioning herself next to him, she pulls her dress over her legs to protect them from the sun and can't help noticing just how topsy-turvy the morning has felt – tranquillity and peace jarring with flashbacks of Christos's lifeless body. The sparkle of fireworks. Xanthos's fearful eyes. Dark secrets and glittering revelations. A lot happened last night and now here they are, washed up on an idyllic cove without a care in the world.

'How is your dad?' She breathes in the scent of his shirt. 'Really, I mean.'

'Better than you'd imagine.' He smiles. 'He's promised he will make the trip to Paphos for The Golden Spoon final.'

Freya's stomach lurches. 'I thought we'd agreed that's a forbidden topic of conversation?'

'Think like a winner, Freeya.' His green eyes blaze through tendrils of dark hair as he shuffles his elbow around in the shell fragments to get comfortable, then props his head in the palm of his hand. 'OK. Are you ready for a lesson in cheese?'

Freya's heart fills with joy. 'Am I ever!'

She looks down at the cheeseboard where a dozen or so cheeses are set out. A soft cheese drizzled with olive oil and herbs sits on the edge of the platter – Anthotiro? Manouri? Certainly not feta. Next to it stands a hulk of crumbly yellow cheese topped with walnuts and grapes, and in the corner alongside two ripe figs is a chunk of what is unmistakably halloumi, but the rest she's not so sure about.

'OK.' He clears his throat with his trademark growl. 'A cheeseboard is like a chessboard . . . The queen, in this case the Ladotyri, is the most powerful player here but never overlook the strength of the other pieces on the board. You should never underestimate the creaminess of Mizithra or the smokiness of Metsovone in the same way a chess player should not disregard the capability of a knight or a bishop.'

Freya feels her skin getting hotter.

Xanthos looks her straight in the eye. 'And just like chess, a cheeseboard needs a king. Kaskavalli. Kaskavalli is always King.'

'Kaskavalli?' she says, disappointed that she's never heard of it.

'It is a Cypriot cheese, similar to Kefalograviera.' Plunging the curved blade of a cheese knife into a small block of smoked cheese, orange in colour, he holds it up under her nose and smiles. 'Do you recognise this one?'

'Kaskavalli? King of the board?'

He shakes his head, flicking small droplets of water over her shoulders which even through the shirt make her skin tingle. 'Kaskavalli is this one.' He prods at a pale yellow semi-hard cheese standing in the corner. 'Belonging to the family of pasta filata, he is made from the milk of sheep. You'll meet him in sandwiches or pastries and we can also pan-fry him and serve as *saganaki*. But this one . . .' He returns the blade of the knife to the smoked cheese. 'This one is metsovone.'

Freya feels like a culinary heathen. She can't pronounce it, let alone pick it out from a cheese line up but it feels liberating not to be judged for it.

'I'm told metsovone is not so well known outside Cyprus. She's from the village of Metsovone in the mountains of Northern Greece – a beautiful, beautiful village.' He holds the cheese to his nose and inhales. 'Made from the milk of cows, sometimes blended with other milks, but always including that of the cow, her taste is unique. Sprinkle cayenne pepper on top and grill her for a short time only and she is perfect.'

There's something about the way he assigns gender to each cheese that holds Freya powerless. She digs her fingertips into the gritty shells and feels herself falling further under his spell.

'This one you may know from the supermarket.' He holds up what she knows from its wheel-shape to be Graviera. 'In Crete, she is made of sheep's milk and has a buttery flavour, but here in Cyprus, we like her rich, sweet and slightly spicy.'

Freya watches, open-mouthed, as his finger travels around the board, a pulse springing up in her groin. 'Feta, Anthotiro, Kaskavalli, Anari—'

'Anari?' she says breathlessly.

'Anari is another Cypriot cheese,' he says, dipping his finger into a soft ricotta-like whirl and offering it to her on his fingertip. 'It is soft and mild.'

It's almost too much. Slowly, she leans towards him and licks it off his finger, her mouth filling with a soft cream that tastes both sweet and salted. 'Oh, wow. That's incredible.'

Eyes shining, he nods. 'Cypriot cheese is the best.'

She doesn't want to swallow for fear of losing the flavour. 'Manouri, Galotyri . . . Galotyri is beautiful for dipping.' As he goes on, the pulse in her groin grows stronger. 'Feta and finally, halloumi. You know halloumi, right?'

'Right.' She smiles.

'Wrong!' He springs to life, sitting up straight and gesticulating flamboyantly. 'You know a plasticky, rubbery poor man's halloumi. A halloumi who has been suffocated and unable to breathe. A halloumi who does not represent the real halloumi of Cyprus. As my dad would say, "you know Santa's little helpers, but you do not know the real Santa Claus."'

Freya is practically on her hands and knees begging for more.

'The real halloumi is the hero of the cheeseboard. Like the knight on a chessboard, he represents the soldier of medieval times who protects his people from hunger and boredom. He may be considered less important than a bishop, a king or a queen, but he is the only piece who can leapfrog another. Halloumi is the dark horse.'

Freya wonders how much longer she can take it without ripping his clothes off and straddling him. This is cheese porn at its finest and she doesn't want it to end. Xanthos explaining the flavours and history of cheese in his strong, Greek accent is so much more sensual than any sex. Give her cheese porn over porn-porn any day.

She watches in a daze as he gets up to comb the beach for small pieces of driftwood.

'What are you doing?' she calls over.

'The thing about halloumi,' he says, gathering up a bundle of wood in his arms, 'is that he only really comes to life when heated up.'

It's almost too much for her to take.

Angled this way and that, the splintered wooden shards stack together nicely to form the basis of a perfect fire which he ignites with a cigarette lighter out of the basket. The driftwood acts as kindling, heat ripping through each piece until a small fire comes to life with the crackle of wood and the flickering of flames. He takes a strip of halloumi and holds it on a fork a few inches away from the flames.

She watches as the cheese relaxes, its ends curling up and its body melting until it is about to drop off the fork. Who cares whether he's a player or not?

'When raw, halloumi is something, but grilled, he is everything.' He carries the fork through the air and guides it towards her mouth.

It feels as though the ground is slip-sliding away beneath

her. Opening her mouth, she engulfs the melted cheese, loving the sensation of it on her tongue, its tangy, salty flavour becoming almost smoky.

'Never underestimate the power of halloumi,' Xanthos goes on. 'He is very versatile. Serve him with fig jam and crackers as an appetiser, or whole as a fondue cheese *kataifi* pie.'

'Mango, chicken and halloumi salad.' Freya volleys back a suggestion.

'Cut him into strips, wrap her in pancetta and serve him as halloumi fries.'

'Halloumi and harissa fatteh,' she counters.

'Halloumi and pea falafel with flatbread.'

'Halloumi and tomato bake?'

'Barbecued halloumi skewers with purple sprouting broccoli.'

She giggles. 'Barbecued halloumi with any type of broccoli!'

'Or add honey and chilli and turn him into a sweet treat,' he says, dipping his finger into the soft cheese and pressing it into Freya's mouth. 'So, are you hungry, or would you like to work up an appetite?'

Her heartbeat quickens. She holds his gaze until her stomach feels all spongy and she dare not breathe, swallow or scratch at the itch behind her ear in case it ruins the moment. And then with soft, strong lips that taste of sea salt, he kisses her. Stomach fluttering, skin tingling, she feels his tongue press against hers, exploring her mouth as his arms engulf her. She breathes him in, running her fingers through his dark hair as he traces the line of her collar bone and kisses her again. She closes her eyes and savours the moment. The taste of his mouth against her tongue. The sound of water rushing over shale. Shells being dragged across pebbles. The squawk of a gull. The warmth of his skin. The gentle sea breeze . . .

He peels off his shorts and throws them down next to the cheese basket whilst she does her best to wriggle out of her dress. Then standing in front of each other, he in his boxer shorts and she in her bikini, he leads her over to the sea. Pulling her through the shallow water, he presses his body against hers and drags her deeper into the surf. A shiver travels down her spine as his hands find the clasp on her bikini and a moment later, they are both naked. The thrill. The rush. The elation. Overcome with giddiness and roused by desire, she allows him to carry her back to the shore where he places her down carefully as though she is treasure itself. Lying like a washed-up mermaid, her hair matted with small flecks of rainbow shale, her eyes connect with his and their bodies share a conversation of their own.

And she doesn't want this to end.

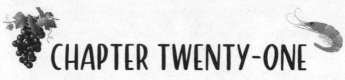

CHAPTER TWENTY-ONE

Banana Man and Bacchus

Khady

> How'd it go with Bacchus!!!?

Freya contemplates this for a moment. It's almost impossible to put into words how off-the-scale amazing the day has been. From the mouth-watering smorgasbord of cheese to the gentle waves lapping at their feet as they lay in post-coital bliss. Everything about that boat trip was heavenly. And although she got burned to a crisp and can now barely move her arms without searing pain shooting through her shoulders, lying there naked was worth every ultra-violet ray her skin has absorbed. Awash with feelings she has never before felt, she returned to her room an hour ago in a starry-eyed,

218

groin-throbbing daze, her mind an endless soundtrack of Beatles ballads. 'Till There Was You.' 'Do You Want to Know a Secret?' 'Across the Universe.'

Freya

> Window-shopping went out of the window . . . and it's fair to say, I bought myself a whole outfit.

Khady

> Parp! Parp!

Freya

> Floating around like a love-struck teenager.

Khady

> Good for you! I bet you feel a million dollars. BTW, I think André may be a sociopath. He's started turning up at my flat . ,

Freya

> WTF?

Khady

> I told him (nicely) I didn't want to see him again and he sent me a pie-chart of his emotions (30% Heartbreak, 20% fury, 10% panic and 40% pain if you're interested)

Freya

Holy shit! Should someone check under his floorboards?

Khady

The other day, he convinced my neighbour he lived with me and had forgotten his keys, so she let him into the block and I found him licking my wellington boots outside my flat when I got back.

Freya

He sounds UNHINGED.

Khady

Then he sent me a matchstick man picture of me and him on our wedding day, entitled 'destiny.' He's already married FFS!!!

Freya

Seriously, Khads. Be careful and don't think twice about calling the police if he turns up at your place again.

Worrying about Khady and wishing she was still with Xanthos, Freya takes her tea onto the terrace to watch the sunset, relishing the sweet smell of honeysuckle on the evening breeze. She squeezes the Lipton Yellow English Breakfast teabag against her spoon, trying to extract as much flavour as possible, chiding herself for not bringing her own stash of PG Tips.

Her thoughts return to tomorrow's cooking challenge. Dubbed D-Day, this is the task which will separate the winners from the losers and ultimately define which two contestants will make it through to the final, the journey over for everyone else. She swallows hard. It's all about having a delicious menu and taking risks – balancing complexity with simplicity by bringing something new to a failproof dish, leaving your nerves outside and giving it your all in the kitchen. Keeping things fresh, experimenting with textures and flavours, daring to splice and spice. Salmon terrine could be a good option – smoked or fresh – it's delicious with a thick, creamy sauce and fresh asparagus and she could add a fennel twist but is it really Greek enough? Lamb *kleftiko* coupled with a courgette, dill and fresh mint salad might be nice. *Soutzoukakia* with wild rice infused with lemon is another option. Decisions. Decisions.

The tag on her teabag flutters in the breeze and a voice calls out. 'Got the place to yourself?'

Freya swivels around to see a young woman wearing nurse's scrubs, her hair a wild frizz.

'Your friend ordered more fabric so I promised my grandma I'd drop it off.'

It's not until a Betty Boop tattoo pokes out from her nurse's sleeve as she drops a bag of emerald silk onto the table that

Freya realises this is Mrs Anastasis's granddaughter, Angeliki from The Fabric Emporium – her unbraided hair makes her look a few years older as do the hospital scrubs and the absent nose ring.

'Take a seat.' Freya smiles.

'Thanks.' Angeliki sits down and surveys her surroundings. 'I always forget how nice it is up here.'

Freya reaches for the teapot. 'You're up early.'

'Or late, depending on which way you look at it. I work at the village hospital. I've just finished the nightshift.'

Freya flinches. 'So you saw Christos then? Is he OK?'

'He's fine.' Angeliki smiles reassuringly. 'He should get discharged today.'

Freya feels her body relax.

Angeliki lowers her voice conspiratorially. 'I'm glad I've bumped into you. I saw you on the step outside the hospital and . . .' She checks behind her before continuing, Freya beginning to feel ambushed. 'My grandmother's right. The Bazigou brothers have a reputation. It's probably better if you don't get involved.'

'Riiight.' Freya's body tightens. That ship has clearly sailed.

Angeliki rummages in the pocket of her uniform and drags out first a spliff and then an inhaler. 'Sorry,' she says, popping the perfectly rolled joint back into her pocket. 'Medicinal, of course.'

'Of course.'

Angeliki shakes her inhaler, places the mouthpiece between her front teeth and shotguns two short, sharp blasts into her mouth before exhaling slowly. 'Dimitri was married to my sister but it didn't last long. He can't seem to help himself . . . not with the steady stream of sun-starved, sex-deprived women coming to the island in search of a holiday romance. Xanthos isn't much better. He was in love with a Scottish girl last time I heard—'

'Helena?' Freya interjects, remembering the story Mrs Anastasis told.

'No, I think her name was Alison. He's no doubt moved onto the next one by now so who knows?'

Freya feels the ground shift beneath her. Is she really just 'the next one'? A sun-starved, sex-deprived statistic? A notch on Xanthos's bedpost? Another name on his list of fresh-off-the-boat conquests? Her face stings at the slap of reality, a knot of jealousy forming in the pit of her stomach – she knows that her inner-feminist should rise above it, but she does not like the sound of this Scottish girl – not one little bit. Shit. How could she have been so naïve to think that she and Xanthos shared a connection and that their time together yesterday actually meant something?

'Hey!' Harj bursts onto the terrace, a smile flickering across his face at the sight of the bag of green silk. 'Thanks for bringing it up the hill.' He grins like a happy schoolboy.

'You're welcome.' Angeliki flicks a small insect off her shoulder.

Freya's mind tips into overdrive as Harj starts blathering on about the health issues associated with undercooked lamb and trying to impress Angeliki with his culinary know-how. She doesn't really hear the details because her mind is busy thinking back to Christos's conversation about a cheesecake and a wedding. What was it again? *'My son picked a three-tier wedding cheesecake. It was wonderful, but it didn't last long – a little like his marriage.'* It throws a whole new light on things now she knows Christos to be their father. And although she'd bet The Golden Spoon that Dimitri is the greater Casanova of the two of them, the whole thing feels messy to say the least.

Angeliki turns to Freya once Harj has finally stopped talking. She taps her inhaler against the table. 'Don't get me wrong, my sister was just as bad as Dimitri. At the end of the day, she ran off with his mate, so she's just as much a slut as he is.'

Harj lights up like a Belisha beacon. 'That's what I was saying to Freya!'

Angeliki's face shimmers with annoyance. 'Listen up, *I* can call my sister a slut, but *you* can't. In the same way as it's OK for me to tell you your tomatoes are an absolute triumph but it's not OK for you to say so . . .'

Harj's face ripples with confusion.

'Self-awareness, that's all I'm saying.' Angeliki takes the joint out of her breast pocket and tucks it behind her ear. 'Sorry, it just really makes me mad the way that it's always the woman who gets a reputation and the man who walks off scot-free. It's almost like sleeping around is expected of a man, but the moment a woman does it, she's a harlot, a harridan, a scarlet woman. Men have indiscretions whilst women are homewreckers. It sucks.' Her eyes narrow in Harj's direction. 'Don't you think it sucks?'

'I suppose,' Harj splutters, a dumbfounded expression on his face.

Angeliki leans over him aggressively. 'Trust me, it sucks.' She turns to Freya. 'I'm serious about those Bazigou brothers. You should stay well away.'

Acid rises in Freya's throat. Is Xanthos really that much of a player? It seems difficult to believe it of a man with cheeseboard/chessboard analogies. A man to whom she has bared both her body and soul over the last forty-eight hours. A man who gazed into her eyes with such magical intensity that she'd felt an ethereal glow about her. How could she have been so gullible and naïve? And just like that her bubble bursts, her inner soundtrack slowly morphing from a timeless Beatles ballad to Alanis Morissette's angst-ridden 'You Oughta Know'.

'I'd better go.' Angeliki gets up and turns to Freya. 'Don't say I didn't warn you.'

Freya watches as Angeliki disappears down the footpath in a cloud of smoke, the smell of marijuana carrying on the breeze. She can't think straight. Surely this is untrue, Xanthos tarnished with the same brush Dimitri uses to paint a picture of promiscuity? But then again, don't the Helenas and the Alisons speak for themselves?

Xanthos's piercing green eyes appear in her mind's eye. A dark tangle of sea-soaked hair. His soft, olive skin. That gentle voice. 'Freeya.' That husky growl. The way he touched her breasts and filled her head with a soundtrack of Beatles ballads. 'And I Love Her.' 'All My Loving'. 'Till There Was You.' How is it possible that the man she spent an idyllic day with only yesterday is a womanising, bed-hopping piece of shit? Impossible.

But why would Angeliki make any of that up?

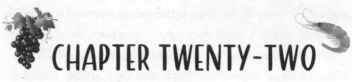

CHAPTER TWENTY-TWO

The Beetroot Thief

Freya	14
Harj	13
Michel	13
Leandra-Louise	11
Hazel	11
Stéphane	8
Kwame	Withdrawn from the competition

Determined to be the first to the taverna, Freya sets her alarm and ambles up the hill at dawn. The sky is the sepia hue of old photographs, the hillside bursting with birdsong and the long grass glistening with dew. Her thoughts ricochet from

Xanthos to Angeliki. From hot melted cheese and sex on the beach to 'beware of this man' warnings. Whatever the truth, a big day lies ahead and if she's to have any kind of shot at reaching the grand final in Paphos, she needs to push aside these distractions and focus on the competition. If she can just maintain her lead, she's through. If not, she could be out of the competition for good. Everything rides on today.

She reaches the taverna door, enters the code on the number lock and relaxes. Like being the first to the beach, it's nice to have the place to yourself and set the energy before anyone arrives, but Michel has beaten her to it.

'*Bonjour.*' He kisses her on each cheek like a friendly host. 'Coffee?'

'Thanks.' She rearranges her face into a smile – the last time she saw him, he threw her under the bus in front of Dimitri, robbing her of her barbecue glory, and although she knows there's no point holding a grudge, she'd be lying if she said she was over it. 'All set for the big day?'

'Getting there!' He sharpens his knife.

'Is that our stuff?' Her eyes flicker to a pile of cardboard boxes brimming with fresh fruit and vegetables.

'Yes. The meat is in the fridge.'

'How come there are only six boxes?' Freya says, counting them again.

'Kwame has gone,' Michel replies.

'Gone, gone?' Freya's forehead becomes a frown.

Michel nods. 'He wrote lots of things on Twitter. I'm not sure he'd be allowed to return even if he wanted to.'

A shudder of discomfort passes over Freya. The whole Golden

Spoon experience is proving to be quite like Charlie's trip to Willy Wonka's chocolate factory, what with people dropping at each hurdle. Thank God she'd been diverted last night and therefore forced to bite her tongue, otherwise she too could have been on an early flight home what with everything she'd wanted to rant about on festival night. She feels the warmth of the sun beaming in through the patio windows and unclasps the glass doors that concertina back on each other, letting the scent of fresh rosemary drift in from the hillside.

'Please, if you can leave it shut.' Michel passes her a small cup of black coffee and returns his attention to his food box inventory, ticking red onion off his list with a flourish.

Freya feels a pang of disappointment. 'Really?'

'I need to be ready before I open myself to the world,' he says flatly.

'Riiight,' she says, sliding the door panels back into place.

Michel affirms his approval with a nod of his head. 'What will you be making today?'

Freya looks through the glass at the turquoise sea and yearns for the fresh, salty air. '*Pantzaria* gazpacho.'

He grimaces. '*Pantzaria*?'

'Beetroot gazpacho,' she elaborates.

'I know what it is. It's just I've never heard it pronounced like that before! *Pantzaria*!' He chuckles under his breath. 'It's *pantz*aria.'

Freya forces a smile. 'How about you?'

'Similar.' He looks away, folding a tea towel into perfect quarters.

'What, *pantzaria* gazpacho?' She frowns.

'*Pantz*aria!' he barks with frustration.

'*Pantz*aria!' she repeats, simmering with exasperation.

He peers into his veggie box. 'Of a sort. You realise beetroot is difficult to prepare under pressure? Make sure you chop it finely.'

Freya swallows hard. Is he really going to mansplain the basics of cookery to her?

'If the cubes are too big, they won't cook as quickly.'

Fire blazes in her eyes: Yes, he is.

'A quick spritz with oil before you drop into boiling water should do the trick!'

'Great advice,' she says, wondering what sound he would make if hypothetically pushed off the cliff outside.

The door creaks open and in comes Stéphane, a broad smile on his face. '*Bonjour, les enfants!*'

'Morning!' Freya chimes.

Michel glares at him across the room and makes a heavy-handed point of leaving through the kitchen fire escape, the door clanging against the spare gas canister outside.

She raises an eyebrow. 'Is he OK?'

'Stressed.' Stéphane makes his way over to the cafetière and turns to Freya. 'What happened on festival night? You should have told them Hazel did *not* run the kitchen.'

Freya channels her breath through her nostrils. 'I did, but then nobody would back me, so it was my word against hers and then the thing with Christos meant that I wasn't around to defend myself.'

Stéphane tilts his head to one side with suspicion. 'Michel was there. He did not defend you?'

'No,' she says.

This is not how she wanted the day to start. Arriving early at the taverna was meant to be like cleansing the palate, arranging the feng shui of the kitchen and clearing the air of bad karma, not building an atmosphere of distrust, resentment and anger. Still, her veggie box has arrived, everything is present and correct, and this time she will not kowtow to treachery, deceit or sabotage. Should anything underhand go on this time, she'll be calling it out the moment it happens at the top of her voice.

'Hi.' Leandra-Louise breezes in. 'Ready for the big day?'

Freya nods. 'You?'

Leandra-Louise shrugs her shoulders. '*Que sera sera.* That's my motto.'

Freya eyes her with distrust. Is it really her motto? How the fuck can anyone be so blasé about something so important? Not only is Leandra-Louise's laissez-faire attitude out of keeping with the nature of the competition, but it's insulting. At least everyone else is open about how much this means to them. An opportunity of a lifetime. One of the toughest competitions in the world. And meanwhile Leandra-Louise is treating it like child's play!

Harj bursts through the doors. 'Any chance we can Irish up the coffee this morning? I'm a bag of nerves, innit.'

Thank God for Harj wearing his heart on his sleeve.

Hazel brings up the rear. 'Could we not open the doors at the back?' she harrumphs, her large wicker bag knocking a small porcelain goddess off the alcove shelf in the wall.

Freya grabs a dustpan and brush and sets about sweeping

up the small pieces of china, Michel appearing from the fire exit smelling of cigarettes.

'Don't blame me if everything blows away.' He steps over the smashed figurine and looks Hazel up and down. 'Why do you need that big bag?'

Hazel jerks her head around like a startled hen. 'I . . . I've just got my stuff in it.'

'What stuff?' His eyes narrow.

'Just a few personal items and a few bottles of water.'

'You really need such an enormous bag for a few personal items?' His words are loaded with suspicion.

Harj peeks between the wicker handles. 'Water. Mobile phone. Purse.'

'Don't go telling everyone where my purse is!' Hazel swats his nose out of the way with the back of her hand.

Pitted against each other, all six of them have become so wary that the light-hearted camaraderie they shared only two days ago is a thing of the past and a groundswell of deceit and duplicity has taken its place. The knives are out, each cook for themselves in a contest that has become every man for himself, friendship forgone for cold, calculated cuisine.

'Does anyone know who the mystery diners are?' Leandra-Louise tries to diffuse things.

Hazel dumps her bag on the table. 'A couple from the village, Christos said.'

'How is Christos?' Leandra-Louise asks.

'All good,' says Freya. 'He got discharged yesterday, apparently.'

'I guess you'd know,' Michel says snippily.

'What's that supposed to mean?' Freya says, feeling a stab of hurt at his accusatory tone.

Hazel looks up from the depths of her enormous bag. 'Tongues waggle, you know, Freya. First Dimitri, then Xanthos.'

'Sorry?' Freya feels her skin prickle.

Hazel carries on regardless. 'There are no secrets here, you know. Getting naked on Dimitri's banana. Tugging Xanthos off the terrace the other night.'

Harj raises an eyebrow and looks up at Freya. 'She didn't mean it to sound like that.'

'I most certainly did,' Hazel quips.

Freya swallows hard. 'The skinny-dipping thing . . . well, I thought I was alone. And I disappeared with Xanthos to take Christos to hospital having found him on the hillside half dead. And just for the record, I DID NOT TUG XANTHOS OFF!'

The door swings open and in walks Xanthos, the room instantly falling silent.

'Good morning.' He addresses the group, his eyes flickering across the room until they find Freya.

Michel coughs loudly for effect.

Freya feels her chest prickle with heat and isn't sure where to look.

'OK, everyone.' Dimitri files in behind Xanthos. 'We'll get started in about twenty minutes. You know the rules. Once the timer starts, you'll have twenty minutes to serve your dish. Help yourself to your food crate. They should all be labelled.'

A murmur of agreement follows, everyone making their way over to the veggie boxes where Harj and Hazel tussle over the same food crate, their initials both H.S.

Freya picks through her veggie box, ticking off the ingredients on her list for the third time – you can never be too careful, especially not in this environment.

Avocado. Tick.

Fresh dill. Tick.

Red onion. Tick.

Garlic. Tick.

Greek yoghurt. Tick.

Sherry vinegar. Tick.

Beetroot. Beetroot?

There's no beetroot. There must be beetroot. It was there a minute ago. It's her nerves, she tells herself. Bloody well calm down and have another look. But a thorough hunt through her veggie box confirms her fears: the beetroot has vanished.

Her throat goes dry. There must be a simple explanation for this. Maybe she's mixed up her veggie box with someone else's. She looks at the side of the cardboard crate – F.B. – no, it's definitely hers.

'Has someone picked up an extra beetroot by mistake?' She tries to conceal the panic in her voice.

One by one her fellow chefs affirm negative.

'Maybe it fell out?' Harj suggests.

She searches the kitchen, casting her eyes over the floor, under the tables and between Dimitri's feet.

She looks up at him. 'You haven't seen a beetroot, have you?'

His forehead creases.

'Beetroot?' She thrusts her list of ingredients under his nose, indicating it on her list and then it hits her: Hazel's bag.

With an accusatory scowl, she marches towards Hazel's wicker carrier. 'Hazel, can I have a quick look in your bag to check my beetroot hasn't *fallen* into it?'

Hazel looks bemused. 'Can everyone leave my bag alone?'

Ignoring her, Freya seizes the handles and yanks them apart. Three bottles of Evian, a large leather wallet and a mobile phone stare back at her. No sign of beetroot whatsoever. 'Sorry,' she says, fire leaving her belly.

Then where is it?

'Seriously, guys. I had a beetroot. I saw it. Twice. And now it's gone.'

Everyone is too preoccupied with their own ingredients to give a shit about the whereabouts of her beetroot and yet one person amongst them is the culprit. How can they live with themselves? Blood drains away from her face and her skin feels clammy. This cannot be happening. Not again. How the fuck is she supposed to make beetroot gazpacho without any fucking beetroot?

Xanthos walks over to her, his khaki jacket bringing out the emerald green pigmentation in his eyes. He puts his hand on her shoulder, sending a shiver down her spine. 'What's the problem?'

'You're a womaniser!' she wants to say.

'I'm cooking beetroot gazpacho and I haven't got a beetroot.' She tries to remain calm.

Dimitri looks over. 'Why did you choose that if you don't have a beetroot?'

She exhales with frustration. 'I *had* a beetroot, but it's gone missing.'

'Does anybody have a spare beetroot?' Dimitri shouts.

Freya's legs starts to tremble.

Dimitri claps his hands. 'Beetroot anyone?'

Stéphane looks up and shrugs whilst everyone else keeps their head down.

Xanthos takes Freya by the arm. 'Come with me.' He leads her out across the gravel. 'This way.' He gestures to a lightly trodden footpath that meanders down towards the valley in higgledy-piggledy twists and turns.

She wants to hammer him with questions – just how many guests has he slept with exactly and who is this Scottish girl he was in love with? But all that will have to wait. 'We don't have the time to go to the village!' She stomps along behind him.

'We're not going to the village.' He assesses her footwear. 'Are you a fast runner?'

'What?' Her heart races. 'No.'

'If you hear a dog – German shepherd, very loud, you can't miss it – then my advice is to run. And if things get too crazy . . .'

'Define crazy!' She tries to catch her breath.

'Then climb a tree.'

'Wait! What are you doing?'

With the agility of a mountain goat, he scrambles up the grassy bank. Tiptoeing sideways, he balances along a narrow ridge, negotiating the blue, feathery fronds of fennel as he goes. She watches as he zigs and zags up the hillside like a pond skater gliding across the water's surface until he makes it as far as a transparent Perspex fence which separates the riotous, overgrown hillside from a leafy private garden.

Gripping the top of the fence, he hauls himself up, drops one leg over and plops down into a vegetable patch on the other side. She watches as he picks his way through a jungle of unruly beanstalks and beckons her over. Pah. Choosing a longer, more forgiving path, she climbs the hill towards him, clinging onto tussocks of long grass for balance until she reaches the fence.

'Jump over!' he whisper-shouts from a row of cabbages.

She laughs. Even if her life depended on it, there's no way she could scale this barrier, not without losing a kidney.

He edges around a rhubarb patch towards what look like giant dandelion leaves. 'How many do you need?'

She looks up at the windows of the stone house for a sign of movement, but all is still. 'Two?'

The buzz of adrenaline fizzes through her as he crouches down and peels back the undergrowth. Whether it's his chivalry or the thrill of indulging in something forbidden and the possibility of getting caught, she hasn't felt this exhilarated since . . . well, since they got naked on the beach together. Her pulse quickens as she watches him dig his fingertips into the soil like a human spade, his eyes shifting every so often to the windows of the house. Loosening the dirt, he unearths a large beetroot, soil clinging to its pale brown bulb, and holds it up proudly as though it is freshly mined gold. She studies the blood-red veins crawling through its tree-like leaves, a burst of excitement rushing through her. Xanthos, her plucky daredevil hero. Robin Hood of the Cypriot countryside. Courageous. Enterprising. Audacious. She his Maid Marion. He drops to his knees and shuffles over to a larger plant at the end of the row. Checking over his shoulder, he plunges his fingers into the earth and is just about to lift out a second beetroot when the front door of the house flies open, and an ear-splitting bark resonates across the land. Freya freezes in horror as one hundred pounds of German shepherd comes hurtling out, its bone-chilling snarl echoing through the valley.

She squeaks with terror as the dog rockets towards Xanthos. He grabs the beetroot and makes to escape, the Alsatian growling and snapping at his heels.

'Run!' he shouts, Freya turning to see the outline of a man standing at the door to the house, wielding an air rifle.

Heart in her mouth, she watches as two beetroots fly over the fence towards her, shortly followed by Xanthos, the dog trapped on the other side, standing on its hindlegs, growling and baring its teeth.

Down the hillside they run, Freya losing her footing and Xanthos grabbing hold of her sleeve in a bid to save her, only for them to tumble over each other a moment later. Down they roll, over and over each other, laughing and giggling as they gather momentum, the German shepherd all the while barking ferociously at the edge of its boundary. Clinging to each other, they at last come to a halt when the ground plateaus towards the taverna, Freya lying beneath Xanthos, his weight bearing down on her.

'You OK?' His eyes sparkle with exhilaration.

'Uh-huh.' Butterflies dance in her stomach as his breath catches against her cheek.

'I got your beetroot.'

'I can feel it,' she says, wriggling beneath him, something bulbous pressing against her crotch.

'That's not the beetroot.' He smiles, holding two bulbs up by their leaves and dropping them victoriously at her side. 'You know, in Greek mythology, beetroots were said to be worth their weight in silver, second only to horseradish.' He laughs as she rolls her eyes. 'It's true! They were offered up to Apollo in gratitude. They're a symbol of love.'

'Really?' She shakes her head.

He brushes her hair out of her eyes. 'At the very least, they're an aphrodisiac.'

She feels the urgent need to kiss him, but she mustn't – not now she knows that he's like this with all the girls. Pinned to the ground by yearning, she lies beneath him, the outside world melting away and a skin-tingling shiver travelling down her spine. She wants him so badly she can barely breathe.

'Xanthos?' A voice calls over from the taverna.

Freya turns to see Dimitri hollering from the terrace. Hurriedly, she gets up and straightens herself out.

Xanthos chuckles, holding up the beetroots for Dimitri to see, as though this somehow absolves him of any wrongdoing.

Dimitri shakes his head and turns away.

Eyes trained on Dimitri's retreating back, Freya comes to her senses. What on earth is she doing? It's not as though she couldn't have avoided that situation, choosing to lie beneath him for no other reason than she was getting off on it. Not only has she become a cliché – falling for a Bazigou brother – but she has put her credibility in this competition at stake. With exaggerated movements, she throws back her shoulders and dusts the dirt off her dress. How is anyone going to take her seriously now that she's been caught romping with the village playboy? Pushing aside the tingling in her loins, she smooths down her hair in an attempt to compose herself.

'I should get back to the kitchen,' she says quietly.

'Aren't you forgetting something?' Xanthos calls after her.

She turns around to see him holding up the beetroots by their muddy leaves.

In spite of herself, she smiles. 'Thank you.'

CHAPTER TWENTY-THREE

D-Day

Back in Nottingham on her way home from work, Freya was often so deep in thought that she couldn't remember having crossed roads, got on buses and navigated major thorough-fares. It's the same with preparing this meal. She has a faint recollection of garlic tadpoles oozing out of the grater and the clink of the sherry vinegar bottle against a metal table-spoon but that aside, she's pretty much been floating around in a bubble, affixing her own endings to her beetroot tumble with Xanthos. Beyond blending the beetroots and adding a handful of chopped parsley to garnish, she remembers nothing about preparing this dish. All she can think about is lying beneath Xanthos in the dirt. A feel-good jet lag takes hold of her as she glides around the kitchen in an endorphin-infused haze. Staying away from him is going to take some serious willpower.

Harj leans over her chopping board and grins. 'All right there, crockpot?'

'Crockpot?' she says, wondering if this is in any way a reference to being spotted romping on the ground with Xanthos.

'Slow-cooker!' He flashes a toothy grin. 'No offence but the speed of your food prep's not going to win you any world records. What are you doing?' He peers over her chopping board. 'Want a measuring tape?'

Freya realises she has been inspecting a single cube of beetroot for what must be over a minute and still couldn't say if it's the same size as the others. Damn. Consistency is key in a garnish like this, the dill, yoghurt and lemon juice unable to do all the heavy lifting. Her breath quickens. It's almost impossible to concentrate though, what with the memory of Xanthos's boat trip. The sun-soaked beach they lay upon. The clear, turquoise waters they frolicked in. And then everything she's learned of since about Xanthos's philandering ways. A girl in every port – or rather, a whole bunch of girls in the same port. She did well not to kiss him just then. Thank goodness he had to see to a delivery and isn't around for this task, otherwise she'd be incapable of doing anything.

Paranoid that she smells of foreplay, her eyes shift around the room in search of sideways glances and knowing smiles, but they're all focused on their cooking, everyone beavering away at the task in hand. Stéphane garnishes his fish kebab and wild black rice with freshly chopped parsley and adds a slice of lemon on the side whilst Michel smiles triumphantly at his spinach and feta *koupes*. Freya feels a surge of panic. Is her food too simple? Her gazpacho is beautifully pink, its nutritional value unrivalled, but will it have the culinary clout it needs to compete with the expertly crafted dishes of her fellow chefs? She glances over at Hazel who is carrying some sort of halloumi pie out of the oven and feels her stomach lurching further when she sees the rainbow of colours exploding out of Leandra-Louise's chicken breasts – courgette greens and bell pepper yellows sandwiched between slices of vibrant red capsicum and fresh tomato – a visual spectacular.

She looks down at the consistency of her cream of beetroot and wonders if it isn't a little runny. It's weird – she's stayed measure for measure faithful to the recipe but for whatever reason it's not as creamy as her last attempt. Dipping her finger into the mix, she taste tests. Too acidic. Adding a little more puréed beetroot and one more teaspoon of yoghurt, she mixes it through. That's more like it. Thicker. Creamier. Luxurious. Always trust your gut. She looks over at Harj who, despite faffing about with an oven glove for the last few minutes, seems to have everything under control, a row of beautifully presented salmon *koupepia* laid out in front of him. Adrenaline pumps. She waits a couple of minutes before ladling the mix into the bowl, carefully transporting each spoonful across as though lowering a sleeping baby into a cradle – if she's too quick off the mark, the colours will run and she won't get that distinct pink crown. Holding her breath, she drizzles the remaining cream in the shape of a heart – something she perfected years ago at catering college – and stands back to assess her handiwork. Not quite perfect, but nearly.

'Hi.' Dimitri appears at her side, flashing a knowing smile and she wishes she could hold back the heat that rushes to her cheeks. 'I know you've had your hands full . . .' He wiggles his eyebrows and waits for a reaction, and although she tries not to give him the satisfaction, she knows her face must look the same colour as her beetroot. 'But could you tell your fellow chefs that your judges have arrived?' He gestures to a middle-aged couple who have taken the table next to the window.

Freya smiles awkwardly before passing on the message, Dimitri returning his attention to his iPad. Craning her neck for a better look at the judges, she catches a glimpse of the woman's steel-grey leather-panelled pullover at odds with statement jewellery made up of angular shapes in bright colours – orange hexagons, lime-green ovals and hot pinks jostling for position around her neckline, an aggressive pair of glasses with rainbow frames balanced on the end of her pointed nose. Propped against the table are a pair of crutches. It's unclear whether they belong to the woman or her male counterpart who sits opposite, sporting the thick, groomed moustache of an army colonel. Freya watches as he fingers the menu with an air of insouciance and returns it to the table unread. Knife and fork held vertically in each hand and serviette tucked into the neck of his shirt, he reminds Freya of her Uncle Harry, an enormous man who used to come to the caravan every other Christmas for a turkey roast, falling asleep in his cracker hat after too many sherries.

'May I introduce your judges for today?' Dimitri says, and

the couple rise from their seats. 'Mr Papastathopoulos, Mr P
for short, and Mrs' Onassis! Both have worked with the
wonderful Talia Drakos, Mr P running her flagship restaurant
in Paphos whilst Mrs Onassis acts in an advisory capacity and
is often involved in recruitment, so play your cards right and
who knows, you might get talent spotted!'

Tension mounts as each contestant is asked to line up in
front of the judges with their dish, Dimitri acting as Anglo-
Greek translator whilst the chefs are quizzed about their food
choices. With unsteady hands, Freya picks up her bowl of
gazpacho and takes her place behind Michel, her head full of
the health benefits of beetroot and the taste of Xanthos.
Gazpacho, for fuck's sake. The taste of gazpacho.

The pastry fork looks tiny in Mr P's bear paw of a hand
as he jabs it into Harj's salmon *koupepia*, a splurge of creamy
dill sauce oozing out between the layer of spinach and dried
apricots. Harj puffs out his cheeks whilst Mr P pokes, prods
and then lifts a forkful to his mouth. They all watch in anticipation as he chews, tilts his head from side to side and
swallows. It's intense. Wiping his mouth on a cloth napkin,
he maintains a poker face and launches into rapid-fire Greek,
his hand waving around as though swatting a fly, Dimitri
reacting with requisite frowns and nods whilst Harj chews on
his lip.

Dimitri looks over to Harj. 'How much cream did you use
in the sauce?'

Harj undoes the top button of his shirt, his eyes shifting
from Mr P to Dimitri. 'Just a smidge,' he says, pinching together
his thumb and forefinger.

The energy shifts as Mrs Onassis hobbles forward on crutches to pass critique. She makes her way over to the salmon and, tongue darting out like a Komodo dragon, takes a mouthful. As the food rolls around her mouth, she lets out a loud 'mmmmm' befitting an orgasm.

Freya stifles a giggle and looks at the floor, trying not to catch Stéphane's eye.

'Exquisite.' Dimitri smiles. 'Though I don't think you need me to translate that.'

They chuckle good-naturedly, nervous tension intensifying when Mr P moves on to Leandra-Louise's orange-glazed chicken breasts whilst Dimitri jots down notes on his iPad. Freya's heart races. Three more dishes and then she's up.

Mr P queries how much honey went into Leandra-Louise's orange glaze whilst Mrs Onassis wants to know whether Michel's spinach is organic and what utensil Hazel used to peel the ginger – highlighting that a teaspoon is preferable to a peeler or knife as most of the flavour sits just under the skin and is not lost to the round contours of a spoon. Finally, it's Freya's turn to be put on the spot.

Slowly, Mr P lowers his nose towards her gazpacho, the expression on his face akin to having toothache.

'What made you choose a beetroot-based dish?' Dimitri translates.

Freya clears her throat which seems to have taken on the texture of sandpaper. 'Because it's flavoursome, refreshing and the creamy pink colour makes me feel happy every time I make it. It always seems to bring joy to those who taste it. It's bold. It's delicious, the sharpness of the lemony garlic offsetting the earthiness of the beetroot and what's more, in Greek mythology, beetroot is the food of love, worth its weight in silver and offered to Apollo as a token of gratitude.' She feels her face burn at the thought of her own Greek god filling her head with all of this only a few moments ago. 'And the other great thing about *pantzaria* . . .' She glances at Michel, half-expecting him to correct her pronunciation mid-flow. '. . . is that it's a great source of fibre. And nutrients. Mustn't forget the nutrients!' She lets out a nervous laugh. 'Oh and the nitrates and pigments contained in beets help to lower blood pressure which is why they're such a great food for athletes.' Her eyes shift to Mr P's bulging waistline. 'And non-athletes . . . not that I'm suggesting you're not athletic . . . either of you. Or you, Dimitri! Oh my God.' She goes to pieces, her words tripping over themselves. 'What I mean is, beetroot is good for everyone.'

'Yes, I saw earlier on your passion for beetroot.' Dimitri grins wryly.

Freya wants to curl up and die but first, she wants Dimitri to translate what she's just said and relay the vital nuggets of information she has just blathered to Mrs Onassis, maybe omitting a few nervous ramblings. The room feels hotter than ever. A trickle of sweat runs down her forehead as Mrs Onassis jots something down in her notebook then winks like a silent murderer, Freya all the while kicking herself for not mentioning detox properties, keto, improved blood flow and gut health: the culinary cornerstones of a nutritious diet.

'The best thing about this dish is that you can leave it for a day and it only gets more flavoursome,' she blurts, unable to suppress her words. What the fuck's the matter with her?

Michel shoots her daggers whilst Mr P mops his moustache with the end of his serviette and mumbles, 'Delicious, thank you.'

Freya knows not to get her hopes up. He has told everyone that their dishes are delicious and seems to be keeping his cards close to his chest. She watches out of the corner of her eye as Mr P presses his lips together and moves them back and forth, reminding her of the Hungry Hippos board game she used to play at Kids as Carers rainy day club. Rubbing his hands over his girth, he mutters something to Dimitri who stands over him, head cocked like an expectant Springer Spaniel.

Dimitri looks to Freya. 'Mr P wants to know how much salt you used?'

'Just a sprinkling!' Freya tries to mask the desperation in her voice. 'You know, to balance out the sweetness of the yoghurt.'

Dimitri parrots this to Mr P who nods, jowls wobbling like turkey wattles.

'I mean the yoghurt is fat-free, so it wasn't that sweet to begin with, so . . .' Again, she can't stop herself.

Mr P looks down at his plate and grunts.

'Thank you.' Dimitri holds his palm up to Freya in a way that a traffic controller might halt cars. 'If everyone wants to go outside and help themselves to a drink, the judges will deliberate and then we'll call you back in once they've made a decision.'

Out on the terrace, everyone is too nervous to make conversation. Aside from the odd bit of small talk about Michel's tailor-made chef top and how much gold thread it took to embroider his initials on the lapel, few words are exchanged. Freya sits on the terrace wall, her legs dangling over the edge, and stares out across the olive groves, her thoughts returning to Xanthos. She closes her eyes and can almost feel his hot breath on her neck. His soft, firm lips. His sexy, low growl. Those strong hands. The smell of his very essence. Remembering the delicious way in which he'd cocooned her in his arms, she squirms with delight and it isn't until Harj is jabbing at her shoulder that she becomes aware that she's spent the last five minutes caught up in that boat trip. Time to move on – there's fun to be had in lighting a fire but you only get burned if you play with the flames.

When called, the group makes its way back into the taverna where each dish is lined up in front of the food critics, Mrs Onassis now propped up on her crutches and scrutinising each one.

Dimitri wrings his hands and looks up at them. 'I appreciate this is a big moment for you all, so we'll keep it short.'

Mr P lets out a belch and consults his notebook, Mrs Onassis glaring at him through her rainbow-rimmed spectacles.

Freya holds her breath, her eyes flickering from Stéphane to Michel and then over to Harj and Hazel, finally resting on Leandra-Louise who has turned a shade of white. Hmm, so she does care?

Dimitri steps forward. 'Stéphane, your fish kebab was perfect in terms of texture and succulence, but the combination of fennel and fresh mint doesn't work for us. One or the other but not both together. Three points; and they are mainly awarded based on presentation – you've done a great job aesthetically.'

Stéphane looks down at the floor and then glances up at the scoreboard which shows that even with those three points, he can't catch anyone else.

'It's with a heavy heart that I have to inform you that your quest for The Golden Spoon ends here, Stéphane,' Dimitri says, his head hung in sorrow.

The atmosphere thins, the group sharing a series of glances, loaded with sympathy, compassion and no small measure of relief that it wasn't them.

Stéphane shrugs his shoulders with acceptance, Michel reaching for his hand and rubbing it consolingly. 'It was a pleasure to be part of the experience,' he says, stoically.

'What a gent!' Harj claps like an excited sea lion. 'I'm sorry, mate.'

'It's OK,' Stéphane says, trying to downplay his disappointment.

One by one, they offer their condolences, Mrs Onassis extending a sympathetic smile and a firm handshake, whilst Mr P slaps an enormous slab of a hand on his shoulder.

Freya bites at her fingernails in trepidation, watching as Mr P glances at the watch embedded in the folds of skin around his wrist and Dimitri takes it as his cue to move on.

'Hazel?' Dimitri glances around the table in search of Hazel who is peering down at her phone, her finger hovering over a voice recording button.

'One sec!' She hits the red button, her tongue darting out between her front teeth like a hungry lizard. 'I'd quite like the recording as a keepsake.'

Dimitri's brow puckers. 'You might not want to—'

'Good or bad, it's a privilege.' She beams smugly.

Mr P and Mrs Onassis share a look and a few raised eyebrows appear amongst the contestants – this is perhaps the first smattering of self-awareness Hazel has shown since they got here.

'OK,' Dimitri says, glancing at his iPad, the glare of its screen illuminating his face. 'Our judges have concluded that whilst ginger aids digestion and reduces gas and inflammation, there wasn't enough of it.'

'Really?' Hazel quibbles.

'And whilst prawns are obviously a rich source of selenium and zinc, great for boosting the immune system, they are also high in cholesterol.'

Tears spring to Hazel's eyes, her finger twitching over the red 'stop recording' button. 'I wasn't aware that it was supposed to be a healthy-eating competition!' She folds her arms under her chest and stares out of the window.

'The dish lacked a little in flavour and its appearance . . .' Dimitri frowns at the iPad screen, holding it under Mr P's nose and highlighting a section of text with his finger. Mr P nods, muttering something under his breath. Dimitri's eyes return to Hazel. 'I'm told it looks as though a dog has been sick in a bowl.'

Harj stifles a laugh whilst Hazel hits the red button, lets out a whimper and buries her mouth in her inner elbow.

Dimitri looks up. 'It's therefore with great sadness that you will be accredited zero points in all categories—'

'Harsh!' Harj tries to compensate for his previous show of disloyalty.

'—and will therefore be joining Stéphane as we say goodbye,' Dimitri adds apologetically.

Whilst Freya sympathises with Hazel – nobody likes to be told the food they have lovingly prepared looks like dog sick in a bowl – she also feels unexpectedly buoyed by satisfaction. Karma is a wonderful thing at times and surely this is universal payback for Hazel's beetroot-hiding, cheesecake-sabotaging, victory-stealing foul play. What goes around comes around and all that.

'Really?' Hazel pulls herself up into a straight line. 'Just exactly how many prawns did they try? If it was just the one prawn, they may have chanced upon one that missed out on the ginger. Could they not perhaps try another?'

'I'm sorry, Hazel,' Dimitri says tersely and shakes his head.

Hazel struts around the kitchen with indignance, then strides towards the door, Mr P shuffling out of her way and peering out of the window to see where she's heading.

Dimitri returns his attention to the group. 'Harj?'

'Oh God, really?' Harj holds his head in his hands.

It feels as though the air has been sucked out of the room and there is not enough oxygen to go around.

Dimitri chews his bottom lip, his eyebrows dipping in the middle. 'Harj, it could be you.'

'Going or staying?' Harj envelopes his mouth between the palms of his hands.

'Either or,' Dimitri says flatly.

'Sorry?' Harj shakes out his feet as though preparing for a sprint.

'He's just trying to build some suspense,' Leandra-Louise says. 'You know, like on *Love Island*.'

Harj's leg trembles. 'OK, so am I through or not?'

'I'm afraid you're not through . . . Leandra-Louise.' Dimitri shifts his gaze to Leandra-Louise who looks bewildered and confused.

'Sorry, I don't understand whether you paused for effect or whether I'm not through?' Leandra-Louise says, quivering like a jelly.

Mrs Onassis eyeballs Dimitri and then looks out of the window.

'OK, OK, no more dramatics, I'll keep things to the point.' Dimitri continues. 'Leandra-Louise, whilst your chicken breasts look spectacular – plump, succulent and very inviting . . .' He all but glances at her chest. '. . . you just didn't quite wow the judges in the taste department. Three points for presentation, two for texture, one for taste.'

Freya peers at the scoreboard and tries to process what this actually means. Her brain goes into overdrive. Is Dimitri announcing them in reverse order of how well they performed in today's task or has he structured the sequence to maximise dramatic tension?

'I'm sorry,' Dimitri says, 'Leandra-Louise, your Golden Spoon journey also ends here.'

Leandra-Louise crumples, her face dissolving into a hot mess of tears as she slides down the lower kitchen cabinet into a pool of crushed regret. 'Fuck, fuck, FUCK! Was it because I didn't come across as wanting it enough? Only I really want it. I mean really, really. Oh God. You know it's all I ever think of. Dream of. Cookery is all I've ever known. It's part of me, part of who I am . . . I know it might not look like it but it's all I care about.'

Harj bends down and strokes her arm. 'Come on, babe.' He helps her up.

Freya watches as Leandra-Louise, a tangle of hair and runny mascara, is led outside by Mrs Onassis who guides her onto the terrace with her crutch, bumping into the wall as she goes.

Dimitri's eyes travel to Freya's gazpacho, her stomach rolling over itself with apprehension, and then over to Michel's *koupes*. 'As Kwame left the competition a few days ago, that leaves Freya, Michel and Harj.' He pauses for effect. 'Congratulations, Michel. You are the winner of today's task earning you a total of eight points – three for presentation, three for taste, two for texture. Many congratulations – you are through to the final!'

Michel dives into Stéphane's arms, then bursts out of them like a jack-in-the-box to leap around the taverna punching the air as he goes, his eyes shiny with tears of joy.

Mr P smiles. 'Congratulations.'

Mrs Onassis shakes his hand. 'Beautiful flavour. Delicious.'

'Thank you, thank you.' Michel bows to them all like some sort of wind-up toy.

Everyone in the room claps, some with heartfelt applause and others with an air of resentment. Freya is somewhere between the two, clapping because it's the right thing to do whilst all she wants to do is curl up in the foetal position and rock back and forth until her frayed nerve endings have healed and she can breathe once more. Everything hinges on this next moment. She looks over at Harj who returns her nervous smile with one of his own. It's either him or her.

Reaching for her hand and squeezing it in solidarity, Harj closes his eyes and rocks back and forth on the gel-cushioned soles of his Nike Airs. Like a baby bird taking its first flight, she knows she is about to freefall from the edge of a cliff. Fly or die? She thinks of Mrs K. She thinks of her mother. She thinks of every batter she's ever mixed, every stew she's ever flavoured. She thinks of sausages wrapped in foil and fried on her uncle's car bonnet when the caravan gas supply ran out. She thinks of Xanthos's naked body pressed against hers. Of the beetroot he dug up for her. Of the Golden Spoon – the actual Golden Spoon – a gleaming gold statue that sits pride of place on only a dozen mantlepieces worldwide. Lucky thirteen? And it's all she can do not to pass out.

Leandra-Louise reappears, having composed herself. Free of make-up, her face has been rearranged into one of solemn acceptance. Blotchy and tear-stained but finally free of the mask she has fashioned to protect her from the outside world and maybe from herself, she makes her way over to Michel and Stéphane who huddle at the window.

'Harj and Freya.' Dimitri returns his attention to the competition.

Freya becomes conscious of her pulse. She balls her fists and stares at the ceiling.

'We have an unusual situation here.' Dimitri taps at the iPad. 'Harj, the judges described your wild black rice and salmon *koupepia* as delectable. The fresh herbs, red onion and garlic really giving it a lift. A full three points for flavour. Presentation, I have a one written down here.' He looks over to Mrs Onassis who explains something in detail, her hands miming what looks like wringing out a cloth nappy and then gesturing for him to continue. 'A little too much black pepper, I'm told. But great in terms of omega-3 fatty acids and DHA. A lovely source of potassium, selenium and vitamin B, and packed with antioxidants, so you've been awarded three bonus points for healthy-eating.'

'Thank you,' Harj says tentatively, clearly unsure as to what this means and whether he has a ticket to the final or not.

Freya's body has become so brittle, it could shatter into a million pieces. Can't someone just put her out of her misery?

'And last but not least, Freya.' Dimitri looks down at his screen and turns to her. 'Your gazpacho has captured the hearts and taste buds of both of our judges today. They declared your dish a taste-sensation. "Fresh, aromatic and tantalisingly delicious." They loved the texture, the flavour, and the beautiful pink colour they described as a piece of art. Alongside Harj's *koupepia*, it was declared dish of the day.'

Freya fills with hope. Like a balloon inflated with as much air as it can take, she's not sure whether she can tie the knot to clinch the deal and float high up into the sky with Michel or whether she's about to pop, her whole world deflating like that of Leandra-Louise. *Cut to the fucking chase, Dimitri and stop dilly-dallying.*

Dimitri looks from Freya to Harj and back to Freya again. 'Which means, ladies and gentlemen, that we have a tie-break.'

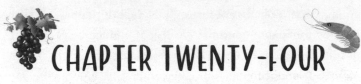

CHAPTER TWENTY-FOUR

Regret

The thought of going head-to-head with Harj in some sort of Greek-Cypriot Bake-Off to be hosted in the village in front of all and sundry makes Freya feel as though she has been poisoned and her internal organs are shutting down one at a time. On the one hand, she's still in the competition and has everything to play for, on the other, she has to go through the torture of another head-to-head all over again and isn't sure her nerves can take it. And if there's one person she doesn't want to be in a Bake-Off with, it's Harj. Nice, supportive, team player Harj.

@TheGoldenSpoon

Congratulations @Monsieur_Michel_Vergnon

  #TheGoldenSpoon FINALIST. Check out the grand final
next week in Paphos!

  #Cooking #Cookery #MasterChef #BakeOff
#GoldenSpoon

@TheGoldenSpoon

@The_Hungry_Sikh and @UtterlyButterly battle it out for

  a chance at the grand final @BakeOff tomorrow!

  #Cooking #Cookery #TheGoldenSpooon

Freya scrolls through the gazillions of comments spurring on
Harj who seems to have a global fanbase out there – a whole
harem of Twitter followers who are liking, retweeting,
commenting and taking the time to append a variety of carefully selected GIFs – the chef from *Sesame Street* beating two
cantaloupe melon drums with a pair of wooden spoons, a
five-second clip of Nigella licking chocolate sauce off her
fingers with pornographic prowess, a dancing Dalmatian in a
chef's hat, and several screenshots of Harpal Singh Sokhi,
India's celebrity chef, who admittedly does bear an uncanny
resemblance to Harj despite being several years his senior.

Meanwhile, Freya has attracted no interest whatsoever. Not
a single tweet – hardly surprising considering how much she
hates social media, sticking her head above the virtual parapet
only when completely necessary and using Twitter more as
a means to stalk celebrity chefs than for anything self-
promotional. Nigella, Raymond Blanc, Gordon Ramsay and

Jamie Oliver; they're all worth a follow, but nobody tops Talia Drakos. A goddess in the kitchen, an angel of invention, it's no wonder she has going on for forty thousand followers (Freya has nine). Top tips on local produce, inspirational gluten-free recipes, newly discovered nutritional facts; the micro-blogging opportunities are endless and it's about time Freya rolled up her sleeves and threw some superficial chitchat into the ether.

@UtterlyButterly
Delighted to be in the @GoldenSpoon Bake-Off along with
@The_Hungry_Sikh

Nothing could be further from the truth. Along with having to play Mary at her Year 3 nativity play and being unsure at what point Jesus was supposed to be born, this is one of the most painstaking, nerve-wracking moments of her life. Since leaving the taverna this afternoon, her chest has knotted and she is permanently on the cusp of vomiting . . . not that she can say any of that on social media. Gah, she's forgotten to add hashtags and attach a photo – both encouraged by The Golden Spoon media team who run a tight ship. Oh and shit, bollocks, fuck; she's only gone and tagged the wrong Golden Spoon which happens to be a California-based Seniors dating website and now everyone is asking if they can reserve a place at the Bake Off and whether, like last time, clothes are an optional extra.

Hunting around for the edit button which no longer appears to exist, she's about to hit the 'Delete Tweet' button but then remembers being told how distinctly uncool it is and that any permanent deletion is a red flag of inappropriate content. Apparently, you should just leave an unwanted tweet to fritter away until, like a banana skin left to decompose on the roadside, it loses oxygen. Oh help, she's stuck in Twitter-purgatory. To tweet or delete, that is the question.

Voices out on the terrace drift in through the window and for a split second Freya considers joining the others for a few evening drinks but then thinks better of it; now that Hazel has beaten a hasty retreat to the airport to catch an early flight home and *les Français* have locked themselves away in some sort of victorious love-in, it feels a little intense when it's just the three of them (Freya, Harj and Leandra-Louise).

A gnawing sensation nibbles away at her. A niggle in her gut. Maybe two niggles. Firstly, that she is up against Harj, who happens to be one of the nicest people on the planet and no matter how much she wants to win, she doesn't want him to lose. Secondly, not knowing what she's got to bake is really stressful. If she knew what was in store, she could plan and prepare, but as the task won't be revealed until she's under the spotlight tomorrow, it's impossible for her to strategise. She draws the curtain with a heavy sigh. What was it Mrs K used to say? *Take your time and enjoy the process. You can't hurry food like you can't hurry love.* Her mind drifts back (fifteen years) to an image of Mrs K spreading pink buttercream icing over a sponge cake . . .

'I think she needs flowers on her dress, don't you?' Mrs K shuffled over to a narrow cupboard exploding with baking supplies – lustre dust, edible glitter, fondant roses, white velvet sugar paste, Disney cake topper figurines, chocolate chips, rainbow sugar strands, edible pearls and diamonds, food colouring pens, snowflake sprinkles – an Aladdin's cave of cake decorations which always made Freya happy deep down inside, a magical glow dancing about her cheeks as she looked up in awe. There was no place like Mrs K's kitchen – the smell of freshly baked pastries, the heat of whatever casserole was on the go in a slow cooker, the reassuring solidity of her smooth wooden spoons – it made Freya feel warm, safe and secure.

'Who's it for?' she asked as Mrs K wedged a Barbie doll into the hole in the centre of the cake and stood back to admire it.

'My daughter. She turns nine tomorrow,' Mrs K said proudly.

Pressing royal iced daisies into the butter cream folds of the sponge cake ballgown, Freya felt a sense of importance. To be trusted with Mrs K's daughter's birthday cake was an honour and a privilege.

'The day after my birthday!' Freya giggled.

A look of concern fell over Mrs K's face. 'Your birthday's today, Freya?'

Freya nodded. 'Yup. I'm a teenager now!'

'Did you get a cake?'

'I'm too old for cakes.' Freya was already indebted to Mrs K and didn't want her feeling awkward.

Mrs K put down her icing nozzle. 'No one is ever too old for cake.'

'Honestly, I—'

'Tell me, are thirteen-year-old's still into Barbie ballroom dancers?'

'No, no, no . . .' Freya crossed her arms in front of her chest. 'It's Laura's. I don't want to—'

'I've plenty more time to make another one.' Mrs K squeezed her shoulder reassuringly.

'Seriously, I—'

Despite her protestations, a few minutes later Mrs K, her husband and children gathered around the kitchen table to sing Happy Birthday to Freya. Driving the knife through Barbie's glad rags, Mrs K pivoted a slice of the delicious, light sponge cake onto a serviette and handed it to Freya, Laura smiling at her throughout. There, in the palm of her hand, it looked so perfect and yet taking a bite of that ballerina cake was one of the worst moments of Freya's life.

Making Laura's cake had been magical. Enjoying the process of mixing, blending and beating, Freya had relished the whole baking experience from beginning to end. Just being in Mrs K's company and creating something special from scratch was enough. Fulfilling. Satisfying. Rewarding. But being given Laura's cake and accorded darting looks of sympathy across the table only said one thing: she was a rescue-project. Pitiable. Pitiful. Pathetic. The caravan kid whose mum was a psycho and couldn't even sort out a cake. The taste lingering in her mouth turned from the lightest, fluffiest, sweet vanilla sponge to one of acidic revulsion. She didn't want pity, she wanted respect. She'd made that cake, so surely she'd earned it? But whilst she was dependent on Mrs K to source the ingredients and provide the recipe, she hadn't really, had she? Self-loathing swam through her veins. One day, she'd be able to afford all the ingredients herself. One day she'd be able to make her own birthday cake. One day she'd be dependent on no one. But in the meantime, one thing was for sure: she could never come back to Mrs K's kitchen.

Freya looks down at the broken skin on her knee that she has spent the last five minutes gouging out with her thumbnail; a habit she can't shake whenever she's under extreme stress. She'll never forgive herself for giving up on Mrs K. It's not like Mrs K gave up on her – persevering at school, at holiday club, and at the caravan. When her mum was too encumbered with her illness to appeal for Freya to re-sit her end of year exams, it had been Mrs K who had filled out the forms and appealed on her behalf, representing her at a board of governors committee gathering and a face-to-face meeting with the headmaster. Dear Mrs K. Every week she'd leave a home-made casserole tucked under the caravan steps with a note. Always cheery. Never intrusive. *Just checking everything is OK? How are you getting on? It would be lovely to see you. How's your mum? You have my number if you need it. Give me a call. You can always find me in the Home Economics kitchen if you fancy a chat.*

Why hadn't she called? Why hadn't she looked for Mrs K in the school Home Economics room? Why had she left it too late to say anything? *Thank you. I'm sorry. I was embarrassed and ashamed.* Pride is a curse at times.

Dabbing at the blood with a tissue, her eyes burn with

shame and regret. If Mrs K hadn't got her through school, she'd have left with nothing. If Mrs K hadn't taught her the art of cooking, she wouldn't have gone to catering college and if Mrs K hadn't taken her under her wing, she certainly wouldn't be here now. Her eyes sting with tears. Mrs K had never given up on her and yet she had given up on Mrs K and by the time she was ready to make amends and put things straight five years ago, Mrs K had left the country. All those years wasted. She looks down, her leg now streaked with blood.

Under the hot spray of the shower, she washes away her childhood and all the shame that goes with it. She is here in Cyprus because she earned it. She is through to the Bake-Off because she earned it. She is a contender for The Golden Spoon because she earned it. God only knows, she'd have been through to the final already had somebody not sabotaged her cheesecake. *I am worthy.* She closes her eyes and repeats the words her child psychologist used to get her to say in the mirror each night before bed. *I am worthy.* Bedtime being quite a solitary affair. *I am worthy.* All those days at Kids as Carers rainy day club. *I am worthy of more.* She thinks about the years she spent working in that rat-infested pub. She thinks about the three jobs she juggled throughout catering college. She thinks about her time at A Taste of the Mediterranean. About The Golden Spoon lighting up like a beacon on Twitter. About the written exam. The oral exam. Are the nutritious benefits of mackerel superior to those of sardine? About the ten-thousand-word dissertation she wrote. The exam adjudicator's feedback. The smile that played on her mother's lips. She *is* worthy. Why wouldn't she be?

Lumbering back to her room, she imagines Harj giving himself the same pep talk in the men's shower block and vows to send him a good luck email. She picks up her phone and finds an unread message.

Xanthos

Her heart flip-flops. That's it? A single 'hi'? Isn't that the lexicon of a physical prod? A 'Hey, I'm here! What are you going to do about it?' She must not respond. If she replies, even if it's with a 'hi back!' then that's only fanning the fire and besides, if he's got something to say, then he should just say it. A single 'hi!' is not enough. *I am worthy of more.* Her finger hovers over the keyboard on her phone. Surely one little text can't hurt.

Freya

She throws her phone down on the bed and breaks open her private stash of Dairylea, then reaches for the miniature bottle of Cab Sav the flight attendant gave her to compensate for the tea he poured down her sleeve when an unexpected bout of turbulence struck. Ripping the foil lid from the plastic tub, she looks down at the perfect circle of cream cheese, its pulpy flesh staring back at her like fresh, unspoiled snow. Her mouth waters. Hopping onto the bed and leaning her head back against her pillow, she twists open the screw-top cap on the wine bottle. Heaven. Plunging the plastic fork (also courtesy of Ryanair) into the soft, creamy cheese and lifting it to her mouth, she relishes the velvet-smooth texture against her tongue. Smooth. Cold. Delicious.

Xanthos

Would you like to meet tonight?

Freya

Sorry, busy x

Delete. Too abrupt. And also not true. And should she really add a kiss? And will he know that an x is a kiss? Only the other night Stéphane was saying that the French don't use an x as a kiss, so maybe it's not universal.

She takes another swig of wine from the bottle and cuts herself another portion of cheese. Slippery. Creamy. Divine.

Freya

Not sure yet. Pretty tired so might have an early night – big day tomorrow!

Delete. Too passive. And dull.

Another swig and another mouthful of cheese. Exquisite.

Freya

I'm not sure it's a good idea.

Delete. Isn't that just opening Pandora's box? Wouldn't it be better to deploy Khady's 'phase them out' tactic, replying hours later with an innocuous 'sorry, missed this' non-committal type message, dialling it down like winding down a business, until all assets have been returned and no further transactions are expected.

Freya

Would love to but . . .

But what? But I found out that you've been shagging your way through your customers and I'm just another conquest? Delete.

More wine. More cheese. Bliss.

Freya

We could always . . .

No, we couldn't. Delete.

More wine. More . . . A tap at the window.

She jumps, spilling Cab Sav everywhere.

'Freeya?'

Fuck, he's here! Outside her room. Fuckety, fuck fuck. She's wearing off-white knickers and has no make-up on whatsoever.

'Are you there?'

She has wine-stain all over the sheets, and her off-white knickers.

'It's me, Xanthos.'

Best to whip them off, surely?

Within seconds, she's yanked everything off – T-shirt, shorts, underwear – and kicked them under the bed. Then, wrapping herself in a beach towel to look like the fresh-out-of-the-water seductive mermaid she needs to be, she goes to open the door.

'Hi,' she says, feigning serenity, one leg cocked as she tries to lean alluringly on the doorpost only for her towel to come loose under her armpit. What is she doing, for Christ's sake? Isn't she supposed to be 'phasing him out'? Determined not to come across as the sun-starved, sex-deprived tourist that she is, she grabs the towel before it descends entirely and gathers it up under her chin.

Xanthos's eyes run over the peeling skin on her shoulders. 'Sorry to interrupt, I . . .'

Paranoid that her neighbouring contestants will see, she bundles him into her room and closes the door.

Glancing around the room, he smiles. 'No rats?'

She smiles. 'No rats.'

He gestures to the burned skin on her shoulders. 'Does it hurt?'

She blows air out of her lips dismissively. 'Nothing a bit of cream won't sort out.'

He sits down on the edge of her bed and glances at the tub of processed cheese spread. Her innards twist with discomfort as his eyes shift to the half-empty bottle of Cab Sav. Were he not a professional viticulturist and cheese connoisseur and she not a food expert up for one of the most prestigious cooking prizes in the world, it would still feel pretty degrading, but oh God, what must he think? She holds her breath in her mouth and blows her cheeks out like a guppy. At least the Dairylea lid has been stripped away and it could just about pass for something more upmarket. Philadelphia, maybe?

Then to her horror, he picks up the tub of processed cheese.

'Do you need some help?' His eyes twinkle and for a split second, she thinks he's going to magic up a packet of bread-sticks and join her for a bedside picnic, but instead he reaches for her hair and guides her long, red tresses over her shoulder. A shiver runs down her spine and for some reason, she has become unable to swallow. Unable to communicate. And unable to tell him that the substance in his hand is not some globby form of After Sun or epidermic burn treatment cream but is in fact a tub of Dairylea cheese. Yet before she can find the words, he plunges his fingers into the soft, springy pulp and . . .

Slap.

A blob of Dairylea hits her shoulders, its coldness soothing against her hot skin.

Gently, he massages it towards her neck, tracing the contours of her collarbone with his fingers until they reach her chest. She should really tell him to stop, and yet it feels so good. He looks at her with shimmering eyes, his fingers finding the edge of her bath towel and just like that, her willpower goes out of the window along with her inhibitions. What does it matter that he's a bad boy? It's not like she's looking to settle down with him and have his babies or anything. Arching her back, catlike, she pulls him towards her, willing the towel to fall to the floor but it has somehow become welded to her body and refuses to shift.

Slop.

A glob of cheese slides down her chest, melting as it disappears under the towel and travels between her breasts. The smell of Dairylea intensifies as he reaches for another handful. At what point should she tell him that it isn't skin cream?

Smack.

He presses his lips against hers and kisses her hard. A throbbing sensation starts up in her groin as his tongue travels down her neck, across her collar bone, her chest and then abruptly stopping.

Licking his fingers, he looks up at her. 'Is this cheese?'

'Urm.' She bites her lip nervously.

'Dairylea?'

Her face burns with humiliation. 'Sorry, I . . . I know it's trashy but . . .'

He pulls her towards him. 'I love Dairylea.'

The towel falls to the floor.

'Come here,' he growls.

She can always start the phasing out tomorrow.

PART THREE

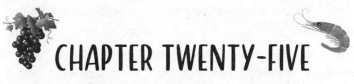

CHAPTER TWENTY-FIVE

 Bake-Off

They arrive at the village, sweaty and thirsty in the late afternoon heat. As tie-breaks are so rare and make for such good entertainment (apparently), Bake-Off is to be hosted al fresco in the village square and, judging by the throngs of crowds hanging out under the shade one of the giant sycamore tree, everyone's invited.

Chakras aligned, goals visualised, energy harnessed, Freya is supposed to feel as though she could walk on water right now. Having spent the last two hours practising Khady's manifestation techniques – envisioning what it will be like to go through to The Golden Spoon final alongside Michel, creating the journey to Paphos for the grand final in her mind's eye and visualising her name at the top of the leader board – Freya should be ready to kick culinary ass, so why does she have that feeling of dread in the pit of her stomach?

In a complete tailspin – what if she has to make a filo pastry-based dessert and her fingers won't work quickly enough? What if it involves skinning fruit really fast? Anything reliant on super-dexterity could destroy her chances – she follows a white-washed wall draped with orange flowers around the crumbling neighbourhood of shaded squares and polished cobbled lanes in search of a toilet. Bougainvillea climbs the sides of the walkway, its striking purple petals fluttering in the sea breeze as she ambles closer to the harbour, the citrus smell of grilled calamari carrying on the air. Picking her way through backstreets no wider than a donkey, she twists and turns, zigs and zags only to go full circle once again, arriving back at the main taverna, its terrace hugging the sweetest spot of the village square and consequently rammed with people. Tourists. Locals. Gastronomes the village over. Shaded by gargantuan sycamore trees planted along the edge of the old citadel wall ruins, the taverna serves something for everyone – coffee in the mornings, lobster at lunchtime and rabbit stew of an evening. She's never seen it so busy.

Out in the village square, a large banner advertises The Golden Spoon Championships – presumably they didn't have a Bake-Off banner at the ready. Team Bazigou has set out several rows of chairs, half of them already occupied. Tables have been set up in front of the audience where Freya and Harj will presumably 'perform', and if that isn't enough to incite bowel-churning nervous tension then the microphone rigged in the stand between them certainly is.

Bolting to the taverna bathroom for the third time today, she gives the waiter a withering look before knocking on the door of the single unisex cubicle, knowing from past experience that the lock doesn't work properly. The door swings open and she comes face-to-face with Harj, a beautiful emerald green turban atop his head.

'Frey!' His face fills with sadness. 'Thank God I got to see you. Can we have a chat?'

'In a sec,' she says, pushing past him and bursting through the toilet door.

Harj stumbles. 'I just . . .'

'Nature calls!'

Hovering over the toilet seat, Freya tries to pull herself together. This is baking a cake just like any other. All she has to do is block out the audience and get in the zone. *Enjoy the process.*

'You OK in there, Freya?' she hears Leandra-Louise say.

How many fucking people need to listen to her shitting her guts out, for fuck's sake?

'*Elle est nerveuse,*' she hears Stéphane add.

Jesus Christ, must a whole scrum of people really loiter outside the toilet and tune into her bowel movements? She washes her hands in the small sink and looks at herself in the mirror. Her skin is more freckled than usual, her hair a lighter shade of red, but other than that, she's the same person that she was this morning and the same person she was when she entered this competition. Ambitious. Focused. Hungry. She can do this.

By the time she lets herself out of the bathroom, a whole entourage has congregated – not only are Harj, Leandra-Louise and Stéphane there, but Michel and Dimitri have also crept into the mix.

Michel reaches out to her and puts his hand on her shoulder. '*Bonne chance.*'

'Thanks,' she says, a shiver of discomfort running down her spine as he turns to Harj and wishes him the same. She dries her hands on the sides of her dress and shuffles over to Harj. 'You wanted a word?'

'Yeah,' Harj says, looking to Leandra-Louise who nods at him, squeezes his shoulder and wanders off.

Out on the narrow pavement, Christos greets them with a smile.

Freya swells with affection. 'Good to see you.' And it really is. Granted he's dropped some weight and looks a bit gaunt, his cheeks sunken and the skin around his chin a little looser than before, but his eyes are clear and the spark which only ever appeared as a vague glimmer when cooking anything lamb (lambassador that he is) shines brighter.

'Hi,' Harj mumbles.

Christos reaches for Freya's hand and cups it between his. 'Thank you for everything.'

Harj fidgets awkwardly.

Freya looks into Christos's dark eyes and nods slowly. 'It's good to have you back.'

'You have a small audience.' He gestures over to the seating area which is filling rapidly as people roll out of the taverna, drinks and pastries in hands.

She takes a deep breath and tries to reason that this is no different to baking at home.

'Fuck.' Harj kicks at the ground.

'It'll be OK,' she says, caught between wanting to bolster him and wanting to retain all positive energy for herself. Harj may have become a good friend to her, a little brother even, but he's also her competitor and she knows he wants this as much as she does, which ups the stakes somewhat. Her mouth dries and she wonders whether this is how Venus and Serena felt every time they had to play against each other in a Grand Slam final. It just doesn't feel right having to battle it out so publicly and that one of them will lose out.

There must be about sixty people seated in all, and families are still spilling out of the taverna and filling the empty chairs. A shot of adrenaline courses through her, her legs feeling all wobbly as Christos leads them to their respective tables, though when she looks over at Harj, he looks to be in a worse state than she is, his arms jittering, terror plastered across his face.

'Come on,' she whispers. 'Forget about everyone else.'

His Adam's apple bulges in his throat as he swallows. 'I...'

She waits for his words until it's clear they aren't going to come, then looks away, her eye drawn to their identical sets of ingredients. Half a dozen eggs. A block of unsalted butter. A thimble of cinnamon. Sugar, salt, honey. Vanilla essence. A pile of pistachio nuts. Chopped walnuts. Two bowls of flour of different textures. White wine vinegar. Olive oil and corn starch.

Harj glances over from his table. 'Baklava?' he mouths.

Freya's heart sinks. It's game over if it's baklava. She looks down at the ingredients. Surely filo pastry would need a couple of hours to refrigerate before it can be layered with any type of filling, in which case that would kind of kill the whole audience engagement thing.

In her peripheral vision, she spots Xanthos arriving and feels hollow all of a sudden. He smiles at her and waves, and although she can feel the corners of her mouth turning up in response, she feels the pressure rise further – here is someone she doesn't want to fail in front of. He takes a seat opposite her, his dark skin offset against his white T-shirt, his back-to-front khaki baseball cap allowing a tuft of hair through the fastener. A roller coaster of emotions twist and turn inside her, lust and trepidation rolling around like aggressive playmates. Just how is she supposed to focus when all she can think about is lying beneath him?

Christos takes to the microphone. 'Ten minutes, everyone. We'll start in ten minutes.'

Freya glances at the audience, watching as two children fight over an i-Pad and a man in knee-length shorts chides them. Further along the row, Mrs Anastasis and Angeliki are engrossed in conversation over a bag of plums whilst Leandra-Louise and Dimitri sit in front of Harj on the front row. Freya looks down at her shaking hands. How the hell is she going to be able to sieve flour and roll dough trembling like this?

Christos carries over a basket of freshly picked oranges, their leafy stalks still attached. He hands them each a dozen or so, and the audience looks on in delight as their tabletops rapidly fill, oranges rolling to the ground and bouncing across the cobbles.

'Not baklava!' Freya whisper-shouts over to Harj, her mind racing to work out what's expected of them. *Revani* cake?

Melopita? Melomakarona? With a whole pot of honey amongst the ingredients, it surely has to be melo-something. Then again, honey is in most Cypriot desserts. What about *milopita?* Although there's no sign of apples. *Yiaourtopita?* Nope, there's no sign of yoghurt either. *Loukoumades?* But surely deep-fried doughnuts would require a fryer and there has been no such talk of anything like that. St Fanourios Cake? But what about all these oranges?

'Ladies and gentlemen,' Christos announces. 'Without the aid of a recipe, our cooks will prepare Cyprus's finest orange semolina cake.'

Freya's heart flutters. Semolina; the coarser of the two flours – of course. She feels her chest constrict. She hasn't made orange semolina cake in years but from memory, it's all about the syrup. Making sure the syrup cools before adding it to the cake so it doesn't go too soggy. Making sure the syrup doesn't thicken too much through over-baking the sponge. Poking holes throughout the cake with the prongs of a fork to allow the syrup to permeate the cake all over   nobody wants a gloopy middle. She takes a deep breath. Just how is she supposed to let the cake cool with a live audience? And what if the cake winds up with a dip in the centre (which she seems to remember her last one did)? She hunts around her table in search of a pastry brush to spread the syrup around in case it pools. There's no way around it; orange semolina cake is a syrup minefield.

Harj puts up his hand as though he's at school. 'Don't we need yoghurt for the topping?'

Christos nods over at the taverna. 'It's chilling.'

'Me too.' Harj reverts to his role of class clown, folding his arms theatrically and smiling, English-speaking members of the audience reacting to his showmanship with a series of chuckles.

Christos laughs. 'Ladies and gentlemen. May I introduce Harjot Sowal.'

Harj bows deeply, his turban nearly scraping the floor, the audience clapping with gusto. He's clearly back on form.

Christos turns to Freya. 'And our other wonderful chef, Freya Butterly.'

Freya is unsure whether to bow, curtsey, wave or smile and does a kind of weird mixture of all four which makes her look like a giant, undulating worm, the audience applause petering out when she knocks her kitchen utensils to the floor with her elbow. Thank God the audience are not judging the Bake-Off, she tells herself, watching as Christos addresses the audience in Greek. Although why is he holding up a large gold card and gesturing to their seats in a way that suggests that the audience *will* be voting?

'The baker with the most votes will be our winner,' he summarises for the benefit of Freya and Harj.

Freya's gut fills with dread. If anyone is going to get the popular vote, it's Harj, what with his playful charm and natural entertainment skills. She closes her eyes, remembering Khady's pep talk at the airport. 'You've jumped through hoops to get here so don't for one second think you're not as good as anyone else. You're the best, and that's final.' At the end of the day, this is a cookery competition, not a popularity contest. All she can do is her best.

Christos turns towards them. 'The taverna ovens are preheated and ready. Are you?'

Another surge of dread. As soon as the clock starts, she'll cream together butter and sugar until it's light and fluffy. Or should she start by juicing and zesting the oranges? Actually yes, the oranges are a better use of time. Oranges first. Mix the juice and zest with the vanilla and then move on to the butter and sugar, before adding the eggs one at a time. As there are no measuring scales, she'll just have to use the cup. No need to get flustered. It'll be fine. The trick is to alternate between the orange juice and the dry mixture. Dry, wet, dry, wet, dry. Layer upon layer.

'Frey?' Harj calls over from his table, his voice wobbling.

Freya turns to him. 'Good luck!'

He fidgets from side to side. 'Frey, can we . . .'

'Your forty minutes start NOW!' Christos takes hold of the stopwatch around his neck and clicks a button. A countdown clock springs up on a huge screen just outside the taverna.

Making a grab for an orange and reaching for the zester, Freya scrapes the metal blade over its puckered skin and, flipping the huge orange globe over and over in her hand, breathes in the sweet, tangy aroma as her hands become sticky.

Scrape, rotate.

Scrape, rotate.

Scrape, rotate until cramp sets in between her thumb and forefinger.

'Keep going!' Xanthos yells as Freya tries to massage out the pain with her thumb, aware of Harj in her peripheral vision who seemingly isn't moving.

She reaches for another orange. Scrape, rotate.

'Frey?' Harj whisper-shouts.

She mustn't lose concentration.

'Frey?'

'Whassup?' Her eyes remain faithful to the oranges.

He doesn't answer.

'Get on with it, Harj!' Leandra-Louise calls out from the audience.

Freya sets about bisecting each orange, one after the other, and their halves falling open like told secrets. Reaching for the citrus squeezer, she squashes the first orange half down and presses so hard, the pointy tip spikes through the peel and pierces the palm of her hand. Bloody nerves! Two, three, four. She glances at Harj who stands hands on hips, surveying the ingredients in front of him.

Christos turns to the audience. 'He likes to build excitement.'

Freya continues to squeeze oranges, her fingers working like pistons. Five, six, seven. She can't look up. Not if she doesn't want to get derailed. And eight. She pours the orange juice into a jug, adding the zest and a splash of vanilla essence. Out of the corner of her eye, she can see that Harj still hasn't started. Should she launch an orange at his head? Fuck it, if he wants to dick about, wrong-footing the audience into thinking he's a hapless fool and then pulling it out of the bag at the last minute, that's on him. Everyone knows the fable about the hare and the tortoise.

'Harj?' Michel calls out.

'Get a fucking move on, Harj!' Leandra-Louise hollers.

Freya reaches for the block of butter, chops off enough to be about 150g, plops it into the bowl and chops it into cubes. Adding a cup of sugar, she takes hold of her wooden spoon, her heartbeat thumping in her ribcage. Like a rugby player with the ball, she tucks the bowl under her arm, creaming and blending for all her worth.

'Go, Freya!' Stéphane shouts.

Ordinarily she'd be beating herself up for not mixing her ingredients fast enough but as Harj isn't providing her with any competition, it's hard to feel pressured.

Christos entertains the crowd in Greek, the audience laughing at regular intervals. God knows what he's saying. Freya's eyes flicker over to Xanthos who runs his fingers over his strong, stubbled jaw and returns her gaze, her insides melting.

'You might want to start now, Harj?' Dimitri yells over.

And just like that, Harj storms off, his ingredients untouched. An audible gasp arises from the audience who break out into pockets and Christos is left standing at the microphone speechless. Freya has no idea what's going on and what she's supposed to do. Should she stop out of respect? Shouldn't they pause the clock? Is this all some sort of staged hurdle she is supposed to jump, Harj in on the whole thing? She glances at Christos who turns off the microphone and watches Dimitri as he chases after Harj through the bewildered crowd.

Nobody has told her to stop. Nobody has told her to continue. Stuck in Bake-Off purgatory and unable to claw her way out, Freya figures that whilst the clock is still ticking, she should focus on the job at hand until somebody tells her not to. She reaches for an egg, its cold shell reassuring against her sweaty palms. To say she's distracted would be an understatement.

People are starting to get up and leave, their chairs scraping against the cobblestones. Christos has abandoned his commentary, and everyone is adding their own. She looks up to see a huddle of people crowded around an emerald-green turban next to the Aphrodite fountain on the other side of the square. Leandra-Louise, Dimitri, Angeliki, Michel and Stéphane – they have all flocked to him. But still the clock ticks and the fat lady has not yet sung. Folding in a tablespoon of plain flour and another of semolina flour, she adds a dash of orange juice. Dry followed by wet; repeating the process until she has a smooth, orange-infused mixture. Dry, wet, dry, wet. She looks up. There are only a handful of people in the audience, Xanthos amongst them.

'Keep going!' he calls out, his voice deep and gravelly.

Her batter has separated slightly, but does that even matter? She looks up at Xanthos and then down at her bowl. It's just a natural chemical reaction, she tells herself. The batter, that is. Eggs and sugar reacting, acids and oils congealing with the orange juice in exactly the same way that her own emotions are colliding and curdling right now. Confusion. Ambition. Panic. What the hell is going on?

This time when she looks up, Xanthos is the only one left in the audience. The last man standing. Hanging on her every move, he waits patiently as though her completion of this task is the only thing that truly matters.

She lets out a laugh. 'Am I supposed to carry on?'

He shrugs his shoulders. 'I guess.'

She sets about greasing the cake tin. Slippery with butter, her fingers find the bowl and pour in the mixture, Xanthos purring with appreciation.

'I guess you've won,' he says, a wide grin on his face.

She looks up to see Christos leading Harj back towards them, a line of people following them like a bridal procession. Her heart flutters. Has she really won this task or are they to perform it all over again because something went wrong? She braces herself as a crowd of people draw around Christos as he takes to the microphone.

'Congratulations, Freya,' Christos says. 'I'm sure your cake will taste delicious . . .'

Her legs become liquid. Has she won? Is the event annulled?

She bites her nails as Christos looks first to Harj and then to Dimitri who snatches the microphone from his father and rattles away in Greek, Freya only understanding the words 'Harj' and 'Freya' amongst the torrent of animated language.

She bites the inside of her cheek. 'Have I won?'

Nobody appears to hear, not whilst Christos, Dimitri and now Xanthos who has just joined them, jabber away in an aggressive tone, arms and hands flying all over the place.

Freya looks at Harj whose shoulders hang low, a deep sorrow weighing down on his facial features that he can't seem to shake. Slowly, he raises his hands to his head and removes his kingly, emerald-green turban. Beneath the layers of silk, his hair is sweaty and bedraggled. Without his crown, he stands a few inches shorter. The fallen prince. Dethroned and devalued.

Freya reaches for his arm. 'Harj?'

He says nothing, his eyes remaining faithful to the ground.

Xanthos glances at her and shakes his head with incredulity.

'What?' she mouths.

Dimitri thrusts Harj towards the microphone. 'Harj has something to tell everybody.'

CHAPTER TWENTY-SIX

The Confession

'It was you all along?' Freya's mind races as she tries to piece it all together. The salt sabotage. Michel's garlic-spiked prawns. Her beloved cheesecake. Stéphane's death by red-hot chilli peppers. Her missing beetroot. Hazel's missing garlic. It feels as though the wind has been knocked out of her. 'You're the saboteur?'

Harj massages imaginary lumps out of the palms of his hands. 'I know it was wrong and I'll obviously leave today.'

'But . . .' Freya can't find her words. 'Why? Why did you do it?'

They sit atop a grassy hillock, Harj swinging his feet and filling her peripheral vision with garish neon leather and a hefty chunk of rubber sole. 'Because I'm a dick.' His Adam's apple bulges with discomfort. 'Because I didn't think I stood a chance of winning without taking someone down. You and Michel were clearly the ones to beat so I kind of . . . It's difficult to explain. My dad always taught me, "All is fair in cookery and war." And I guess I just thought—'

'That nobody would guess it was you?'

'I . . .' He shakes his head and releases a long drawn-out exhalation of breath.

'Because to be honest, you were right,' she continues. 'I've always thought of you as the nicest, friendliest, kindest—'

Pain slices across his face. 'Don't!'

'You're a dick, Harj, but only because you've ended up sabotaging yourself.'

He pops a tab of chewing gum into his mouth and laughs. 'If you and Xanthos hadn't dug up your own beetroot, I'd be through to the final!'

'Where did you hide it?'

His eyes flicker from his crotch to his feet. 'You don't want to know.'

Digesting his confession, she rolls her tongue around her mouth and stares at a blot on the horizon – a bird? A ship? 'And what would you have done if you *had* got to the grand final?'

His face becomes an unconscious smile. 'How do you mean?'

'Well, how would you be able to cheat in front of all of the cameras?'

'Oh God, I wouldn't cheat at the final!' he says with a rush of indignance. 'I'd have thrown myself open to the hands of fate at the final.'

She plucks a blade of grass from the clump that they are sitting on and, sliding the inner bud out of its sheath, chews on the tip until her mouth fills with the sugary taste of sap. 'You really screwed me over with the cheesecake, you know.'

He busies himself with a daisy chain, threading the stem of one through the eye of another. 'In fairness, you deserved that one.'

Irritation catches in her throat. 'How?'

'Persuading Christos to replace *galaktoboureko* was bang out of order!'

'I . . .'

'I saw you,' he says, huffily. 'We all saw you. Wiping *galaktoboureko* off the board and replacing it with cheesecake. I cyberstalked you. I know cheesecake is your thing.'

Freya fills her lungs with air. 'I changed it because Christos told me to! They were out of semolina so we couldn't make *galaktoboureko*.'

Harj looks at her for a second. 'Really?'

'Yes!'

'I'm sorry, Freya.'

She turns to him. 'You realise The Golden Spoon is just as much my dream as yours? Just as much as it was Hazel's and Leandra-Louise's and . . .'

'Shit, I thought you'd take it better than this.' He adds another daisy to his chain. 'You have no idea of the pressure I'm under back home. I'm sure you get hassle from your parents, but I swear to God my dad is a food Nazi. If I don't come back with The Golden Spoon, he'll disown me.'

Freya watches as a butterfly dances over the yellow petals

of a nearby gorse bush and thinks of her mother who doesn't even know she's here in Cyprus. 'It's highly unlikely that any one of us will go home with The Golden Spoon.' She kicks off her flip-flops, Harj's words sticking to her like oil to a bird's wing. In many ways she would love to have parents so engaged in her life that their hopes and dreams are projected onto her. A set of parents who believed in her and dared to fan the flames of her ambition. Unconditional support. Hell, she would even settle for a pair of functioning parents who were ambivalent about her dreams, but then again, the other man's grass is always greener and flying solo at least means she has the freedom to be herself and drive her own destiny. Unbridled. Uninhibited. And if anything, underestimated.

'It's not like I can't cook.' Harj wipes his nose on the back of his hand. 'I *could* have legitimately won. It's just that so could you lot and I needed to make sure you didn't.'

Freya turns to look at him. 'Only you've confessed to us all now so it's kind of a moot point. You had a real chance and now you've gone and thrown it all away.'

He lets out a cry of pain and a snort of laughter 'Don't say that, it makes me think of "Bohemian Rhapsody".'

'What?'

He gathers up his phone and jacket. 'Anyway, I just wanted to say sorry and it was nice knowing you and thanks for not making me say all of that over the microphone.'

'So what happens for you now?' Freya says, pinning down the edges of her dress which balloons with the westerly wind.

'Me? I guess I'll go off travelling for a couple of weeks before I wind up back in Brum with my tail between my legs and wait for my dad to start speaking to me again.'

She digs her fingernails into the dirt. 'He honestly won't speak to you if you don't win?'

Harj nods. 'Threatened to disown me. Means it too.'

Freya stands up, a wave of impatience overcoming her. 'And what sort of a man do you want to become?'

'Chuffing hell, Frey. That's a bit deep!'

'It's just that from an outsider's point of view, it looks like The Golden Spoon is your dad's dream rather than yours.'

Harj looks down at the ground and then out to the sea. 'You've *nearly* got a point.' He shuffles around as though trying to get comfortable. 'Cooking is my thing; not just my dad's. It really is,' he says as though trying to convince himself. 'I love preparing food, I love the taste of food . . . I love the way people react to food. I just don't care about awards. The moment it becomes a competition, I lose interest. It's like football. I love having a kick about but the moment everyone wants to play a match, it's no fun anymore. Jumpers for goalposts – that's more me – but I get lost on a full-sized pitch with a uniformed ref. Know what I mean?'

Freya searches for the ship on the horizon but it has disappeared from sight. 'Kind of. Though if I'm honest, pressure makes me up my game.'

'I'm sorry I screwed you over, really and truly I am, but at least it means you're through to the final.' He looks at her with puppy dog eyes. 'If there was any way I could make it back up to you, I obviously would.'

Freya looks down at her ugly big toes and has a flash of inspiration. 'Well actually, there is one thing . . .'

CHAPTER TWENTY-SEVEN

Food Rocky

'Fine motor skills, innit.' Harj passes her another carrot.

'It's the way they reset my wrist. I just can't seem to hold it at the same angle as you.' Freya pushes her sweaty hair out of her face and takes hold of the knife once more. 'OK. Let's go again.'

Harj gathers up the stopwatch that hangs around his neck. 'On your marks. Get set. Go!'

'Ah!' she cries, the carrot catapulting off the table and into a plant pot of geraniums before she's even made the first incision of the rose petal she is meant to be carving. How the hell does Harj create flower buds so fast and so skilfully? This is the third time the carrot has rolled away mid-slice and cramp has already set into her hand which has taken on the form of a claw, her fingers hanging limply. Picking the carrot out of the soil, she massages the spot between her thumb and forefinger, and returns to the chopping board where Harj has lined up another.

'You've got to grasp the knife tighter and keep your thumb tucked back,' he advises from the shade of the crooked olive tree.

She stares at the pile of carrots heaped up on the edge of the chopping board and prepares her grip.

'Knuckles forward,' Harj orders.

She repositions her hand, the carrot starting to roll adrift again. 'I've told you, my hand just won't do what yours does,' she says with an air of exasperation.

'OK, let's change things up a bit.' He takes hold of the knife, this time grasping it at an entirely different angle. 'Chip chop flick. Chip chop flick.' He motions, moving the knife forty-five degrees and flamboyantly skimming the blade against the edge of the carrot. 'Chip chop flick.'

Freya does as she's instructed, but it's no use. She can chip. She can chop. But no matter how much she twists her wrist, she just can't flick.

'Think of it as performing a lunge—'

'I never perform a lunge.'

'OK, imagine if you were to perform a lunge, your knee works as a hinge. You never straighten out fully in the same way that the knife should work as a hinge against the chopping board, the tip of the blade never leaving the board and gently pivoting to slice, slice, slice. Forget the flick, just slice, slice, slice.' He makes it look so easy, the petals of a carrot rosebud forming before her very eyes. 'OK, again.'

Freya takes hold of the knife and pictures the mind-boggling speed at which Michel can thinly slice a courgette. It might only be the odd ten second saving here and there, but it all adds up, and if her calculations are correct, she stands to lose about three minutes to Michel on each task purely because it takes her longer to cut things up. Her damned hand.

'I know you can't hold it in the same way as the guy in the YouTube video because—'

'Because I am not the guy in the YouTube video!' Freya spits with annoyance, calling to mind the overzealous P.E. teacher they had at school who would spend the entire tennis lesson talking theory and correcting their racquet grip, so they never actually got a hit of the ball.

Harj sighs with more volume than is necessary. 'Maybe you should try the other hand.'

'No.' She picks up the knife once more, a sharp pain returning to her hand as she grips the handle. Grasping the carrot with her good hand, her attention is diverted to a group of tourists who arrive on the edge of the terrace, red-faced and sweaty, flanked by Stéphane and Michel. Wheelie cases. Backpacks. Water bottles. Cameras. It's clear they're not just day-trippers.

'*Mesdames, messieurs, je vous présente l'équipe Cuillère d'Or,*' Michel announces to the people who stand and stare as though Freya and Harj are about to perform some kind of show.

'*Bonjour, bonjour.*' Stéphane greets Freya and Harj. 'Friends of Michel's.' He gestures to the group who huddle like penguins and blink back in wonder. 'They arrived for the final.'

'Hi.' Freya's heart freezes over as he introduces them one at a time.

'Sylvie.'

Michel has an entourage of people to support him at the final?

'Jean-Luc.'

Whilst she has nobody.

'Raphael.'

People who can hop on a flight to Cyprus at the drop of a hat.

'Marie-Hélène.'

Who have the time, money and fundamentally the belief in him?

'Xavier.'

And have come all this way to champion him.

'Leo.'

Support him.

'Jean-Matthieu.'

Root for him.

'Manu.'

Fill him with the confidence that he can win.

'My mother and sister can't make it until the final, so they'll join in Paphos.' Michel swabs his glasses on his sunhat and looks at Freya. 'You have family arriving?'

Freya squirms. 'Yeah,' she says emptily. 'In Paphos, for sure.'

He waits for her to elaborate, then realising the conversation is over, turns back to his disciples, ushers them over to the outdoor tap for a water bottle refill and leads them up to the top barn where they will apparently be staying the night.

Freya looks down at her carrot, a metallic taste in her mouth from biting her lip so hard, she's drawn blood.

'Don't let them rattle you.' Harj picks up on her anxiety.

'I've got nobody coming out,' she says flatly.

'What about your parents?'

'No.'

'A friend?'

Freya contemplates this. She could have asked Khady to come out – or at least hinted at it – but it's too big an ask. Flights alone are over £300, and she couldn't expect Khady to eat into her savings and travel all this way just to watch a cookery event for two hours max. Besides, Khady has a business to run back home. Clients to train. And with marathon season approaching, everyone wants a bit of Pump's number one P.T.

Harj is still looking at her. 'You didn't ask anyone, did you?'

Freya remains silent. It's far easier not to ask anything of anybody. To depend on nobody. That way nobody can let you down. Choosing to go solo is a whole lot easier than the loneliness and abandonment that comes with being forced to go it alone. If she asks nobody, it won't hurt when they say no, or worse than that, say yes and then forget to come, too caught up in their own life – imagined or other.

'It's not a big deal.' She tries to push away the emotion that rises in her chest. 'I think I'd feel too pressured if I knew the people watching.'

'You know me, and I'll be watching,' Harj says.

'That's different. I've met you since coming here.' She looks down at the carrot and shoves it back in the bag, her thoughts drifting to a summer when she had been made to sit a dexterity test before being hired to pick strawberries at a local fruit farm, aged eighteen. The woman had made it look easy, fitting the small wooden pegs into a block puzzle within seconds. Yet when it came to Freya's turn, try as she might, the pegs just wouldn't fit. Her fine motor skills have always been a problem since the pen incident. 'Listen, sorry to be a defeatist but I'm just not fast enough.'

'Yet.' Harj takes the carrot back out of the bag and slams it down in front of her. 'You're not fast enough *yet*. But you will be.'

'I've got two days, Harj!' she growls with frustration.

'Two days is plenty of time,' he reasons. 'This time, picture the person you are dedicating this to.'

'Sorry?' she says.

'It's something my sister does with yoga. She's dead spiritual, my sister. Her yogi always says you should dedicate the practice to someone you care about. I heard him on her video. He says it's like giving them a gift and hoping they will feel the benefit of the session as well as yourself. May as well try it with vegetable chopping.'

Freya reaches for her glass of water. 'Have you been drinking?'

'No harm in trying, is there?'

'OK,' Freya says, closing her eyes tightly and trying to picture Mrs K, though all she can visualise is Xanthos. His wet black hair dripping with sea water. His emerald-green eyes gazing into hers. His salt-stained shirt. The way he takes great care to pronounce her name, massaging each vowel in his mouth before releasing it. Freeya. His strong, athletic thighs. His gentle growl. The shape of his—

'Ready?'

Freya nods, fixing an image of Mrs K in her mind's eye. A mass of unruly dark hair. Olive skin. Pearly white teeth. Kind eyes.

'Go!' Harj clicks the button on the stopwatch and looks up with expectation.

Holding the tip of the knife blade against the chopping board, Freya drags it down through the carrot. Again and again, she chops and chops, picturing Mrs K in the school Home Economics kitchen, her upper arms wobbling as she folds flour into eggs. Mrs K's face pressed against her caravan window checking for signs that Freya was still there. Still alive. A steak and kidney pie left on the fold-away doorstep. An apple crumble stashed behind the gas bottle. Always in sealed Tupperware, so the foxes wouldn't get to it.

Shuffling her hand backwards as the cold blade touches her knuckles, the knife pivoting up and down like a hungry hinge until the whole length of the carrot has been fashioned into a rosebud, its stem leafy and thorny. The amount of Tupperware boxes she never returned to Mrs K. Total bad manners. She shakes her head in self-disgust and grabs another carrot, chopping it into a cuboid and setting the knife to pivot. Again and again. Carrot after carrot. Rosebud after rosebud. Faster and faster. Until her fingers become a blur.

'That's it!' Harj all but squeals. 'Keep going!'

Freya carves and slices for all she's worth. She thinks about

Mrs K slicing green beans in the school dinner hall. Mrs K slicing red peppers at her own kitchen table. Mrs K slicing and slicing to a rhythm of her own.

'Boom!' Harj says as soon as she's finished chopping the last one. 'A new P.B. You were a whole forty seconds faster that time.'

Freya flexes her fingers to dispel the pain.

'OK.' Harj looks down at his notepad. 'Next up, grating . . .'

After two hours of food prep bootcamp, Freya is ready to drop. The skin on her fingertips feels raw and her knuckles are bleeding. She closes her eyes and plunges her hands into a basin of warm water, picturing The Golden Spoon trophy in her mind's eye.

Has she got what it takes?

CHAPTER TWENTY-EIGHT

A Surprise Guest

Freya scrambles up the hillside in the morning sunshine in search of the others. Past violets and windflowers, blood-red poppies and golden mimosa. Water drips down her spine, her hair still wet from the shower. How the hell has she overslept again? Following the sound of chatter, she sees Xanthos addressing Michel's family and friends beneath an apple tree.

'You may have heard of the Apple of Discord which indirectly started the Trojan War, or the Golden Apples from the Garden of the Hesperides which gave immortality, or maybe you just love the taste of apples.' He reaches up to the low-slung branch of the nearest tree and grabs at a yellow-green apple dotted with dark brown spots. 'Delicious Pilafa.'

Dimitri sidles up behind her. For some reason, he's butt

naked save for a novelty Christmas elf apron. She looks down. Oh shit. She's naked too, and she hasn't got Santa's little helpers to protect her modesty.

Xanthos's eyes flicker first to Freya and then to Dimitri, his face becoming crumpling into a frown.

'I . . . it's not,' Freya splutters as Dimitri kisses the back of her neck.

Xanthos glares at her, clearing his throat with one of his trademark growls as he holds up the apple. 'Delicious Pilafa. Their name does not disappoint. The flesh is juicy yet firm, sweet yet acidic and you may notice that they smell more of banana than of apple.' He looks over at Freya. 'I know some of you go crazy for banana, especially my brother's.'

Heat shoots to her face. Does everyone know she's sleeping with Dimitri? Why is she sleeping with Dimitri? Before she can think it through properly, her attention is diverted to a loud banging noise. She looks up to see another busload of Michel supporters, all of them hammering on the window, demanding to be let loose. Hundreds of them.

Bang. Bang. Bang.

Freya startles awake and sits bolt upright, her hair stuck against her head. Her throat is dry and her skin is clammy. The murky shapes dotted around the room morph into familiar items as her eyes become accustomed to the dark. Her jacket hanging on the back of the door. The wardrobe. The curtains. The pile of cookery books. The laptop case strewn on the floor. Her heartbeat slows as she reaches for the glass of water on her bedside table, the vivid imagery of her nightmare evaporating into an indistinct haze. And there it is again, that banging at the door. A real noise which isn't part of her dream. Bang, bang, bang. Is it really her door or is it Leandra-Louise's?

The garish digits on her phone suggest it is 6 a.m. She sits up and throws her legs over the edge of the bed, her bare feet finding the smooth floor tiles.

'Hello?' She pads over to the door and prises it open, letting in a stream of sunlight and there, in its golden haze, stands Khady, all oversized sunglasses and baggy yoga pants, a single sports bag slung over her shoulder and a map of the island in her hand. Her hair is off-the-scale cool – tight spirals of caramel and burgundy, naturally tapered into her long, slim neck – and the huge pair of tortoiseshell earrings dangling from each ear matches the frames of her sunglasses. Always the Style Queen.

'I was going to rock up in Paphos tomorrow but figured you might need some pre-match support.' Khady drops her bag to the floor and wraps her arms around Freya.

A warm, fuzzy feeling takes hold of Freya. She presses her cheek against Khady's and holds her tight. It feels so good to hold the warm hulk of a friend despite Khady's perfume being so overpowering that she can't help but waft her hand back and forth in front of her nostrils.

Khady laughs. 'There's not a lot to do in Larnaca Airport at 4.30 a.m. other than spray yourself stupid with duty-free eau de whatever it was.'

Freya checks to see if anyone else is outside. 'How did you . . .'

'I recognised your swimming costume,' Khady says, nodding to the flowery bathing suit hanging under the window box and leaning her chin on Freya's neck – something of an accomplishment what with her being a good foot taller than Freya and having to widen her stance like a giraffe straddling its legs to reach down for grass.

Freya leads her inside. 'You must have travelled all night.'

Khady shrugs her shoulders like it's nothing. 'I slept on the flight and then in the taxi. Apparently, I got lucky with the tide.'

Peeling off sunglasses the size of dinner plates, Khady's face is as beautiful as ever; her skin as silky smooth, her cheekbones as attention-grabbing, the violet contact lenses she's wearing giving her eyes a mesmeric appeal. Looking into them, Freya feels a bit like Mowgli gazing into the swirling, hypnotic irises of Kaa. Striking. Powerful. Enchanting. Certainly not the eyes of someone who has travelled thousands of miles and hasn't slept, but as Freya looks a little closer, there's a hint of something heavy Khady is carrying. A lingering insecurity. A niggling worry. A trace of apprehension that has crawled into the small lines around her eyes. A flicker of something bigger.

Freya wriggles her feet into flip-flops. 'You OK?'

'Never been better.' Khady flashes a broad smile, showing a row of perfectly aligned pearly white teeth. Maybe it's just jet lag.

Rummaging in the drawer of her bedside table for teabags, Freya gets out two sachets of Lipton Yellow and plugs in the travel kettle.

'Wait.' Khady dips her hand into the pocket of her bag. 'I know how important a proper cup of tea is to you.' She drags out an envelope of Yorkshire Tea.

Freya feels a surge of happiness. There is tea and there is Yorkshire Tea. She hasn't had a decent cuppa since she's been out here and like watching *Friends* or flicking through *Grazia*, sometimes you need a familiar pleasure, and that's where Dairylea cheese and Yorkshire Tea will always sort you out.

Khady throws the teabags into the stainless-steel camping mugs Freya has lined up. 'I figured you'd never ask me to come out, so I thought I'd surprise you.'

'Sorry, I . . .'

'You *are* worth it, you know.' Khady squeezes Freya's shoulder. 'You can ask.'

Freya looks down at the floor. 'Thank you.'

The kettle boils, steam crawling against the window, allowing Freya to make tea for two whilst Khady touches up her mascara, kicks off her leopard-skin boots and heads out onto the terrace.

'It wasn't easy finding this place,' Khady says, taking in the vineyards below.

'Yeah, it's pretty remote.'

'Remote is good, mind. I need remote.'

Struck by how at odds this is to the city-loving, always-on Khady she knows and loves, Freya flinches. 'Are you OK?'

Khady opens her mouth to speak but then pauses at the arrival of Angeliki who appears on the stone steps in her nurse's scrubs with an armful of fabric.

'Hi.' Angeliki's eyes shift from Freya to Khady and back again. She places the material down on the table. 'Your friend ordered another length of silk. Can you tell him I—'

'Hey!' Harj emerges from his room, eyes still crusty with

sleep. 'Thanks for carting it up the hill. I thought I'd treat myself to another new turban for the final. I trust you'll be cheering on Team Freya?' He looks at Angeliki who stares at him blankly.

An awkward moment follows which is finally broken by Khady who clicks her fingers at Harj. 'You must be The Hungry Sikh? You've got quite the following on Twitter!'

'At your service, ma'am,' Harj says, offering a soldier's salute and then trying to fumble his way out of it. He turns to Angeliki. 'So, I was wondering if you'd like to . . .'

Angeliki fixes him with a thousand-yard stare. 'No.'

'You've not even heard me out yet!' Harj says, a curtain of disappointment drawing across his face.

'The answer's still no,' Angeliki says.

Harj goes to speak and then thinks better of it.

'I'm just saving you your pride,' Angeliki says, glancing at the watch face pinned to her nurse's scrubs and attaching a receipt to the bag of fabric. 'It's just that guys aren't really my thing.'

A smile plays on Khady's lips, Freya instantly recognising a flirt of admiration. She's seen that look before – in response to the beautiful Indian girl who used to come into the restaurant on Friday lunchtime to write her book over steak frites to escape the strict vegetarianism of her home life. In response to the Swedish waitress at Old Market Square's Pret A Manger who gave them free coffee whenever the manager was out. And in response to her hot-shot lawyer neighbour whenever they'd share the apartment lift.

Harj peels a twenty euro note out of his wallet, accepting

that the only transaction he is going to complete with Angeliki is financial.

'Nice fabric.' Freya remarks, unsure what else there is to say.

'Thanks.' Harj runs his fingers over the silver-flecked white silk before scuttling back to his room with it, shoulders sagging with defeat.

Khady reaches over to shake Angeliki's hand. 'I'm Khady, Freya's friend from home.'

Freya watches as the two women press their cheeks against each other in a kiss salutation that takes longer than necessary and feels somewhat of a spare part.

'I'd better go.' Angeliki sees Harj returning to the terrace.

'It was nice meeting you.' Khady grins. 'Maybe we could . . .'

'Sure.' Angeliki tucks her hands into the pockets of her cotton trousers and smiles. 'You can find me at The Fabric Emporium down in the village. I work nights so my schedule's a little upside down.' And with that, she turns on her heels and disappears back down the footpath.

Harj holds his hands up in disbelief. 'How the . . .' His voice trails off.

Khady and Freya share a laugh as he retreats to his room once more, tail well and truly between his legs.

Freya chuckles under her breath. 'Seriously, Khads. How do you do that?'

'Do what?'

'The whole femme fatale thing. You've been here for what, fifteen minutes and . . .'

Khady straightens herself out and takes a gulp of tea. 'I'm not here for the women or the men. I'm here for my brilliant friend, Freya Butterly.' She holds up her mug and chinks it against Freya's. 'Here's to you winning tomorrow.'

Freya's stomach drops. *Tomorrow*. It makes everything sound so imminent. And whereas the final in Paphos was always in the offing, on the cards, at hand and just around the corner, *tomorrow* is an altogether different proposition. Tomorrow is definitive. Saturday 30th June to be precise.

'You'll be grand.' Khady reaches for her hand as though reading Freya's mind.

That warm, fuzzy feeling returns. Her mother may not be flying out to Paphos as Michel's family are, but she at least has Khady at her side. Strong, loyal, dependable Khady.

Thelma to her Louise.

Rachel to her Monica.

Elsa to her Anna.

Spirit lifted, the wind of solidarity beneath her wings, maybe tomorrow won't be that bad after all.

CHAPTER TWENTY-NINE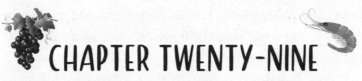

Grand Final Preparation

In Paphos, Freya will be asked to prepare a three-course meal that showcases the flavours and traditions of Cyprus, combining fragrance with substance, succulence with presentation and subtlety with spice – each dish nothing short of simply delicious. All this, in front of television cameras and an audience, not to mention sharing a stage with the one and only Talia Drakos. No pressure! The one saving grace is that the show will be sold to a small British television channel and therefore everything will be in English – a good job as Freya doesn't speak a word of Greek and it wouldn't just be her red pepper that'd be stuffed.

Freya stares at her laptop screen and assesses the form in

front of her, the words ballooning and shrinking before her eyes.

'Come on, Frey. If you don't submit it in the next ten minutes, there's no guarantee of getting all of your ingredients.' Khady shifts her wooden bangles up her arm and reaches for the keyboard. 'OK,' she says, fingers poised. 'Name of starter you are going to cook?'

Freya's throat dries. Starters are a problem. As Dimitri pointed out when they first arrived, you should never under-estimate a starter – they carry as much heft as a main and like the first page of a novel, can either draw you in or turn you off entirely. Choose the wrong starter and you could write yourself off lock, stock and barrel. Starters are your calling card, designed to show what you're capable of without going too over the top. Nobody wants death by flavour. It needs to be bold without being overpowering. Adventurous without being too risky. Eye-catching but also mouth-watering. Dilemmas. Dilemmas. Lamb *keftedes* are an obvious choice but may not have the wow factor considering how much time the whole team has spent perfecting it over the last week. *Kapnista loukanika* is another option, but you could argue that smoked sausage might be too heavy before a main. And although *elies tsakistes* is listed as a starter in *The Golden Spoon Guide to Mediterranean Cookery*, surely, even when accompanied by crudities, olives are more of a side dish?

'Come on, Frey. We've been through this a million times. All those years we should have spent binge-watching Netflix true crime series or trawling the internet for archive footage of Tom Hiddleston, we obsessed over this. Or at least, you did. You always said it had to be halloumi if you got through to the final,' Khady says, waggling her teabag back and forth through hot water.

'As a starter?'

'Why not?'

'Halloumi's difficult. Undercook it and the cheese goes all rubbery. Overcook it and it burns and loses all its flavour.'

'Then cook it just right. You're overthinking it. I'm going to submit what you came up with earlier else you'll miss your deadline.' She glances at the envelope Freya scrawled over yesterday and types in all of the ingredients that make up:

Starter: Halloumi and watermelon salad with fresh mint, pomegranate and smoky aubergine

Main: *Spanakopita* with lemon drizzled asparagus and green beans

Dessert: Cypriot lemon cheesecake

'Wait!' Freya lunges for Khady's fingers which hover over the 'send' button. 'Do you think it matters that it's an all-vegetarian menu?'

'No.'

'They might think I can't cook meat!'

'This is Talia Drakos, Frey! Isn't she like a huge supporter of vegetarian food?'

'Yeah, but . . .'

'Well then.'

Freya's heart plops into her mouth as she watches Khady hit the 'send' button, her menu and ingredients disappearing into the ether.

'OK, outfit?' Khady says.

Freya claps her hands against her breasts and hips. 'What I'm wearing now.'

'Frey, you cannot share a stage with Talia Drakos looking like that! She'll have some designer jumpsuit and you'll . . .'

'What? I'll have an apron on over the top anyway.'

Khady shakes her head. 'Come with me.'

An hour later, Freya barely recognises herself. Wearing Khady's Adrianna Papell puff sleeve moonlight blue jumpsuit (surely Talia will recognise it as homage) coupled with glittery platform trainers – powerful yet practical – she practises bending and stretching to ensure the fabric has enough give in it for her to butter and blend. Hair straightened. Eyebrows volumised. Lips accentuated. Cheeks bronzed. A pair of statement earrings dangling from each lobe, at last she is ready to kick culinary ass.

The sixty-seater coach that Xanthos has hired comes with a designated driver. It sits in the village square, gathering sap from the overhead branches of a sycamore tree, villagers treating it as a free courier service and loading its underfloor luggage compartment with packages destined for Paphos-based businesses, friends and family. Angeliki has wedged three rolls of bubble-wrapped silk behind a vat of plump nectarines and the waiter from the taverna has boxed three pairs of shoes to be professionally shined. Christos is also getting his money's worth, lugging a broken microwave he can't fix down the hill on the back of a donkey and sliding it in next to Mrs Anastasis's box of silk handkerchiefs.

Freya climbs aboard, grateful that the air conditioning has got some kick to it once the engine turns over. The back seat is occupied by Stéphane's family – three siblings, his mother and an aunt – and the left-hand side is rapidly filling with Michel supporters. The mayor of Narbonne and his wife. Two of Michel's sisters and their respective husbands. Friends from the cookery school he runs in Narbonne and an entourage of men from his tango club. Bags are crammed into the overhead luggage shelves and a packet of home-made liquorice sweets is doing the rounds, courtesy of Mrs Anastasis who stumbles towards the rear of the coach with a pair of knitting needles and a ball of baby blue wool. Freya bags a window seat at the front of the bus which smells of carpet cleaner and tries to keep her head straight whilst Khady squeezes in next to her, attracting the attention of almost everyone that boards the bus, their eyes falling first to the psychedelic spirals of hair and then to her catlike eyes.

So far, so good. Despite her knotted nerves, Freya managed to get a decent night's kip and the central team has already confirmed that all of her ingredients are ready and waiting at the cultural centre studio in Paphos. The coach has turned up on time, and she's remembered to wear her lucky knickers – not her 'get lucky' knickers which are black lace and as flattering as a pair of tanga summer briefs can be, but her 'lucky' knickers which her mother bought her as part of a lingerie set for her eighteenth birthday along with a gift-wrapped bottle of Issey Miyake perfume.

No woman should have to buy herself perfume, the tag had read, Freya intrigued by her mum's change in handwriting which had taken on a few more loops and squiggles since she'd last studied it – she knew deep down that the perfume was Eau de Recycled Gift, her mother the intended recipient, but she chose not to ask questions or make a song and dance of it. After all, if she said anything, she'd be forced to acknowledge the weekly visit from her mother's married boss, who'd call around on Thursday evenings in tennis whites, the two of them disappearing for an allotted sixty minutes and re-emerging with a post-coital glow – something Freya preferred to ignore. Surely it was better to see the good in her mother who at least remembered her birthday and, unable to afford her own gift, was thoughtful enough to relinquish one of her own?

The perfume bottle was empty within six months and the teenage push-up bra (at least the undies were bought especially for her) disintegrated in the campsite tumble dryer the following summer, and although the knickers should probably have been slung in the bin a few years ago, she can't bring herself to chuck them away. Good things have happened in those pants. They were instrumental in losing her virginity (Hamish, seventeen, apprentice bricklayer) and went on to bring her luck at all sorts of events – catering college assessments, The Golden Spoon exam, a bridesmaid speech she'd delivered at a friend's wedding. Important pants indeed. She feels through Khady's slouch dress for the elastic, her thoughts evaporating when she sees Xanthos chatting to the driver outside. Smart casual in dark indigo jeans, white trainers and a simple khaki T-shirt, he looks effortlessly cool, Freya's stomach squirming with delight each time he glances up at the bus and catches her eye.

'What's going on there?' Khady nudges her in the ribs and smiles.

'What?'

'Come the fuck on, Freya. I've seen that look before!'

'What?' She turns her attention to the bag on her lap, and tries to extinguish the glint in her eye.

'He's nice.' Khady nods with approval and gives Freya's thigh a friendly squeeze. 'And so are you.'

Freya exhales sharply. 'It's complicated.'

Khady awaits an explanation but the moment is lost when Harj boards the bus. 'Ready for the big day?' he says to Freya.

Her nerves cascade like falling leaves.

'Ready as a ready meal, eh?' Leandra-Louise says, squeezing in next to Harj on the seat behind, make-up smudged from the morning heat.

Harj eyes her overflowing bag. 'What have you got in there?'

'Stiletto-heeled slingback shoes, a floral dress with straps, a floral dress without straps, a black velvet tuxedo, slim-cut black trousers . . .'

'What's this?' Harj holds up what looks like a dead rat in a hairnet and pinches his nose with embellished disgust.

'A girl can never have too many wigs.' Leandra-Louise snatches it back.

'We're going to a cookery final, not the Oscars,' Harj says.

Leandra-Louise dabs at her face with a wet-wipe. Superdrug. Lightly fragranced. Cucumber. 'Are you kidding? The Golden Spoon *is* the Oscars.' She snatches the wig out of his hands and strokes it smooth until it takes on the form of a groomed, dead ferret. 'Talia Drakos will be there, isn't that reason enough? Oh my God, do you think we'll get to meet her? Backstage I mean?'

Freya's heart jackhammers in her chest. She has so far managed to push Talia Drakos out of her mind, the pressure too much to handle, and now here she is about to share a stage with her all-time hero. A woman superior to all other beings. Glamorous. Glorious. Gifted. A woman who inspires others – what she can't do with a ripe courgette is not worth thinking about. Freya swallows hard. The thought of having to cook in front of this superhuman gives her the shivers. She reaches for her water bottle, her neck prickling with heat, and wonders whether Talia Drakos will be in one of her shoulder-padded trouser suits she is famous for sporting on special occasions. Sassy. Stylish. Sublime. Or maybe she'll favour one of her floral, cotton jumpsuits with an accompanying apron. Pretty. Playful. Perky. And just how hands-on with the food will she get? Will she run her fingers through Freya's lentils as she did Rod Stewart's on *Saturday Kitchen*? Will she dip a teaspoon into Michel's sauce and slowly devour its contents, enticing viewers with a close-up shot of her gratified face as she did on *Friday Night Live*, Twitter blowing up a few minutes later with #*foodporn* memes?

'Ready?'

Shaken from her reverie, she looks up to see Christos

standing in the aisle, his trembling fingers holding onto the opposite headrest.

Freya nods tentatively. 'I guess.'

He taps his head with the suggestion that it's all mind over matter. 'Very good,' he says, shuffling off down the bus in slippered feet.

Angeliki appears in the space that he has just left, looking more goth than nurse, black miniskirt, ripped top, heavy black boots and nose ring. Surely the Cypriot climate with its unrelenting dry heat is not conducive to being a goth? She looks straight at Khady and smiles. 'Thanks for the invite.'

Freya elbows her friend in the ribs, wondering just how and when this little rendezvous was arranged and hoping that the tiny ripping sound was the zip of Khady's bag rather than the split of her puff sleeve.

Khady remains unflustered. 'I'll save you a seat at the venue,' she says to Angeliki who twizzles the skull skeleton embedded in her ear cartilage round in circles and totters off to the back of the bus all sparkly-eyed.

'You don't hang about, do you?' Freya laughs.

'*Carpe diem.*' Khady wiggles her eyebrows and is just about to say something when rapturous applause erupts as Michel climbs aboard.

The coach fills with animated chatter, feet drumming against the floor and the whole vehicle shaking as team Michel unites in a frenzy of thigh clapping, whooping and cheering.

'*Vas-y, Michel. C'est bon. Vas-y, Michel. C'est bon, bon, bon!*'

Michel lifts the trilby hat from his head and salutes his

followers.

'*Fais un discours, Michel!*'

'*Dis-cours. Dis-cours. Dis-cours!*'

Khady reaches for Freya's knee. 'You've got this. Hare and the tortoise, remember?'

'I'm the tortoise?' Freya frowns.

'I'm just saying he can get all the glory he wants but he hasn't won. Let him carry the pressure of being the favourite.'

She's right of course, Freya thinks. Let him carry the pressure. She watches as Michel launches into a speech, choreographed with his hat – something about *chef de cuisine*, something about the tango, something about the Cuillère d'Or. Freya's throat tightens as Stéphane joins him, thrusting Michel's arms into the air and coercing him into a deep bow. Thunderous clapping and foot stamping starts up, the whole coach rattling and swaying as a tuneless song is belted out with gusto. Mrs Anastasis turns off her hearing aid and glares at the French contingent.

'Holy fuck!' Khady lurches over Freya's lap towards the window and whips the pleated orange curtain across its wire runners.

'Khads?' Freya shouts over an explosion of laughter.

Khady's head remains in Freya's lap. 'André's here!' she hisses.

Freya sits bolt upright, shock rocketing through her veins. As another eruption of laughter gets underway, she slowly peels back the curtain.

Striding towards the coach in a grey linen suit, mirrored sunglasses tucked into the V-neck of his white T-shirt, a look of urgency etched on his face, is a man that indeed resembles André. But it can't be André. How can it be André? They're on a remote Cypriot islet and he . . . . She looks at the huge bouquet of flowers he carries in one hand and then at the wheelie case that he is dragging over the cobbles, a TASTE OF THE MEDITERRANEAN sticker gummed across the pocket. Freya's throat fills with acid. She watches as he walks towards the coach driver who is still in conversation with Xanthos and, in what feels like slow motion, sees Xanthos's face crumple as André approaches the driver who nods him over to the coach and more specifically to Freya, pocketing the twenty-euro bill that is being thrust at him.

A moment later, Xanthos appears at the top of the steps of the bus.

'Freeya?' His voice is lost to the chanting and whooping, and although she is already halfway out of her seat, he takes it upon himself to stick his fingers into his mouth and let out an ear-splitting whistle. The chanting stops dead.

'Freeya, you have a surprise guest!' he announces to the whole coach.

A collective gasp of intrigue fills the bus, faces pressing against the window for a closer look.

'He can't know I'm here.' Khady ducks down in the footwell.

Angry at the sight of him, Freya rises to her feet. 'You've always protected me. It's about time I did the same for you,' she says to Khady as she climbs over her, trying not to split the loaned jumpsuit.

'Thanks,' Khady whispers.

Shuffling into the aisle, Freya reaches for Xanthos's hand. 'It's not what it looks like. He's not here for me!'

Xanthos looks at the expensive bouquet of flowers André is clutching and pushes her away, a look of disdain flashing over his face as he edges back towards the driver's cabin, allowing her access to the steps.

Alighting the bus, she turns to Xanthos and reaches out to him once more. 'It's not what you think!'

He snatches his hand away and shoves it deep into his pocket.

Bile rises in her throat as her feet hit the tarmac. How dare this man stalk her friend? How dare he turn up like this and ruin her big day? Pumped and primed, she charges towards André who rearranges his face from one of abject terror into one of serenity in a matter of milliseconds, smooth criminal that he is.

'Here she is!' André says to nobody, opening his arms to Freya as though he's her biggest supporter. 'Golden Girl Extraordinaire.'

'What are you doing here?' Freya spits.

'I've just come to offer my support. To cheer you on at the final. To . . .' He adopts the body language of an injured puppy. 'We need you at the restaurant, Frey. It's not been the same since you left. Standards have slipped and—'

Anger burns in her veins. 'It's got nothing to do with you coming out here for Khady?'

'We're in love, Freya. Khady and I. We've been trying to make a go of things, but Sindy hasn't been able to let go. It's been so difficult, and I swear to God I'm . . .'

'Here to stalk her?' Freya offers. 'Only that's what this is.

Harassment.'

'No, no, no, no. I didn't come out here for Khady.' He buries his head in his hands. 'I came out for you!' He steps back as Xanthos thunders between the two of them, Freya's heart somewhere in her mouth as Xanthos turns to glare at her before heading into the taverna.

Filled with frustration, Freya snarls at André. 'You're ruining everything!'

'Don't be silly,' he says condescendingly. 'I'm here to support you.'

She glances at the closed curtain on the coach and then turns back to him. 'Stay away from Khady and stay away from me.'

A look of satisfaction spreads across his face. 'So she *is* here then . . .'

Every fibre of her body burns with fury. 'Piss off back home. You're not welcome here.'

'It's a free country. I can do what I want.'

The driver beeps the horn, Xanthos jogging out of the taverna and jumping onto the bus. He turns to her. 'Are you coming or not? The tide is on its way.'

André looks up at Xanthos, an everything-is-fine grin on his face. 'Of course we are. Come on, Frey. You can't miss your big moment.'

And then to Freya's horror, he strides towards the bus.

'No!' Freya shouts. 'You are not getting on that bus!'

'Don't be silly!' André says, passing her the bouquet. 'Hold these for a second, I need to show you something.'

And somehow she is now holding the flowers and André

is reaching into his pocket and dragging out a ring box purely for the benefit of Khady who he knows will be watching from the window, positioning himself closer to the bus to give her a better view. Freya turns to see Xanthos standing inside the bus at the top of the steps and feels sick to the very core.

'Frey, I've never loved anyone like it before. It's real. It consumes me. My heart bursts. I can't live without—'

She looks to Xanthos who shakes his head and disappears inside the coach.

'Do you think she'll like it?' André opens the box to reveal a square-cut diamond ring, a Cheshire cat grin plastered over his face.

'No, André.' Freya tries to sound forceful but her voice wobbles all over the place. 'You're already married and even if you weren't, Khady wants nothing to do with you.'

'You're coming or not coming?' the bus driver yells over.

'One second!' Freya yells back. 'Look, André. What you're doing is harassment. You had a fling. She doesn't want it to go any further and you have to respect her wishes. You can't just turn up in her flat, at her work, on her holiday. Now if you'll excuse me . . .'

The bus rumbles, a plume of smoke phut-phutting out of the exhaust pipe and to her horror, starts to pull away. She watches as Xanthos, rolling his arms, encourages the driver to hurry up and looking back at her, shakes his head with narrow-eyed disappointment.

'Wait!' She runs after the bus, still clutching the bouquet.

'You don't think I should have gone for a sapphire?' André

shouts over the noise of the engine.

She watches as the back of the bus disappears out of sight, the faces pressed against the back window getting smaller and smaller. A high-pitched ringing invades her ears, and her legs turn to liquid. This cannot be happening. It doesn't make any sense. Without her, there's no final, right? And even if Xanthos is hell-bent on punishing her, surely Khady will stop the bus for her?

Surely Harj will stop the bus for her?

Surely Michel will stop the bus for her?

But then again, who has the authority to stop Xanthos?

'Look what you've done!' Freya smashes the bouquet of flowers over André's head, white rose petals falling to the ground and lily heads rolling into the gutter.

André looks down at the okra stain of pollen smeared across his white T-shirt, anger flashing across his face. 'What the fuck, Freya? It's a brand-new T-shirt.'

Freya's face twists with who-gives-a-shit fury.

'Look, the next bus will be fine.'

'The next bus?' she cries, a hot mess of rage. 'This isn't bloody Nottingham. There is no next bus! We're in Lappo, André! Lappo doesn't even have a bus stop.'

'I'm sure there—'

'There is no other fucking bus!'

Unable to process what's happening, she splays her arms out and roars as loudly as she can, a flock of pigeons taking flight and an old man dropping his bag of groceries, tins of processed meat rolling down the street and a box of eggs smashing against the ground. She picks up a flower head from the gutter and launches it at André's head. 'You sleazebag shithead!'

He stands there, stupefied.

She bends down and gathers up a whole handful of flowers and then, aiming at his head, she launches each one like a poisoned dart, one after the other, a machine gun round of flower head bullets smacking him in the face. 'You've ruined everything, you mother-fucking bitch-tit cockwomble!'

'Cockwomble?' He frowns with confusion.

'Look it up!' She turns away and runs.

Sprinting through back alleys, she finds herself cornered in the labyrinth that is Lappo. Dead end upon dead end. Finally, she navigates her way through the maze and reaches the water's edge only to see the coach ploughing towards the main island on the raised bridge, sea gulping up the causeway behind it.

'Stop!'

In the hope that she'll awaken from a bad dream, she pinches at the flesh of her thigh but moments later, she is still very much awake and staring at the disappearing bus which has now become a small dot on the horizon. So much for her lucky pants. Collapsing onto the crumbling coastal wall, she runs her fingers over the smooth glass of her empty bottle of l'eau d'Issey, and sobs.

The tide has come in and she has lost everything.

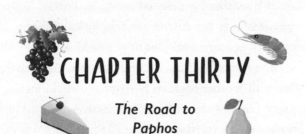

CHAPTER THIRTY

The Road to Paphos

Half an hour later, Freya looks out to sea, a fireball of white-hot anger. Anger at André for showing up, ruining everything and making her miss the bus. Anger at Khady for not stopping the bus. Anger at the bus driver for leaving without her. Anger at Xanthos for not seeing the whole thing for what it was, clearly instructing the bus driver to close the doors and go. But mainly, she's angry at herself for wasting this opportunity of a lifetime.

With each sob, her body convulses. How is this fair? How the hell did none of them not stop the bus? Khady could have at least got off and helped her deal with André . . . Head hung between her knees, she lethargically casts a stone into the water. It lands with a despondent plop. Knowing that all is lost, she thinks she's hearing things when a voice calls out her name over the growl of an engine.

She wipes away tears to see Dimitri's jet ski bouncing over the waves towards her, a deflated synthetic banana following in its wake. He cuts the engine, and the vessel floats towards the shore. 'My brother said you might need a lift!'

Freya's heart leaps with joy. Never has she been so happy to see Dimitri's flaccid banana. She jumps off the stone wall. Maybe there is a God after all, but, like an over-inflated balloon that's lost its elasticity, she dares not spring back into shape just yet. They're cutting it fine and even if they make it over to the other side of the water, there's no guarantee she can cross the island fast enough to reach Paphos on time. Stuffing her empty perfume bottle back in her bag and wiping her nose on her sleeve, she takes off her sparkly trainers and rolls up the legs of her jumpsuit. 'Thank you.'

'We'll get wet, but we might just make it,' he says as she wades through the water towards him, losing her trouser legs to the waves.

'Freya!' André appears out of breath and panting on the other side of the road.

Dimitri wraps his hands around the handlebars. 'I don't have space for your boyfriend.'

'*Not* my boyfriend!' she says, grazing her shin on the side of the jet ski as he pulls her up and almost welcoming the physical pain that rips through her bone – sweet relief from her mental anguish. Blood trickling down her leg, she hops onto the seat behind him. 'Thank you,' she sobs. 'Thank you so much.'

Dimitri glances back at her. 'Xanthos will get over it.'

'I'm not so sure,' she says, recalling Xanthos's steely glare through the bus window.

'He called me, didn't he?' Dimitri says, handing her a helmet.

Dragging the helmet over her head, she feels pulled between hope and uncertainty. Is there still a chance she can make the competition on time? Is there still a chance with Xanthos? She slams the visor shut, dizzy with the emotional tug of war that is playing out in her head.

'Hold on tight!' Dimitri grabs her hands and thrusts them around his waist.

She closes her eyes and prays.

'Tighter!' He revs the engine, the motor responding with a roar.

Thrown backwards by the G-force as they lurch forward, she clings onto him for dear life as he points the nose of the jet ski out to sea and squeezes the throttle, clicking through the gears. Engine roaring, the vehicle rockets forward, Freya paralysed by a mix of feelings. Fear. Exhilaration. Impatience. Desperation. If she makes it on time, she'll be forever grateful to Xanthos and Dimitri. If she doesn't, she'll never forgive herself.

Burning through the surf, the wind in her hair and the salt spray against her face, they plough through the deepening sea, Freya reminded of the white-knuckle water ride she got pressured to go on at a 'Kids as Carers day trip to Alton Towers and had promptly thrown up after. Pain slices through her shin with the sting of salt and sand in her fresh wound. They are about halfway across when she finally dares to open her eyes, her visor so splattered with wet sand that she can hardly see a thing.

Torpedoing towards the main island, they slice through the water, the rocky coastline expanding before them. The jumpsuit is a mess of congealed silt and saltwater, and her beautifully straightened hair has become a backcombed tangle of muck and grime, but what does that matter as long as she gets there? The shallow waters of Cyprus come into view, a sandy beach opening up before them and they're about to reach dry land.

Dimitri steers them towards a small jetty where a man helps them tether the jet ski to a wooden structure, Freya's heart racing. They have reached Cyprus, but now what?

Following him through the shallow water, she crosses the beach, her feet sinking into the soft sand before hitting the car park where a gleaming red Yamaha motorbike waits.

'Jump on!' Dimitri instructs, throwing another helmet at her.

Freya pulls the helmet over her head, buckles up the chin-strap and climbs onto the motorbike behind him. Her leg has now seized up and it's difficult to bend her knee.

Dimitri revs the motor. 'And now, the road to Paphos!'

Freya wraps her arms around his waist, closes her eyes and hopes for the best.

The road to Paphos is a road in parts, but mainly constitutes a meandering dirt track, with grit spraying up from every lump and bump. Tarmacked in places, pot-holed and rubble-ridden in others, it makes for a bumpy ride, especially when bouncing on two wheels of a motorbike, hanging on by a thread. Arms wrapped around Dimitri's waist, engine snarling beneath them,

Freya tries to appreciate the architectural majesty of the perfect rows of cypress trees that rush by on either side but screeching through villages, splashing through fords and taking hairpin bends at fuck knows how many miles an hour is doing nothing for her nerves. Are they really in that much of a hurry that they're prepared to risk life and limb?

Every part of her screams for him to slow down, but either he can't hear her or he's ignoring her, refusing to respond to her tightening grip, so instead she closes her eyes as they take yet another death-defying blind bend at a fifty-degree lean angle and prays that she won't become another roadkill statistic, noting the flowers taped to the previous set of traffic lights they jumped.

Engine at full throttle, they speed through a pretty village where elderly ladies congregate on the stone steps of a silver-ware shop, baskets brimming with home-made sweets, a look of shock etched on their faces. Through narrow alleys lined with overflowing flowerpots. Past traditional brick dwellings with red tiled roofs. Along a dusty track where pencil-thin fir trees frame the entrance to a sandstone monastery, and beyond a small, stone church. Freya tunes into her heartbeat, trying to slow it down by controlling her breath.

She *will* get there in one piece.

She *will* be at her best.

She *does* deserve to win.

Ha!

No really. She *will* get there in one piece.

She *will* be at her best.

She *won't* have died on this journey.

Picturing Michel arriving in Paphos with his boisterous entourage, she digs her nails into Dimitri's waist and bites her bottom lip, trying her best to manifest an image of her arriving alive and unflustered, a relaxed smile on her face. Sweat trickles down the side of her nose and into her mouth, her hair getting damper by the second. The sponge padding of the helmet is oppressively hot, an itch manifesting itself behind her left ear which she can't get to – not without letting go of Dimitri.

A sign for Paphos finally comes into view, the streets widening as they enter a built-up area of boxed apartments stacked one on top of the other. Bicycles. The odd balcony. A row of battered cars. A mangy dog. The air thickens and although her mouth remains clamped shut within the confines of her helmet, her nostrils fill with the smell of petrol. Squeezing the accelerator until the engine whines, Dimitri clicks through the gears, overtaking a school bus, a lorry and a truck full of oranges. He turns sharp left, the tyres screeching against the tarmac, cutting up a silver Mercedes, the old man at the wheel giving them the bird.

Up a cobbled backstreet they climb, Freya holding onto Dimitri with one hand and using the other to cling onto the back of the motorbike for dear life. Through alleys and side-streets with overhanging balconies, beneath washing lines and telegraph wires, bumping and jerking over missing cobblestones until they come out in a town square that isn't quite a square. A triangle rather. People sitting on park benches around an ornate fountain, making the most of their lunch break, the pigeons strutting around their ankles scruffier and skinnier than those of Lappo. A large white building. A small orthodox church with a gold steeple. Dimitri pulls up alongside a row of parked cars, tyres screeching to a halt.

'See, plenty of time!' He grins, showing her his watch face.

Swinging her leg over the back of the motorbike, she peels herself out of the saddle and lands on the pavement with a small thud. Scrambling for the chinstrap with one hand, and holding onto Dimitri with the other, the jitters take over, her arms and legs trembling like jelly. She pulls the helmet off her head and runs her fingers through her sweaty, tangled hair, looking up at a modern building with smoked glass panelling, arthouse posters plastered over its noticeboard. Recognising the icon of The Golden Spoon, she tries to catch her breath.

'I'll catch you up once I've parked!' Dimitri shouts after her, turning towards the motorbike.

'Thank you.' Freya turns to smile at him. He may be Lappo's Don Juan, but he is also a man with a kind heart who loves his brother and for the first time, she can see the soft side which goes hand in hand with him caring for a gerbil.

On Bambi legs, she climbs the steps and reaches for the door. In the foyer, the large digits of a huge designer clock flip over. Searching the foyer for The Golden Spoon's logo, she spots a woman with severe eyebrows manning a table of name badges.

'Freya Butterly. Golden Spoon finalist,' she says, out of breath.

'You're late.' The woman's heavily-pencilled eyebrows form deep arches as she gives Freya the once over, her eyes flickering over her helmet hair and grimy skin.

'I'm sorry.'

Slowly, the woman hands over a visitor pass attached to a

golden lanyard. 'They'll meet you on set. Down the long corridor, first left, then right, and right again. Go, go, go!'

'Right,' Freya pulls the lanyard over her head and runs down the corridor as fast as she can. First left. She tries to comb her fingers through her matted hair, sand showering the carpet. She should really sort out her shin. Then right. Her legs feel crusty with grime, and sweat patches have formed under her arms. Then right again. She looks down at her wound. She should really mop up the dried blood that has trickled down her leg and ankle . . .

'Free the Butterfly?' A production assistant with a clipboard and a Bluetooth headset shouts over the hullaballoo of people falling out of the bar.

'That's me!' Freya yells.

'Free the Butterfly?'

'I'm here!' She hurtles towards the studio door, stopping just short of the production assistant and nearly falling on top of her.

The production assistant looks her up and down. 'You're Free the Butterfly?'

'Yes.' Freya pants. 'Freya Butterly.'

'This way.' The woman leads her through a backstage room and stops outside a set of double doors opening directly onto a brightly-lit stage.

Fizzing with happiness, Freya smiles. She has made it to The Golden Spoon final.

'Ready?' the production assistant says.

Pushing aside every emotion that curdles in her gut, Freya rearranges her face into a smile. 'Ready as a ready meal.'

CHAPTER THIRTY-ONE

All Set on Set

A large kitchen with several cooking stations sits beneath a lighting grid as long as it is wide. At the back is a fridge area set alongside kitchen cupboards and a sink so sparkling, Mrs Hinch would be impressed. Freya's eye trains across a long row of appliances and appliances – blender, kettle, mixer, spatulas, colanders, fish slices and wooden spoons hanging from giant fishhooks – all obviously brand new and gleaming under the bright studio lights. She follows the production assistant up the steps, her rubber soles squelching on the vinyl sheeting of the stage which feels even bigger now that she's standing on it.

'Wholemeal. Stoneground. Malted wheat grain . . .'

It's difficult to take in the guided tour of ingredients when each cupboard is full-to-bursting with God-knows-what. Never has Freya seen so many different types of flour or strains of olive oil. Extra Virgin. Extra Virgin fig leaf. Extra Virgin *kalamata*. The options are endless. Thank goodness everything is labelled and filed in alphabetical order, or she'd never be able to find anything.

On the back wall, a wooden rack is loaded with every spice imaginable, some of them instantly recognisable and others a complete mystery. Cloves the size of mushrooms. Dark red sun-dried chilli peppers. Cinnamon sticks. Bay leaves. Sesame seeds. Marjoram. Tarragon. Dried herbs. Fresh herbs – the air an aromatic swirl that reminds her of Christmas. The fridge is similarly well stocked and organised – ready-to-eat food at the top, dairy products on the shelf below with a rack of perfectly symmetrical eggs (surely selected for geometry alone) sitting in the top shelf of the door. A choice of raw meat sits above a salad drawer bursting with vegetables and fresh leaves.

'What happened?' The production assistant circles her finger at Freya's bloodied leg, her eyes travelling over the grit-splattered jumpsuit to the upside-down bird's nest that is now Freya's hair – a sort of copper, helmet-head frizz in which a whole family of sparrows could reside without anyone, Freya included, noticing.

'Ah yes, slight plan B getting here.' Freya takes the packet of wet-wipes she is being offered and winces at the sting of the soapy liquid against her raw shin. Unsure what to do with the soiled wipe, she balls it in her fist.

'Let's get you changed properly.'

Thirty minutes later and Freya is showered and looking good as new in a pair of floaty black culottes and a polka-dot T-shirt provided by the backstage crew. Her hair has been gathered up in a loose bun and her make-up has been reapplied by a professional. She stands in a small dressing room and catches her reflection in the mirror, a smile spreading across her face. Only minutes ago, all hopes were in the gutter and now here she is at The Golden Spoon final looking brand new and shiny, a real contender for the much-coveted prize she has dreamed of winning for most of her life. It's almost too much to take in. She runs her fingers over her new hair and smiles again, trying to work out whether her toothy grin is cute or disturbing – better go for closed lips in front of the cameras. The cameras! She throws her head back and laughs. Freya Butterly, in front of the cameras! If Mrs K could see her now . . . *The only person you're in competition with, is the best version of yourself. Don't let nerves get the better of you. Enjoy the process.* She takes a deep breath and fills her lungs with positive energy – against all odds, she is here now, and so it follows that against all odds, she can win this.

'Ready?' The production assistant raps on the door.

She pops the empty bottle of perfume into her pocket, throws back her shoulders and, caressing the smooth glass with the tips of her fingers, strides out. She can do this.

'And here is the performance area.'

Freya glances around the stage. Three seats are lined up on the diagonal, presumably for the judges who are yet to arrive, Talia Drakos no doubt destined for the chair in the middle. Ooof. A wave of nervous excitement rushes through her. She is about to share the very same stage as her all-time hero! Breathe. Breathe. Breathe. Further downstage, Michel stands at his workstation, eyes closed in meditation, a set of cameras pointing at him as he mentally prepares himself.

Making her way towards her designated workstation, Freya can't ignore the camera training on her as she limps across the stage, her shin on fire. 'We're not being filmed yet, right?' she asks nervously.

'Not until the big green light flashes,' the production assistant assures her. 'The cameraman is just lining up the shot. Try to take no notice.'

It's difficult to pay no attention to the cameras when a great honking one is being wheeled over on a trolley to sit right next to her, the lens glaring down her top with an over-the-shoulder shot. She looks down at her workstation. Like a surgeon's gleaming operating theatre, the counter is laden with every knife, peeler and grater possible, metallic blades reflecting the studio lights like murder weapons. The drawers beneath hold a tray of cutlery and several rolls of baking parchment, tin foil and cling film. Freya feels a sudden wave of panic. What if the watermelon they've sourced is overripe?

Or even worse, underripe? Her mouth dries and she can't stop her hands from jittering.

The murmur of voices and the shuffle of feet filter in from above as the audience take their seats on the mezzanine gallery overlooking the stage. Freya looks up at the sea of Michel supporters – brothers, sisters, aunties, uncles, nieces, nephews, sous-chefs and plongeurs, pupils and protégés, mayors and mayoresses who have all flown over from France to watch their fellow countryman win The Golden Spoon. It has the feel of playing at an away match, a handful of home supporters dwarfed by a sea of spectators all routing for the opposition. Combing through each row, she searches for Xanthos.

'Up here, Frey!' Khady waves at her from a side mezzanine she wasn't aware of, Angeliki on one side, and a row of elderly ladies behind them. Khady leans over the balustrade. 'I'm so, so sorry, Freya! I tried and tried to stop the bus driver, but he just ignored me and then we had to pick up another guest!'

'Sure,' Freya says quietly, watching as Dimitri and Christos take the seats next to Angeliki. The heightened state of anxiety she has been in for the last God-knows how long has taken its toll and she is by no means ready to forgive – Khady's quantum entanglement with André nearly cost her this opportunity of a lifetime and she's not quite over it.

Shaking out the nerves in her arms and legs, she continues to scour the steady flow of incomers for Xanthos, her eye drawn to the mayor of Narbonne who unravels an enormous banner stretching across five people. MICHEL, C'EST NOTRE CHEF D'OR. Further along, Stéphane also has a sign at the ready. MICHEL À GAGNER! It isn't until her eyes travel to the other side of the narrow aisle that she spots him. Olive T-shirt. Chiselled jaw. Overnight stubble. A stern look on his face as he lifts his picket sign. 'GO, MICHEL!'

Freya's stomach turns to stone. Xanthos would really do that to her?

'*Allez, Michel!*' a voice croaks from the back.

'*Vas-y, Michel. On compte sur toi!*'

She presses her palms against the workstation counter and tries to dislodge the staple that has just been punched through her lungs, blood swooshing around her body and everything turning to liquid. He certainly knows how to stick the knife in. But you know what, she tells herself, fuck him if he wants to behave like that. And fuck him some more. Or no more! He can clutch the Michel sign all he bloody well wants but she is damned well going to win this competition. Fair and square. For herself. If they want a fight, that's exactly what she'll give them. She hasn't clawed her way out of the gutter for nothing and here she finally has the opportunity to show everyone what she's capable of. Breathe in, two, three, four. Out, two, three, four. She closes her eyes, thanks her lucky knickers for getting her here on time (see, they never let her down) and opens them again (her eyes, not her lucky knickers).

Michel's mother – it must be; she looks the spitting image, minus the facial hair – looks down at Michel from the balcony. '*Bonne chance, chéri!*'

'*Merci, maman.*' Michel paces around the stage.

Freya flashes him a conciliatory smile.

'*Et n'oublies pas de sourir de temps en temps. T'as la gueule d'un chameau!*'

'*OK, maman. Ça suffit!*'

The production assistant fixes Michel with a glacial stare.

Determined not to let Xanthos get the better of her, Freya restricts herself to looking up only at the side gallery where Khady is seated. Negative energy will get her nowhere and there is too much at stake to indulge any of these mind games.

'Ladies and gentlemen.' A voice comes over a loudspeaker. 'Welcome to the grand final of The Golden Spoon.' The salutation is repeated in Greek.

'*Bonne chance!*' Michel says to her.

'Good luck!' she replies, flicking out her fingers to dispel her nerves.

'If you could all take your seats and settle down, we will be starting in three minutes.' As the voice booms over the sound system, it takes Freya a moment to realise it is coming from the small man downstage in the dicky bow and tuxedo who never introduced himself.

Like a stone on elastic, Freya's stomach drops and then is catapulted back up again as the director, a hairy man with tinted spectacles, looks up from the monitor of a camera installed down in the stalls, facing the stage.

'Camera one?' The director looks up towards the left of the stage.

'Rolling.'

'Camera two?' He looks up towards the right.

'Rolling.'

'Camera three?' He glances at the chairs set for the judging panel.

'Rolling.'

'And camera four.' He looks to the camera operator next to him, who nods.

'Judges at the ready?'

The production assistant gives him the thumbs up from the wings.

Freya's stomach feels like a yo-yo on a string.

'OK, scene one, take one. We are rolling and . . . action!'

CHAPTER THIRTY-TWO

Talia Drakos

A trickle of sweat runs down Freya's temple. The last time she felt this level of anxiety was when her period started in a Zumba class, and she was wearing her favourite pale-blue leggings. She reaches for her glass of water and tries to get a grip.

Downstage, in a sparkling glass cabinet sits The Golden Spoon: a gleaming gold statue set in a marble base sculpted to look like a pile of cheese, the spoon itself a gold-plated vertical structure in the shape of a wooden, stirring spoon. Oh to be able to reach out and touch it. To hold it in her hands and feel its cool, metallic weight. To cradle it to her bosom. To have it standing on her mantlepiece (OK, she's not sure where she'll be living beyond this trip but small details and all that). To be able to cherish and worship it.

The small man in the tux waves up at the audience, a smile so broad it looks painful running across his face. Like a chipmunk on acid, he chunters away, his chubby cheeks inflating along with his ego. 'Welcome, welcome, welcome to The Golden Spoon Grand Final brought to you straight from the heady heights of Paphos.' He makes his way over to centre stage. 'Three courses selected by our chefs. Each judged for taste, texture and presentation by our esteemed panel. Ladies and gentlemen, put your hands together for super-chef judges Tameka Adeleke and Yiannis Moustakas!'

A statuesque woman in a figure-hugging gold-flecked dress and swingy bob jogs on set stage left, mirrored by a large man with the body shape of a large bear appearing stage right. He wears dark jeans, a dark shirt and the bandana tied around his neck looks like something a pesky but loveable Alsatian might wear. Still, who is Freya to judge? She's still clutching a bloodied wet-wipe and half her leg is hanging off.

The judges make their way over to the centre of the stage, wave at the audience and take to their panel seating. Freya looks down at her cheese grater and tries not to vomit.

'And now, ladies and gentlemen.' Mini-Tux launches into action once more. 'The moment you've all been waiting for . . . It gives me great pleasure to introduce the one and only Talia Drakos!'

Freya feels as though her heart may burst with joy. Holding her breath, she turns around to see a bone-thin version of the Talia Drakos she has idolised over the years. The tappety tap of stiletto heels accompanied by an overpowering smell of hairspray makes its way across the stage, Freya watching as the stick woman she has worshipped for so long totters towards the microphone in six-inch heels and a full-length, black sequinned jumpsuit to rapturous applause. Bowing first to the left, then to the right, her one-piece glitters under the studio lights, the muscles of her back flickering with each movement.

Freya fiddles with her apron as the goddess of cuisine stands before her. If only her mother could see her now – on stage with Talia Drakos. *The* Talia Drakos. Someone who has so far been more of a mythical creature than a real, walking, talking human being. A star who has inspired chefs the world over and given so much joy to foodies all around the globe, capturing their hearts and taste buds with her *Especially Tasty* range of Greek meze. A woman who has invested herself in the future of cuisine by coaching junior chefs and championing the up and coming. A woman so warm, so personable, so—

'I can only stay for half an hour, so you'll just have to work your magic in the edit.' Talia Drakos glares at the director and then, as though flicking a switch, turns to the autocue and, with a smile that could melt the most cold-hearted, launches into her TV personality, her voice becoming honeyed. Soft and silky. Like red velvet cake mixture. 'Ladies and gentlemen, it is an honour and a privilege to be here tonight for The Golden Spoon finals. Nurturing talent is something I feel very strongly about. From small acorns grow mighty oaks.' She looks up from the autocue and scowls. 'What the fuck is an acorn?'

'It's the nut from which an oak tree grows.' The director smiles through gritted teeth.

'Is it a nut or a seed?' Mini-Tux says quizzically.

Talia Drakos pivots on one heel. 'Whether it's a nut or a seed, I'm not saying it. Acorns. Oaks. Ridiculous.'

Mini-Tux opens his mouth to correct her and then, seeing how Talia is crunching her knuckles with exasperation, thinks better of it.

'I'll say it in my words. OK, get filming again!' She waggles her finger at the nearest cameramen. 'We must nurture talent. Support our successors.' She turns on her charm. 'Encourage their passion for food and promote traditional recipes to our younger generation. OK, cut!' She flutters her fingers at the autocue. 'It says something about tasting a meringue here. I'm not tasting a meringue. Do you know how many calories are in a meringue?'

The director removes his glasses and swabs them on his shirt.

Mini-Tux presses his finger against his earpiece. 'I'm told it's a low-sugar recipe of yours.'

'Never heard of it.' She snaps her fingers. 'Get me my keto cookies instead, please.'

Freya watches as a small, leopard-skin print clutch bag gets passed from one production assistant to the next until it reaches the guy in the tux. Snatching it out of his hands as though it's about to expire, Talia opens the clasp and pulls out a handful of what look like small meringues whirled and whooshed into the shape of a flower.

'Nobody will know the difference. Let's go!' She holds them up to the camera. 'Like these meringues I prepared earlier. Light as a feather and melt-in-the-mouth!' She pops one onto her tongue and chews erotically, licking her glossed lips before biting into another. 'Sumptuous.' She looks to the director. 'Got that?'

He gives her the thumbs up and she promptly regurgitates the lot into a paper serviette handed to her by the production assistant who seems well versed in dealing with the requirements of a diva. Then brushing the crumbs off her hands, she takes her seat between the other two judges.

Freya shifts her weight from side to side, trying to ease the downward pull of disappointment that tugs at her limbs as the woman she has had on a pedestal for so long disintegrates into a mere mortal before her very eyes, and a not-very-nice one at that. How can The Golden Spoon mean so much to everyone who strives to win it and yet so little to its founder? She glances up at Khady who returns her look with one which says, 'Yup, Grade-A asshole.'

'OK.' Mini-Tux steps back into the spotlight, relishing his opportunity to take centre stage. 'Ladies and gentlemen, the moment you have all been waiting for. Michel Vergnon versus Freya Butterly in the Grand Final of The Golden Spoon.' He looks down at his cue cards. 'Freya, I'm told, is an award winning cheesecake champion and owner of Taste the Mediterranean, an Anglo-Greek taverna back in London. Give us a wave, Freya!'

Freya isn't sure that she can correct him. Not in front of the cameras.

'And Novelli Academy graduate Michel here has a string of accreditations and awards to his name. Michelin star of Europe. Raymond Blanc's Chef d'Or three years running. Viticulturist. Cuisine minceur specialist. Guy Savoy's protégé . . .'

Freya starts to zone out, Mini-Tux's voice becoming fainter and fainter. How the hell is she expected to win against someone of Michel's culinary standing? And if he really has this many qualifications, can't they just paraphrase to make it sound a little more even? Talk about David and Goliath. She racks her brains, trying to remember how David actually defeated Goliath and recalls something about a small rock, a slingshot and an accurate aim, but how does that translate to cookery? Surely catapulting a boiled egg into his eyeball with a serving spoon would only get her disqualified.

'Chefs at the ready!' Mini-Tux says.

Freya tunes back in and wonders if Xanthos is watching her. It takes all the willpower in the world not to look up and comb the seats for him.

'Five, four . . .' With wafting hand movements, Mini-Tux encourages the audience to join in.

A sinking feeling takes hold of Freya which dissipates as quickly as it came on, only to be replaced by a burst of adrenaline. She reaches for the edges of her apron and gets ready to channel her inner Mrs K. *Enjoy the process. You are only in competition with the best version of yourself. You deserve this.*

'Three, two, one.' The studio echoes.

'And your time starts . . . now!'

CHAPTER THIRTY-THREE

Cut!

'*Allez, Michel!*'

'Silence, please.'

'It's not fucking Wimbledon!'

A laugh.

Blinded by the studio lights, Freya clutches the lip of the solid granite workstation, the audience snaking and bending, contorting and twisting, looking down on her like circling predators, waiting to pounce on her misfortune. An undercooked bean. Too much lemon zest. And then there's the panel of judges lined up like a team of evil aunties, collating notes and clocking judgement, keepers of the keys to the kingdom she so wishes to inhabit. Out of the corner of her eye, she can see Talia Drakos swinging her foot back and forth under the table and glancing at her wristwatch.

With lightning speed, Freya moves to the stainless-steel scratch-free sink, pours an inch of water into a bowl and then makes a beeline for the fridge. Grabbing hold of the green beans, she scurries over to the sink, runs them under the cold tap and returns to her workstation. Withdrawing a knife from the wooden block, she tries to conjure an image of Mrs K in her mind's eye to put Harj's slicing technique into practice but it's difficult to concentrate with a busload of Michel supporters shouting out encouragement for the French man every few seconds.

'*Allez Michel!*' a man calls out from the gallery above.

She must not look at Michel.

'Freya!' Khady's voice calls out from the other side.

She must not look at Khady.

'Freya!' another familiar voice calls out from the same area of the gallery.

She must not look at anybody.

'Enjoy the process!' the same silky soft voice cries out.

Freya freezes, everything grinding to a halt. It feels as though the globe has spun off its axis and is freefalling through orbit. It can't possibly be. Slowly, she raises her head to look up and there she is, sitting next to Khady: a tiny, birdlike woman with a silk scarf tied around a mass of unruly dark hair. The same gravity-defying posture she always had, her upper and lower back perfectly aligned. Proud. Noble. Engaged. As though sitting up and listening to the speech of a king. It can't possibly be . . . but it is. Freya's arms and legs start to tremble, a torrent of emotion rushing up through her core and catching in her throat. Mrs K waggles her fingers at her just like she used to do in the school playground all those years ago and Freya's heart could all but explode. Tears of joy escape from the corners of her eyes and she feels as though her whole body has turned to plasticine.

Mrs K is here. In Cyprus. In this auditorium. Freya's heart sings a thousand hallelujahs. Mrs K has come all this way to watch her? Mrs K still cares? Empowered, emboldened, energised, she slices through beans like a chopper on steroids. Mrs K is the additional guest Khady and Xanthos conspired to pick up en route? Faster and faster. But how did they – ouch! A sharp shock of pain shoots through her finger and the knife clatters against the chopping board, a collective gasp filling the auditorium.

Grabbing the tea towel, Freya wraps up her finger and mops the blood off the counter. The production assistant runs on set like a medic to an injured player on the football pitch, slamming down a first aid kit as large as a suitcase and spilling its contents all over her workstation.

'Cut!' the director cries.

'You can say that again!' Mini-Tux jibes.

A laugh, followed by a that-was-below-the-belt 'ooof' as Freya is being cajoled onto a stool, her finger throbbing like billy-o and told to sit with her head between her legs whilst the production assistant looks for an appropriate dressing. But still the clock ticks, and out of the corner of her eye, Freya can see that Michel has not stopped working, moulding his lamb *keftedes* into small, neat balls and dunking them into a pan of hot oil.

'Stop the clock!' the production assistant cries, administering a bandage and holding up three or four fingers (it's difficult to differentiate when your vision is so blurred) for Freya to count.

'I'm fine.' Freya pulls herself up, her head spinning with dizziness, searing pain jetting through the bone of her finger.

Through blurred eyes, she holds a 'thumbs up' in the vague direction of Mrs K and Khady and staggers back to her workstation. The beans, thankfully, are unscathed. Clean, chopped and unbloodied.

'Are you OK to continue?' the production assistant says, looking at Freya with concern.

Freya nods. There is no way she's got this far without seeing it through.

'Are you sure?'

'One hundred per cent,' Freya says, though her body is telling her otherwise.

'Very well. Scene two, take two and action!' the director yells.

Fingers shaking, Freya pops the beans into a bowl and heads to the sink, a surge of nausea coming on thick and fast when she sees blood seeping out from under the bandage. Focus. Focus. Focus. With trembling hands, she wraps a brand-new dishcloth around her finger, the pressure at least providing some relief from the pain that surges through her.

Moving over to the oven, she sets the grill to 'high', grabs the block of halloumi from the fridge and returns to her workstation. The room spins. Steadying herself against the unit in front of her, she grabs a knife. This one is bigger than the last one. Taking care that each sliver is equal in thickness,

she cuts through the cheese with jittery hands. *She is worthy.*
She can do this. Lying the halloumi slices on the brand spanking
new baking tray, she settles her nerves with a gulp of water
and places the cheese under the grill. One elephant. Two
elephant. She counts down the seconds in her head whilst
setting the oven timer for one minute fifty-seven seconds.
Accuracy is key. Pushing aside the pain that zigs and zags
through her body like shockwaves through the earth, she heads
to the fridge for the watermelon and, gathering up the heavy
bowling ball of a fruit, crosses the stage.

'I carried a watermelon!' Khady shouts.

A trickle of laughter carries over the audience from those
that are *Dirty Dancing* fans.

Focus. Focus. Focus. Now is not the time to get distracted,
not now that another knife is in her hand. Finger throbbing,
she hacks through the centre of the watermelon until it falls
open into two halves, then sets about digging out its pink,
pulpy flesh. The oven timer lets out a shrill jingle, and Freya
legs it over to the grill. A camera follows her closely as she
slides out the tray of halloumi, flipping over the golden strips
of cheese with a fish slice and resetting the timer for – three
elephant, four elephant – one minute and fifty-six seconds.

'*Mais bouge-toi le cul, Michel!*' Stéphane shouts from
the gods.

Freya glances over at Michel who appears three-fold in her
vision, his outlines fuzzy and indistinguishable from each other.
With three hands, he squirts the juice of three lemons onto
three plates of *keftedes* and adds parsley. All those hands
adding all that parsley.

Freya sets about chopping the mint. Not too finely. Not too coarsely. What was it Mrs K used to say again? *A hint of mint is refreshing. Add too much, it gets distressing.* Difficult when you can barely see but, that should about do it. The microwave bleeps.

'Three minutes remaining!' Mini-Tux declares.

Only three minutes? Wasn't there supposed to be a five-minute alert? Blood starts to seep through the dishcloth. Did she really tune out that much that she didn't hear an announcement? She glances over to the row of Michels who stand hands on hips, making a point of having finished early, a sprig of parsley atop his perfectly presented lamb *keftedes*. Her heart pounds in her chest as though it's trying to escape. She should have two slices of pitta bread warming right now and she doesn't even know where the pitta bread is. Fuck. Fuck. Fuck. Pitta? Pitta? Pitta? Like a frenzied jack-in-the-box, she opens and shuts cupboard doors, evoking a couple of chuckles from the audience, before remembering that she saw them in the door of the fridge.

'Two minutes remaining!'

Focus. Focus. Focus. But Freya cannot focus, her eyesight is so blurred. Blood trickles from beneath the dishcloth and is on the verge of contaminating her food. This cannot be happening. Should she shout, 'Stop the clock?' What is one supposed to do in this scenario? But with just two minutes to go, she should probably stick it out. Screw the pitta bread, she'll never be able to stuff it without being able to see properly. Muscle memory alone allows her to drain the beans, run them under the cold tap and mix them with the watermelon and mint. Squeezing the lemon (she's already sliced it, thank God), she adds a squirt and oh the fucking pain as lemon juice finds its way into the gash on her finger.

'One minute remaining!'

A drizzle of olive oil. A pinch of sea salt. A handful of pistachios. Thank God she can do this with her eyes closed. She goes through the motions on autopilot and arranges the strips of halloumi over the salad as an audience of two hundred counts down the seconds.

'Three. Two. One. Stop the clock!'

Everything turns to slow motion, Freya's heartbeat somewhere in her ears. She looks over at all the Michels – God knows how many times he has multiplied by now – then down to her psychedelic salad. Normally, she would feel a sense of satisfaction at the way the beautifully charred halloumi has further melted over the heat of the beans to give a creamy effect that contrasts nicely with the crunch of pistachios and the sweetness of the watermelon, but who knows what it looks and tastes like.

The room spirals. Voices become distant. The lights fade.

And blackness takes over.

CHAPTER THIRTY-FOUR

Judgement

Freya comes round to the smell of antiseptic cream and the glare of stage lights. The blurry faces of half a dozen people loom towards her and the heavy throbbing pain in her finger is now a dull, pulsating ache. Distant voices slowly morph into clear, articulated commands which, she comes to realise, are all being directed at her. Why does she feel so desperately tired?

'You OK?' Angeliki feels for her pulse, a first aid kit at her side.

Xanthos and Khady crouch either side of her, sharing muted looks of concern.

Freya goes to nod but her head has taken on the characteristics of a pumpkin skull and lolls all over the place, her neck seemingly unable to support it. Xanthos strokes her hair out of her face.

She looks up at him. 'I thought you hated me?'

'I could never hate you, Freeya,' he says gently.

'I thought you thought . . .'

His eyes twinkle and his whole face smiles. 'Relax. You have bigger turnips to grill. Khady has explained everything.'

'But you . . .'

'Relax.'

'You had a Michel banner,' she mumbles.

He frowns. 'That was Stéphane's. I was holding it for all of three seconds whilst he tied his shoelace.'

Freya smiles weakly and then remembers her surprise guest. 'Where's Mrs K?'

'Goodness gracious, Freya. You had us all scared!' Mrs K's head pops up behind Angeliki and Khady. She chuckles, the laughter lines around her amber eyes deeper and more pronounced than all those years ago, but still those same eyes. Kind. Intelligent. Caring. 'It's wonderful to see you again though I'm sorry the circumstances are as they are.'

Overwhelmed, Freya crumples into Mrs K's soft, warm arms. Arms that held her all those years ago. Arms that whipped, blended, chopped and buttered alongside her. Arms that she could have been held by countless times growing up but chose not to and all because of misguided pride. She breathes in Mrs K's scent and thinks of freshly made pastries. If kindness had its own smell, it would be that of Mrs K.

'Come on, we can't have you go to pieces in the middle of the competition, can we?' Mrs K says softly.

A tornado of guilt and happiness whip-whirls in Freya's chest, sucking long-harboured feelings out of her gut and forcing them to the surface until they erupt out of her with such force that she can no longer hold them back. Shame. Love. Regret. Joy. Remorse. Gratitude. So many feelings she can't harness or begin to understand, all slip-sliding faster and faster until she spins completely out of control. She looks into Mrs K's eyes. 'I . . .'

She wants to say sorry. Sorry for everything. Sorry for turning her back on Mrs K time and time again. Sorry for pretending not to care. Sorry for not saying thank you for the food parcels. Thank you for teaching her how to cook. For welcoming her into her family. For taking her in. For looking out for her. For making her the person she is today. For giving her the maternal support she so desperately needed but didn't dare ask for. For championing her through school. For not judging her. Or thinking less of her. Sorry for throwing it back in her face and moving to Nottingham without saying goodbye. For being angry. And then too proud to then get in touch even though she'd wanted to. For everything. But although she wills the words to form in her mouth, they will not come. Sorry. One simple word that she cannot muster. Instead, her protective wall is starting to crumble just when she can't afford for it to. Brick by brick. Stone by stone. Her barrier falling away. Tears well in the corner of her eyes. She can't fall apart right now – not when her dish is about to be judged.

'Is she OK?' Dimitri peers through the group of people clustered around her. 'I got her more water.'

'OK, if we can have everyone off the stage, please!' Mini-Tux commands.

'Good luck.' Mrs K pats Freya's hand in the way you might

a good dog. 'I know if I were a judge, your dish would have won me over.'

Freya smiles. 'You think?'

A twinkle appears in Mrs K's eyes. 'You had me at halloumi.'

Freya looks into Mrs K's face. A kind face that would never let you down. Never leave you at home on your own aged nine. Never cause havoc at your parents evening. Never re-gift her married lover's perfume as your birthday present. Never forget to attend important meetings about your exam results. Never let you go hungry. Happiness glows throughout her core. 'Thank you.'

'Ladies and gentlemen, given Freya's injury, we have made an executive decision not to progress to the main and dessert,' Mini-Tux announces over the PA system, a murmur of discontent rippling through the auditorium. 'We apologise that this won't be the usual three-course meal competition, but these are not usual circumstances, and therefore our judges will base their decision solely on the starters prepared by our contestants today.'

Michel sighs with exasperation and mutters something about starters, mains and desserts complementing each other on a journey to culinary heaven, food utopia only achievable through a balance of all three courses and then something about needing the toilet, which leads to the production assistant escorting him off backstage. He's not the only one who's frustrated, crew dashing this way and that and earpieces being pressed in and pulled out in response to producers threatening to pull out now that airtime has been cut. It's chaos.

Freya feels a surge of disappointment. She wanted to do this competition properly. The whole nine yards, the whole three courses. Nobody gets to taste her cheesecake this way. Her head spins and a rush of nausea rushes up her windpipe, the pain in her finger intensifying – on second thoughts, maybe this is the right decision after all.

'Ready in five for feedback on the starters, judges?' Mini-Tux looks over to the panel.

Tameka Adeleke looks up from her phone, tucking her bobbed hair behind her ear and holding up a gimme-one-second finger whilst Yiannis Moustakas twirls his thick moustache.

'Where's Talia?' Mini-Tux taps at his earpiece, his eyes darting around the stage.

Talia Drakos reappears out of the wings. 'All shots strictly above the waist only.' She scowls at the nearest cameraman. 'Any footage with my hips in, and I'll sue your ass.'

Freya swallows hard. To think she has idolised Talia Drakos for all these years. Unreal. After much rearrangement of Talia's jumpsuit and repositioning of her pose to provide the most flattering angle, the cameras start to roll once again.

Michel returns to his spotlight and turns to look at Freya. 'He's OK, your finger?'

Freya holds up her finger for him to see in all its bandaged glory, the hefty stump of bloodied cotton gauze doing all the talking. Satisfied that the dressing alone would indeed hamper her performance, he nods and returns to his workstation. Freya sighs. Being encumbered by the dressing is nothing; she's been encumbered by her hand for most of her life, but it's the fact that she can't apply any pressure to it without feeling like she's going to pass out that's the problem. She cradles her pulsating finger and looks up at Mrs K who returns her glance with a glittering smile. Dear Mrs K.

'And action!' the director shouts.

Mini-Tux reinstates his chipmunk grin. 'OK, the moment of truth. Our judges here are primarily looking for taste and nutritional value, but presentation also has a key part to play – as my mother used to say, there's no point in serving up high quality grub if it looks like a dog's dinner . . .'

He moves over to the judging panel where Freya's halloumi and watermelon salad sits alongside Michel's *keftedes*, both dishes looking drained of colour under the studio lights; something they'll apparently touch up in post-production. She chews on the inside of her cheek. Surely she's already leapfrogged Michel in terms of nutritional value what with his choice of fatty lamb? Or has she? His accompanying Greek salad is doing some heavy lifting in the healthy-eating stakes.

'Each judge will sample both dishes and then be asked to note down their scores out of ten which means that in a few moments' time, either Freya Butterly or Michel Vergnon will be pronounced Winner of The Golden Spoon!'

Freya's heart flutters with hope and dread.

'Judges, take it away!'

An out-of-body sensation overcomes Freya as she glances at Michel who clutches the edges of his apron with apprehension. Whether it's the rhythm of the throbbing of her finger or the adrenaline rush of the last few hours, she doesn't know, but all nervousness has dissipated and instead she feels strangely sedated by an unfamiliar inner peace. Maybe her adrenal glands are burned out and have nothing more to give. Maybe it's the presence of Mrs K, but whatever it is, a calm serenity has swept over her now that she is in the hands of fate (well, the hands of three world-class chefs).

Yiannis Moustakas is the first to sample Michel's *keftedes*. Leaning over and spearing the lamb, he loads a stack of salad onto his fork prongs to create a mini kebab and slowly transports it towards his bushy beard.

'Exquisite,' he says, between mouthfuls, making a ring with his thumb and forefinger. 'The meat is succulent, and the mixture of oregano, parsley and mint brings just the right balance of fragrance. A perfect blend.'

Freya feels a twinge of unease.

Talia Drakos looks down at the plate that has been shunted along to sit in front of her and claps her hands at a production assistant who scurries off stage left.

'Talia, if you can give us your verdict?' Mini-Tux clutches his cue cards nervously.

'The presentation is fabulous. Such a kaleidoscope of colours in the salad.' Talia lowers her fork towards the lamb and snatches at the bundle of kitchen roll being fed to her under the table by the production assistant. 'Wonderful. Melt in the mouth. You can feel how much love has gone into this. They say a picture can paint a thousand words – well, let me tell you, a dish like this can evoke a million sensations. I can feel the explosion of taste on my tongue and . . .'

Each compliment is like a stab through Freya's heart. Maybe she hasn't reached enlightenment after all. It would be OK if the effusiveness was in relation to her halloumi salad but gastro-orgasming over her rival's dish whilst a camera trains on her for a reaction shot is almost too much to bear.

'Honestly, my taste buds are having a party in my mouth right now,' Talia continues.

Can't she rein it in a bit?

'Truly magnificent.'

Apparently not.

'The best lamb *keftedes* I've ever had.' Talia turns to the director. 'You can cut there, right. Nobody needs to see me swallow. The Golden Spoon is not the Gestapo, right?' She promptly regurgitates her whole mouthful into a sheet of kitchen roll and surreptitiously balls it in her fist.

Freya and Michel share a look.

Mini-Tux interjects. 'And finally, Tameka?'

Tameka straightens herself out, inflates her chest and dips her chin towards the dish of lamb. 'The fragrance is heavenly.' She swirls a forkful beneath her nostrils. 'And the taste . . .' She takes a mouthful. 'Nothing short of wonderful. Everything you would want and more from such a local delicacy.'

Freya's confidence crashes down around her ears. This is way more painful than chopping off a finger.

'Are we sure Michel isn't Cypriot?' Tameka goes on.

A murmur of laughter ripples across the audience.

'Thank you, judges. And moving on to Freya's halloumi and watermelon salad.' Mini-Tux guides them along.

Freya's stomach lurches. A nearby cameraman glides over to Freya for a tighter reaction shot, swishing the lens so close to her face that every pore of her skin must look like a giant crater. She starts to sweat.

'Beautifully presented,' Yiannis Moustakas kicks off the discussion. 'A veritable rainbow of colour. It makes me happy just looking at it. Joyous.'

'Although I can't help but think that you missed a trick with the pitta bread,' Talia interjects. 'The pitta bread would earth it somewhat. Provide a canvas on which to paint.'

'I disagree,' Yiannis says. 'I like my starters light. The whole point of an appetiser is to have your appetite whetted rather than sated. It's about being teased. You don't want to feel full before you get to the main.'

Talia Drakos shoots him a piercing glare. 'You want a bit of something to sink your teeth into.' She growls at the camera playfully.

Yiannis digs his fork into a slice of halloumi-smeared watermelon with more force than necessary, the metal prongs scraping against the crockery. He lifts it to his lips. 'Nice.'

Nice? *Nice?* Freya wants to scream. What was it her English teacher at school used to say about the word 'nice'? Insipid. Bland. Non-descript. Greggs' sausage rolls are nice. Processed Bourbons are nice. Luke-warm tea is nice. But her best halloumi and watermelon salad? How dare he!

He passes the dish to Talia.

'The presentation is a little haphazard,' she remarks. 'I like to see symmetry and style. I like to know that it has been constructed with care.'

'There's a beauty to its chaos though, don't you think?' Yiannis says.

'No. I do not think.' Talia Drakos lowers her fork into the salad.

Freya holds her breath. Talia Drakos is about to taste her food. *The* Talia Drakos. The one and only Talia Drakos (even though she is a dick).

Talia takes a mouthful of halloumi-coated green beans and watermelon. Chewing like a llama, she goes back for a second forkful, this time dislodging a pistachio nut from the bed of salad. 'Delicious.'

Only delicious? Not exquisite? Or divine? No explosion of flavour in the mouth?

Talia passes the dish to Tameka.

That's it? The entirety of her review. 'Delicious?' Not sumptuous? Not to-die-for? No gastro-orgasm? No nothing? Freya feels brittle. As though her bones might just shatter into a million fragments. She looks up at Mrs K who holds up two sets of crossed fingers and beams like the sun itself, before returning her attention to the judging panel.

Tameka closes her eyes to inhale the sweet fragrance of the watermelon. 'Beautiful.'

A good start.

'Wonderful flavours. The sticky fig dressing is remarkable – a beautiful blend of sticky fig wine vinegar and syrup – sweet but not too overpowering and the balsamic drizzle sets it off nicely.' She swallows. 'There are some wonderful textures going on there. The pomegranate is deliciously sweet and the pistachio magnificently salty – a beautiful counterbalance there, and the halloumi is nothing short of melt-in-the-mouth world class, which isn't easy . . . We all know halloumi can be difficult to get right. You want soft and squidgy rather than hard and rubbery. This though, is a triumph.'

Freya feels a surge of hope. A triumph. That's more like it.

'And now it's crunch time.' Mini-Tux leaps back into action. 'Judges, you will now be asked for your scores. A simple marks-out-of-ten system. The contestant with the highest score will become Winner of The Golden Spoon.'

Blotches of Freya's face go missing, her skin a mosaic of sweat patches.

'Come on, Freya!' Khady's voice chimes from the balcony.

'*Allez, Michel*,' Stéphane counters from the other mezzanine.

'Quiet please.' Mini-Tux clutches his cue cards to his chest. 'OK, the moment you've all been waiting for.'

A shiver runs down Freya's spine.

'Without further ado, Freya's magnificent halloumi and watermelon salad. Yiannis, if you can start by revealing your score, please.'

Freya's stomach flip-flops, dread and hope competing to sit on top of each other.

Yiannis clears his throat. 'The presentation was a beautiful abstract mishmash. Lovely colours going on. The halloumi was delicious. The concept was great, scoring high on the nutritional value chart, but there was a bit of a metallic aftertaste.'

Dread tugs her in the direction of doom.

'It's a seven from me,' he says.

Hope pulls her back over the line. Seven isn't too bad for a competition as strict as this, is it?

'Thank you.' Mini-Tux turns up his kilowatt smile. 'Next up, the wonderful Talia Drakos . . .'

'It's a five from me,' she snaps. 'Lovely dish but I have to agree with Yiannis, it did have a taste of metal in places.'

Freya closes her eyes in horror. A metallic taste? Her finger must have bled into the dish.

'And Tameka?'

'Loved it.' Tameka smiles. 'I'm a big fan. I didn't taste anything vaguely metallic. The halloumi was sensational. The watermelon so sweet and flavoursome. It's a nine from me.'

'Fabulous.' Mini-Tux presses on his earpiece. 'So an average score of seven for Freya. Well done!'

Everything slows. Is that a loser's 'well done'? A conciliatory, please-try-harder well done? The sort of 'well done' you get on a school report which insinuates that although you tried your hardest, you will never really amount to anything? Should she mention the probability of the metallic taste being her blood? And if she does, will that help or hinder?

'And on to Michel's lamb *keftedes*.' Mini-Tux steers the judges towards the next dish. 'Yiannis, if I can have your scores, please.'

Yiannis twiddles his moustache. 'Again, it's a seven from me.'

Freya exhales sharply as Yiannis recounts his reasons. She and Michel are neck and neck. This could still go either way.

'Thank you, Yiannis.' Mini-Tux grins. 'And over to you, Talia.'

'Simply sensational.' She effuses. 'It's a perfect ten from me.'

Freya feels her stomach solidify. She looks down at the floor which rushes towards her. It would take Michel getting a ridiculously low score from Tameka for her halloumi salad to stand any chance of winning. If only her finger hadn't bled.

If only . . .

'And finally, Tameka?' Mini-Tux continues.

Tameka smiles. 'I'm going to go all out and give it the perfect ten too! Perfection on a plate. Never tasted anything like it.'

Freya's heart plummets as an avalanche of hopes and dreams come crashing down and a life-long ambition evaporates before her very eyes, the taste of defeat bitter on her tongue. To think that Mrs K has travelled all this way to watch her lose. Khady too. Crushed by disappointment, her arms hang limply at her sides as the crowd roars in celebration of Michel's win. She wonders whether the result would have been the same if her finger hadn't bled and concedes, in her heart of all hearts, that although she may have gained a few extra points, she was up against one of the most highly skilled chefs in the world and realistically, Michel and his *keftedes* would have still won. Men and their bloody balls!

'Michel Vergnon, the judges have declared your food exquisite, divine and unbeatable. Not only are you the winner of the competition, we would like to honour you by awarding you with The Golden Spoon!' Mini-Tux announces to squeals of delight.

Freya sucks in her cheeks and isn't sure what to do or where to look and although all eyes are on Michel, she knows that they'll be darting to her in sympathy.

'*Oh mon dieu.*' Michel makes his way over to the microphone, glancing back at her with a look of apology. '*Merci.* Thank you.'

She watches as her competitor accomplishes her dream.

Mini-Tux presents Michel with The Golden Spoon trophy that gleams under the spotlight, laughing and joking as he goes. The actual trophy. He's only gone and won The Golden Spoon. Her throat constricts and her ears feel hot, but she must not cry. She needs to hold it together for the cameras, a model of stoicism and strength, humble in defeat.

'I have been working towards this moment for what . . .' Michel looks up at Stéphane who stands at the edge of the balcony. 'Twenty years?'

'Ooh, là. Trente, quand même,' Stéphane replies.

'OK, thirty,' Michel says. 'It is a great honour and a privilege. Thank you to Talia Drakos for founding the competition. Thank you to the organisers and the judges. To Christos, Dimitri and Xanthos for teaching me so much about Cypriot food, and also to Freya for being a fantastic opponent.' He turns to look at her. 'I could not have produced the quality of food that I did today without Freya. She has been a formidable contestant during the competition, and I knew from the start that she was the person that I needed to vanquish . . . to beat, sorry. So talented. So spontaneous. So young. If you ever have the opportunity, you must taste her cheesecake – she made one the other evening for our team of chefs and it was possibly the most delicious dessert I have ever tasted. She's a real talent. I also find it intimidating that she knows so much at such a young age. I have twenty years' more experience in the kitchen and yet she is my equal. I'm just sorry that the thing with her finger . . . I'm just . . . Sorry, Freya.'

A tear rolls down Freya's cheek. She tries to look gracious in defeat but her whole body is trembling, and she can no longer hold back her emotions. There's nowhere to escape to. There's nowhere else to go. She is duty-bound to take it on the chin and own defeat as she would victory. It's galling to watch though – Michel parading the trophy back and forth across the stage and thrusting it up towards his swathes of fans who hammer their feet against the floor in deafening glory.

'Michel D'Or! Michel D'Or! Michel D'Or!'

Slowly, Freya slinks off to lick her wounds in private, her head hung low, tears rolling down her face and her heart in tatters.

'You were amazing. Your food was amazing.' Khady insists. 'To get to the final is a huge achievement in its own right.'

'One swallow does not make a summer. There's always next year,' Dimitri reassures her.

'Maybe next time.' Mrs K's eyes twinkle as she envelopes Freya in her tiny, strong arms. 'But first, let's get you to hospital and sort out that finger.'

Freya closes her eyes and allows herself to freefall into self-indulgent disappointment. If there was ever a safe space to feel sorry for herself, it's here in the maternal embrace of Mrs K.

'I'll take her.' Xanthos appears amongst them. 'I'll take her on the bike. I know all the shortcuts.'

Mrs K looks up. 'I'm not sure a motorbike is a good idea. Not when she can't grip properly. Can you call a taxi?'

Ten minutes later, Freya is sitting in the back of a taxi,

wedged between Khady and Mrs K, whilst Xanthos directs the driver from the passenger seat through the urban back-streets of Paphos towards a four-storey pyramid-shaped building. They pull up in the hospital car park, Xanthos paying the driver and ushering them all into A & E. Inside, the hospital is overcrowded, every seat taken in the atrium waiting room and people spilling out onto the floor, lying on makeshift pillows of bags and coats.

Mrs K finds Freya a seat on a low windowsill near the reception and squats down next to her. 'I'm sorry about your finger but I'm very glad we got to spend some extra time together.'

'Me too,' Freya says, wondering how many hours it will take to get seen by a doctor and whether it's worth it.

'I wanted you to have this . . .' Mrs K pulls a small scrap-book out of her large handbag and rests it on Freya's lap.

'What is it?'

'Open it.' Mrs K twinkles.

She peels open the pages to see photograph after photo-graph of herself. Making a pineapple turnover cake, aged eight. Kneading bread dough, aged nine. Frying her first kipper, aged ten. An article from the *Nottingham Post* with a 'Local Lass wins Junior Bake Off' headline sitting above a picture of Freya proudly holding up a winning strawberry cheesecake. A warm glow fills Freya's heart as she flicks through more pictures – photos of her chopping, slicing and peeling. A handwritten (Freya's junior scrawl) recipe for home-made pizza and umpteen menu planners in the same pen. She flicks the pages over and over, pausing on another

Nottingham Post newspaper article entitled 'Oops, she did it again!' and running a piece on her winning the following year's British Junior Sous-Chef. And finally, on the last page, her Golden Spoon qualifier results.

'You knew I'd qualified to enter The Golden Spoon?' Freya says, aghast.

Mrs K wraps her arm around Freya's shoulder. 'Of course I knew. You didn't think I'd given up on you, did you?'

Freya wipes the tears out of her eyes. 'But I was rude. I was . . .'

'Just because somebody is out of sight doesn't mean they are out of mind . . . which reminds me.' Mrs K plunges her hand into her handbag and drags out a small, gift-wrapped box. 'Your mother gave me this to give to you.'

'You saw my mum?'

Mrs K nods. 'She's sorry she can't be here and is so immensely proud of you, Freya.'

Freya panics. 'She knows I'm here?'

Mrs K nods. 'She wishes she could be here too.'

'She wasn't funny about it or anything?'

'Why would she be funny about it?' Mrs K reaches for her hand. 'Freya, she's delighted that you're living your life. That you're . . . what was it she said again, "going for gold." She wants you to enjoy yourself. I'm sure there's a big part of her that lives vicariously through you.'

Freya feels her heart swell with a bittersweet surge of joy and sadness. If only her mother could have been there today, but obviously that's totally unrealistic. She looks down at the gift-wrapped box and reads the tag.

So very proud of you and wish I could be the mother
you deserve. Live life to the full for you and for me.

Mum x x
PS Time for a refill. You can't run on empty forever!

Freya's throat tightens. She runs her fingers over her mother's handwriting and tries to imagine where her mum was when she wrote these words. Was she sitting in her favourite chair next to the window in the communal lounge? Or on a park bench on one of her mornings out? Or maybe she penned it from the make-believe imaginings of a white sand beach next to turquoise water – thank goodness for the power of imagination. She sprays the perfume against her wrist and breathes in the fresh, floral scent of lotus flower, freesia and white lilies. A smell she associates with her mother. Resolving to pour the contents of the new bottle of perfume into the old one which still feels better somehow, the glass smoother, stronger and more reassuring, she watches as Xanthos returns from the cash machine. She knows she shouldn't like Xanthos half as much as she does, but there are certain things that are outside of her control.

He strides towards them. 'You OK if I take a seat?' he says, gesturing to the windowsill alongside her.

'I'd better make sure your friend hasn't got lost.' Mrs K takes this as her cue to leave and glances around for Khady who disappeared a good fifteen minutes ago for the toilet and hasn't yet returned.

Freya smiles, slipping the perfume into her bag and making room for him.

He grins. 'How's the English patient?'

'The English patient is good,' she muses, leaning back against the window and taking in the frantic goings-on of the waiting room. 'The English patient would be even better if she didn't have to go back to the UK.'

He takes hold of her uninjured hand. 'I'm sorry I didn't stop the bus. I'm sorry I caused you all this crazy panic, but I am not a perfect man, Freeya. I was jealous. I was hurting and I wanted you to hurt a little too, but only enough to give you a little shock. I knew Dimitri would get you there.'

'You could have let me in on that little nugget of information.'

'I'm really sorry. And I'm sorry you weren't the lucky one today.' He rubs her hand against his stubbly chin. 'But you'll always be my winner.'

Freya looks around the waiting room, anticipating the wave of hurt and disappointment that's about to come crashing over her but instead a sense of peace kicks in. 'It's funny.' She turns to him and looks him in the eye. 'I've spent my whole adult life thinking that all I ever wanted was The Golden Spoon and yet getting so close today made me realise that it's been a surrogate dream the whole time.'

Xanthos frowns. 'A surrogate dream?'

'You know when you think you want something but really you wanted something else all along?'

'No.'

Freya laughs. 'If I'd have won The Golden Spoon today, my name would be in the paper, I'd have a shiny trophy to my name, a slightly different Twitter bio, a glamorous title in my auto-signature and sure, it would have been a ticket to a better job, but would my life have changed really? I mean, I'd have the fame and glory but beyond that, I'd still be the same as I am as runner-up. It's only now that I understand that it wasn't about winning; it was about getting to the final.'

A curtain of confusion falls over Xanthos's face.

'Cooking out here in Cyprus has been the dream. Living in Lappo and waking to the warmth of sunshine, the sound of the sea and the fragrant smell of the hillside is the dream. Cooking all those wonderful dishes and competing in every challenge was the dream. I don't mean to sound smug, but I'm proud of what I achieved. It pushed me out of my comfort zone and made me both a better chef and a better person. Obviously, winning would have been the ultimate bonus but getting to the final was actually the most important part because it brought a very special person back into my life. Someone who is worth a million Golden Spoons.' She looks over at Mrs K who stoops down to retrieve a bottle of Evian and a packet of Maltesers from the vending machine.

'Freeya.' Xanthos places his hand on her thigh which ignites something deep inside her and she's not sure where to look. 'You realise that people see you as a Very Special Person too?'

Freya picks at the cotton gauze swaddling her finger and bristles with discomfort.

'People like me,' he says, looking at her with an intensity that unsettles her.

She doesn't know what to say or where to look. She'll be flying home tomorrow evening so what's the point in embarking on some deep and meaningful heart-to-heart? Better to keep her thoughts to herself, leave intact, build a new life when she gets back home. Golden Spoon Runner-Up should at least earn her some kudos on her CV and open doors that were firmly closed to her previously.

'Spend the day with me tomorrow.' His blistering green eyes connect with hers.

'I . . .' Freya would love nothing more than to hang out with Xanthos tomorrow. Chillax under the Mediterranean sun. Goof around in the turquoise waters. Feel the touch of his soft, olive skin and the resonance of his husky growl. Allow him to take her to places she has never been before, both actual and metaphorical.

'Please?' He looks at Freya imploringly until her internal organs start to melt and a thousand tiny fireworks pop and fizz in her stomach.

'I . . . Look, I'm probably invested in this way more than you are,' she blurts.

'I don't understand.'

She gathers her strength. 'I like you, Xanthos. I like you a lot.'

'I like you a lot too,' he says, smiling.

'Freh Yah Butterly?' A nurse appears in the waiting area.

'Come on, just a few hours?' He places his hand on hers. His touch is electric.

The nurse gestures towards the corridor with the suggestion that Freya should follow.

She gets up, his hand still in hers, and spots Khady through the window in the ambulance bay with her tongue stuck down

Angeliki's throat. A smile plays on her lips. Isn't life for living? She turns to Xanthos. 'Pick me up at nine?'

His dazzling green eyes smile. 'I'll be there.'

CHAPTER THIRTY-FIVE

The Real Winner

The next morning, Xanthos pulls up outside the villa in his truck at nine o'clock on the dot. Freya grabs her stuff and leaves, smiling as she closes the door behind her. He pats the passenger seat and gestures to a paper bag full of pastries and two keep-cups of coffee propped up behind the handbrake.

'Good morning,' he says, kissing her on the cheek.

'Hi.' She wears the same strappy sundress she wore on their island boat trip, hoping that it might invoke the same reaction as last time, although her club finger and its dressing is probably a bit of a mood-killer. 'Where are we going?' she says, plucking her dress away from her sweaty armpits and trying to assess whether the damp patches are visible without drawing attention to them.

'To my place.' Xanthos parks up at the edge of a small olive grove she hasn't seen before.

He helps her down from the truck and leads her over to a footpath, the land opening up to reveal steep, terraced vine-yards that stripe the hillside in neat, narrow lines. Gnarly branches rise out of the ground like old chiefs, their limbs twisting and turning under a headdress of vivid green foliage. She pictures Xanthos tending to each vine, pruning it to perfection, his jeans rolled up to his knees in preparation for treading grapes in a huge wooden vat. She'll miss him, along with this beautiful island. His funny sayings. His soft growl. The way he runs his fingers over his stubble before he says anything of significance.

Sand, grit and stone crunch underfoot, a light breeze fritt-ering on the air as the sun peeps through the cloud, casting shadows across the valley and lighting up the ruins of the old Greek temple further up the hill. Behind them, the dark firs of an evergreen forest sway forebodingly, calling to mind sombre fairy tales.

'This is proper Hansel and Gretel territory. You're not kidnapping me, are you?' She tries to pretend that she's not out of breath.

He squeezes her hand. 'Not my style.'

Uncomfortably hot, she becomes aware that her knickers have curled up and are embedded somewhere in her arse crack ('chewing toffees' to coin Khady's phrase) and although she's tried a casual swoosh of the arm to redeploy them, the sweaty lace has found its way back into her bottom crevice and it feels as though she's being cut in half with a cheese wire.

It turns out that Xanthos lives neither in the Bazigou residency at the top of the cliff nor at Villa Katarina and has shunned both comfort and space for a small, solar-powered shack he describes as a large garden shed. They amble down a narrow path towards the cliff edge where the grass becomes longer and wilder and soil gives way to sand.

'Careful,' he says as she's about to tread on a small, delicate purple flower.

'Violets?'

'Cyclamen. The national flower of Cyprus.' He bends down to touch the petals and something inside her melts. 'Free-ya?' he says, rising to his feet. 'It's important that you know I do not have many things.'

'OK,' Freya says slowly. 'Because obviously, I was walking down here with you just now thinking, "Oh, I hope Xanthos has many, many things!"'

He chuckles, tapping the rim of her cap with his finger and pulling her by the hand.

As they descend the craggy path, she realises that they are approaching *her* beach but from a different angle, the horseshoe-shaped limestone cliffs coming into view, but it's not until they make their way around a single olive tree and along a narrow ravine that she realises how high up they are and how sheer the drop is.

'You OK?' he says. 'Your skin is a little green.'

She returns his look of concern with a nervous nod and squeezes his hand a little tighter.

As they make it around the corner, she has the distinct impression that she's been here before. Call it déjà vu but this limestone ledge feels familiar even though she knows in her logical brain that this is her first time up here and she has only ever been down on the beach. The expanse of cliffs opens up and a flock of seagulls fly overhead, and it's not until they've rounded a huge bolder covered in bird poo that she understands why this is all so familiar. For there in front of them is the small wooden hut that she spotted when bathing in the waters below for the first time, its red and yellow vertical stripes giving off a lifeguard vibe. She holds her breath with anticipation as Xanthos takes a key out of his pocket and leads her down three stone steps, along a narrow ledge ('always face the cliff and don't look down') where the rocks jut out further to provide a small stone terrace in front of the beach shack. Granted, it's bigger closer up but he wasn't lying when he said it was no bigger than your average garden shed.

'This is your place?' Freya grins.

'Yes. I ate the whole world to find it.'

Freya smiles. She does so love his Greek expressions.

He opens up the shack, its garage-type door folding back on itself.

'I always wondered who this belonged to.' She peeps inside.

The interior of the hut has been designed to provide both a sleeping and living space using a clever combination of hidden storage units and multi-purpose furniture – the bed is high enough to double as a table once the mattress has been harnessed to the back wall by leather straps, and the bottom of the mattress has been decorated in a seascape print that has the look and feel of an acrylic painting. Beneath the bed-cum-table are a set of slide-out drawers containing cooking equipment and kitchen utensils, everything having its set place – chopping boards at the back and teaspoons bound together by an elastic band at the front.

'I have solar-powered electricity,' he says proudly, flicking on the light switch next to the bed, small spots of light appearing in the ceiling though hardly visible through the blazing sunshine. 'And here is the bathroom.' He edges down the side of the bed and up three stairs leading to a tiny wet room – a sink built into the top of the toilet and a shower head fixed to the ceiling. 'Everything you need to survive.'

Behind the partition wall where the mattress leans is a walk-in cupboard containing a fridge and several food cupboards.

'Where do you cook?' Freya says, observing that there are no kitchen surfaces on which to prepare anything and more importantly, nothing to cook with.

'Outside,' he says. 'I have a gas hob I take out onto the terrace. Like a kick-ass camping stove.'

'Kick ass, hey?' Freya teases.

He disappears into the cupboard. 'Let me fix you a drink.'

Freya glances around the shack in awe. Everything is so carefully thought through, it's like a boat with all its secret compartments and dual-function, nautical nattiness. A pull-out chopping board with a removable circular piece of wood acts as a chute into the bin below. Several spice racks have been converted to hold a small set of crockery and glass tumblers. Fold-away this, that, and the other. Bistro tables. Dining chairs. She takes the opportunity to dislodge her knickers from her arse before he reappears with a bowl of olives and two glasses of sparkling water.

'Does it upset you that I don't drink?' he says, earnestly.

'Not at all,' she says. 'It certainly makes the mornings less bleary.'

'Good.' He moves her to one side to lever out a section of the floor. Dragging out deckchairs and a fold-up table, he replaces the floor panels and leads her to the terrace.

'Give me two minutes without looking.' He spins her around to face the bay below, her back to his home. 'Don't look!'

She grins to herself, taking in the endless blue sea and craggy cliffs. If one thing's for sure, this is certainly the perfect ending to her holiday here.

'OK,' he declares. 'You can look now.'

She turns around and there on a fold-out table is a Golden Spoon trophy built entirely from cheese, its Kefalotyri base draped with grapes and engraved with her name which stands out in creamy white lettering.

FREEYA

It even has the extra 'e' which she's keen to keep forever.

His kindness unsettles her. It's so damned adorable, she's lost for words. 'You made me a Golden Spoon trophy out of cheese?'

'Take a seat.' He pats the chair next to him.

'Thank you.' She flings her arms around him, her heart bursting with joy.

He smiles. 'I added a new cheese to the mix.'

'I saw. Kefalotyri. Hard, salty yellow cheese made from cow's milk. See, I've done my homework.'

'No.' He points to the creamy italic font that spells out her name and pulls out a tub of Dairylea cheese. 'I will be insisting that Dairylea has her own place on the cheeseboard from now on. She may only be the common pawn on a chessboard but let's not forget how strategic she is to the game. After all, if she can successfully make it to the other side, she can become Queen,' he says, crowning her with a ring of grapes.

Freya glows from within.

'Congratulations.' Xanthos takes hold of her hand.

She laughs. 'You do know I lost, right?'

'You may have lost the competition, but you won everything else. The hearts of the audience, the minds of the judges. This beautiful trophy and . . . a contract at the Bazigou taverna.' He grins from ear to ear.

'Say that again!'

He leans forward, taking her hand in his. 'How would you like to work at the Bazigou Taverna?'

A rush of warmth run through her. 'Are you serious?'

'Deadly.' His eyes twinkle like jewels. 'Head chef. What do you say? My dad wants to retire, and Dimitri and I would love you to take it on.'

'Whooah. Wow. I don't know what to say,' she says, her stomach fizzing with excitement.

'Think about it,' he says.

'I . . .'

It's been a long-term dream to be head chef. And she certainly loves the island. Wasn't this the idyllic paradise she dreamed of waking up to every morning only a few days ago? And yet, she can't conceive of living here with her mum being so far away. God only knows how her mum would take it if she announced she wasn't coming back. But coming back to what? She doesn't have a job. She doesn't have anywhere to live. And although she has Khady and her friends from the restaurant, there's nothing really tying her to Nottingham. The streets are polluted. The food is very rarely fresh. And the weather is crap. There's no smell of wild oregano and sunshine when you fling open your doors in Nottingham. There's no endless turquoise sea to swim in. No beaches to picnic on. No hillside herbs to dine on. Birdsong replaced by police sirens and chugging engines.

'It would have to be a bona fide contract,' she says, 'No disrespect but I could never be reliant on you.'

'Of course.'

'And there's just one more thing,' she says, wondering how to bring up his womanising ways. 'I'm sorry to have to ask this, but how many of your clients have you slept with?' The words tumble out of her mouth, tripping over each other without rhyme or reason.

Xanthos stares at her as though she has just revealed herself to be a small, green alien.

'I just . . . it was something Angeliki said. The other day on the terrace. And I . . . I'm sorry,' she says, her thoughts a jumble of confusion.

His eyes narrow. 'Is this why you've been avoiding me?'

Freya's face becomes a stretched-out affair made of play dough. 'Kind of.'

He clears his throat with a snarl. 'You didn't think to ask me this before we . . . you know, the thing with the Dairylea?'

Freya gathers her knees to her chest. 'I'm sorry. I just . . .
I thought it might kill the moment.'

'Like it has now.' He squints up at the sun.

All she can hear is the rush of the sea and the hammering
of her heart. He's right. Of course, he is. If she really wanted
to raise the subject, she should have done it before clothes
were abandoned and passion took over, but that would have
jeopardised getting naked in the first place and if she's honest
with herself, she wanted to sleep with him no matter what
skeletons lurked in his closet. Rather than ask her conscience
for permission, she'd ask for forgiveness. Live for the moment
and worry about the consequences later. No strings attached.
What was it Khady had said? 'A summer fling is just the
thing. Anything more becomes a chore.' The plan was to have
a bit of fun – release the pent-up sexual tension that had been
simmering between them and indulge in a bit of a holiday
romance. Getting laid without getting stung, trapped or
embroiled in island politics. But now it feels wrong. As though
she has unfairly accused him of something. As though she has
crossed a line she can't uncross, revealing herself to be an
ethical fraud. What good are pseudo-principles and a retro-
spective moral compass? Grrr. If she could take back the
words, she would.

He looks her straight in the eye. 'A few years ago, I had a
small romance with a girl from Scotland – Alison. She accompanied me to Dimitri's wedding.'

'Right,' she says, feeling her insides twist. She's never liked
the name Alison.

'She was not happy with me because I left her with my

family when I had to help my brother with the wedding because I was the godfather.'

Freya lets out a snort. 'The godfather?'

He frowns, the sun dancing in his eyes. 'Isn't this what you say?'

'You mean *best man*?' Freya laughs.

'Best man?' His brow puckers further. 'Surely, the groom is the best man?'

Freya considers this. He does have a point. 'Go on then, how do you say best man in Greek?'

He leans back and looks down at the sea below. '*Koumbaros* for a man. *Koumbara* for a woman. Usually the bride and groom choose one of their godfathers as best man, but Dimitri and I were not baptised and neither was his fiancée . . .' He shrugs his shoulders and plucks a grape off the base of the cheese trophy. 'Alison farted on me.'

'Riiight,' Freya says slowly, wondering if this is a fetish thing.

'She wrote me on my butt,' he goes on, rearranging the cushions behind him.

Freya giggles. 'I'm not sure I'm following.'

He stands up and gives her his full attention. 'She went back to Scotland and never spoke to me again. I was a fool to think it was anything more than a holiday romance.'

'And Helena?' Freya suddenly remembers the other woman Angeliki mentioned.

'Helena?'

'Apparently you stole her away. I'm not sure from who or what but . . .'

Xanthos throws his head back and laughs.

'What?' says Freya, dumbfounded.

'*Helena* is a boat! Not a person. She was a wedding gift.'

'What do you mean she was a boat?' Freya tries to process the information, her mind loop-the-looping.

'I made a boat for Dimitri and Cassandra as their wedding gift,' Xanthos says.

'Hang on, hang on, you made a boat?' she says, struck by the enormity of this endeavour.

'For them to sail away for their honeymoon.'

Freya feels her body turn to liquid. Here is a man who can build his own boat. A man who can create an actual mode of transport from raw materials. Who can hammer and weld, saw and solder. A man with vision, innovation and skill. Winemaker. Love maker. Boat maker. Is there anything that he *can't* make? A shiver runs down her spine and it's all she can do not to pin him to the ground and mount him, *the man that can.*

He mistakes her look of horniness for one of disdain. 'You don't like boats? I took you out on a boat and you don't like them?'

'I *love* boats.' She slips her hand into his and smiles.

'The boat was named after Angeliki and Cassandra's mother, Helena, who sadly died a month before the wedding. When Cassandra left Dimitri, I took the boat back. My poor brother was heartbroken. Devastated. Ashamed. He was the talk of the village. The gossip of the island.'

'Dimitri was heartbroken? But wasn't he the one who left her?'

'No . . . She left him for his friend.'

'But Mrs Anastasis—'

'Mrs Anastasis sees what she wants to see. Her grand-daughter left him shortly after they were married, but he still got the blame – it's always the men who get the bad reputation! It was unbearable around here with everyone stopping and staring, so I took him on a boat trip, and we sailed to the mainland. Athens is a handsome city.'

'I've not been,' she says, quietly mortified that she could think so badly of him and his brother. She squeezes his strong, rough hand – worker's hands – and tries to piece it all together. The scorned grandmother. The angry sister. The way they'd spoken about Helena being stolen away and all this time, *Helena* is a fucking boat?

'So why does Mrs Anastasis bear such a grudge? The way she talks about you and Dimitri, it's as though you kidnapped and murdered her grandchild.'

'Dimitri was angry. He told old Mrs Anastasis that her granddaughter was a whore. She still likes to think that if Dimitri wasn't here, her granddaughter would come back. The reality is that Cassandra has made a new life in Armenia with his friend, Alec. They have two children now.'

'And she holds you responsible too?'

'She holds me responsible for taking the boat. Her husband is a fisherman and he was going to use it every day to catch sardines. Over the years, the story changes. Xanthos took the boat. Xanthos stole the boat. Xanthos stole my husband's boat. Xanthos stole our fishing business. Turkish whispers. This is why I choose not to live in the village.'

Freya's skin tingles under the sun. 'You weren't tempted to stay in Athens then?'

'Athens is great for a hit of energy. Busy. Noisy. Bright lights. But I prefer the peace and tranquillity of the island. The fresh fish. The fresh fruit. The warm sea. The vineyards. I came back after two weeks whilst Dimitri stayed for three years. This is why his English is so much better than mine. He had to speak English all of the time at business school. That's where he met Mrs Drakos and had the idea to set up The Golden Spoon holidays.'

'Mrs Drakos.' She raises an eyebrow with newfound cynicism and kisses him. Not so much lustfully but lovingly. Tenderly. His mouth is soft but firm and tastes of the sea. Her eye is drawn to his arms as they flex this way and that, the markings of his tattoo sleeve flickering in the sunlight.

'I was wondering,' she says coyly, 'how that table can possibly convert into a bed?'

A twinkle appears in his eyes. 'You were?'

'Uh-huh,' she says, her stomach squirming with desire.

He takes her by the hand and leads her inside.

'Pull that!' he says.

She licks her lips and then realises he's pointing to a thick leather strap.

As instructed, she tugs at the fastening, the bed springing down in front of them. Scooping her up in his arms as though she weighs nothing more than a bag of shopping, Xanthos lowers her onto the mattress.

Looking into his sea-green eyes, a volcano of desire erupts from within her. She wraps her hands around the back of his neck and guides him towards her, his lips finding first her neck and then her shoulders. Sunlight streams into the room and the gentle rush of the sea over the shore below fills her with a deep sense of calm and for the first time in her life, she feels truly free. Not only does she have Mrs K back in her life, a Golden Spoon trophy made of cheese and a Greek god at her side, but something much deeper. A burden she didn't realise she'd been carrying for all this time has been lifted and she feels at one with the world. She places her leg over Xanthos's, relishing the touch of his skin against hers and no longer caring how milky-white her thighs look in comparison to his olive complexion.

'Freeya, I'm glad you came to Cyprus.' He traces the contour of her chin with his finger.

'I'm glad I came to Cyprus!' She smiles.

She thinks about everything Mrs K said about her mum being proud of her for seizing opportunities and living life to the full. About 'going for gold' and her mother living vicariously through her adventures. She thinks about Cypriot sunsets and the thrill of waking up to Xanthos every day.

'Yes.' She gazes out at the Mediterranean sun reflecting on the rippling blue sea. 'I'd love to take the job.'

'Freeya?' He growls, hugging her tightly.

And she does feel freer: free to fly.

ACKNOWLEDGEMENTS

Firstly, I'd like to thank my agent, Felicity Trew, for matchmaking me with Bonnier. I feel very lucky to have been paired with such an expert team throughout the editorial process. Thanks in particular to my editor, Sarah Bauer for allowing me to run whole-heartedly with my storyline and characters, and for encouraging me to 'turn up the smut' rather than remove it! It was great riffing with cheese puns in our emails back and forth, and I hope we'll Brie friends for Cheddar! Thanks also to Katie Meegan for catching me in the copy edit and to the whole team at Bonnier for coming up with the artwork and having fun with the concept. Thanks also to Bonnier for engaging Jane O'Connell RNID/RGN to check through my schizophrenia storyline and to Jane herself for her investment in mental health over the years.

I'd also like to thank my sister, Roz, for reading my first draft and offering up encouragement and feedback. It's nice to get that early pat on the back from someone unconditionally Team Ginger. Thanks also to Carlie Lee for reading my opening chapters and offering words of wisdom. Most of all, I feel indebted to my fellow writer, Bruce Jones, who took the trouble of giving extensive feedback on my manuscript and turned out to be a bloody brilliant beta-reader. Thanks, Bruce!

Thanks also to my Trinity Book Club ladies for always being super-supportive and getting excited on my behalf. I'm lucky to have you all in my life and don't know where I'd be without you. To the brilliant Miss K who we miss dearly at my boys' school for letting me borrow her surname and to the Alison Hurrells and Rani Padayachees of the world, who have helped children find their way in the world when the odds are stacked against them – thank you for having big hearts.

Writing *Halloumi* during UK lockdown whilst juggling a job and home-schooling two primary school aged boys was a challenge like I have never before experienced and hope to never experience ever again! However, creating a storyline based in the heart of Cyprus and its Mediterranean waters was fantastic escapism. Although Lappo is a make-believe island just off the coast of Cyprus and its village, surrounding vineyards, beaches and hillside forests are fictional, they are very real in my imagination and I hope you have enjoyed spending time in them as much as I did. Who knows, maybe one day we'll get to go out there and find this paradise, hey Adam?

On that note, I've saved the best 'til last and I'd like to thank Adam Simcox, in the capacity of both fellow author and husband. Thank you for being so positive about *Halloumi*, for reading and feeding back on the manuscript and for allowing me to get Alfie his dog with the advance! (I was going to call her Halloumi but figured I'd feel too silly shouting that in the park, so it's shortened to Lulu – we all love her!). Thanks also for still being my husband in spite of the turmoil of last year.

And a great big THANK YOU to you, the reader, for taking a punt on this novel. I hope you enjoyed it, and if you did, I'd be delighted if you could leave a review. Thanks a mill!

Love, Ginger xxx

PS I don't know if I'm allowed to say this, but I have a follow-up novel coming . . . Prepare yourselves for another holiday romp – this time set in Italy: *What the Focaccia?* is due out in 2023.

PPS Sorry to my boys, Alfie and Oscar, who will no doubt be mortified later on in life that I have written sex scenes! Please forgive me and remember it got you Lulu!

If you enjoyed *You Had Me At Halloumi*, then keep your eyes peeled for Ginger Jones's next book . . .

WHAT THE FOCACCIA?

Coming 2023